Hashtag Islam

ISLAMIC CIVILIZATION
AND
MUSLIM NETWORKS

Carl W. Ernst and Bruce B. Lawrence, editors

Highlighting themes with historical as well as contemporary
significance, Islamic Civilization and Muslim Networks
features works that explore Islamic societies and Muslim
peoples from a fresh perspective, drawing on new interpretive
frameworks or theoretical strategies in a variety of disciplines.
Special emphasis is given to systems of exchange that
have promoted the creation and development of Islamic
identities—cultural, religious, or geopolitical. The series
spans all periods and regions of Islamic civilization.

*A complete list of titles published in this series
appears at the end of the book.*

Hashtag Islam

How Cyber-Islamic Environments Are Transforming Religious Authority

Gary R. Bunt

THE UNIVERSITY OF NORTH CAROLINA PRESS

Chapel Hill

This book was published with the assistance of the
Anniversary Fund of the University of North Carolina Press.

Manufactured in the United States of America

Designed by Jamison Cockerham
Set in Arno and Klavika
by codeMantra, Inc.

The University of North Carolina Press has been a member
of the Green Press Initiative since 2003.

LIBRARY OF CONGRESS CATALOGING-IN-PUBLICATION DATA
Names: Bunt, Gary R., author.
Title: Hashtag Islam : how cyber-Islamic environments are
transforming religious authority / Gary R. Bunt.
Description: Chapel Hill : The University of North Carolina Press, [2018] |
Series: Islamic civilization and Muslim networks | Includes
bibliographical references and index.
Identifiers: LCCN 2018005190 | ISBN 9781469643151 (cloth : alk. paper) |
ISBN 9781469643168 (pbk : alk. paper) | ISBN 9781469643175 (ebook)
Subjects: LCSH: Social media—Religious aspects—Islam. |
Mass media—Religious aspects—Islam. | Islam—21st century. |
Technology—Social aspects. | Jihad—History—21st century.
Classification: LCC BP185.7 .B86 2018 | DDC 297.0285—dc23
LC record available at https://lccn.loc.gov/2018005190

For Yvonne and Kane and my mother, Elizabeth

In memory of Derek Bunt

#Contents

#Illustrations

#Acknowledgments

This development of this book would have been impossible without the help of many people, some in cyberspace and others closer to home.

The University of Wales Trinity Saint David supported my research. Thanks are due to all the staff and students who encouraged me and discussed their interests in this field. I am indebted to the organizers of the numerous UK and international workshops and conferences I participated in for providing the opportunity to test-drive aspects of this work. Special thanks are due to Carl W. Ernst and Bruce B. Lawrence, series editors, for allowing me the privilege to contribute again to the Islamic Civilization and Muslim Networks series. Bruce and I maintain a long-standing trans-Atlantic dialogue on cyber-Islamic issues, and I have welcomed his perceptive insights and encouragement at every stage in this book's preparation. The readers and editors of this book provided thoughtful feedback that contributed to the final version. I particularly appreciate the advice of Elaine Maisner and the team at the University of North Carolina Press.

Throughout the time-consuming research and development of this project, my wife, Yvonne, provided patient support and an invaluable sense of perspective. My son Kane gave his own insights into technology use, as well as virtuoso musical accompaniment. My mother, Elizabeth, and late father, Derek, consistently encouraged my work in this field from its early days. Other members of my family offered their own enthusiastic support.

Despite the input of all of the above, the contents and shortcomings of the book remain entirely my responsibility.

#Note on Transliteration

Within the main text of this book, I decided not to burden the reader with a complex system of transliteration of "Islamic" and other terminology from Arabic and other languages into English, which I thought was unnecessary and damaging to the flow of the text, especially for nonspecialist readers outside the fields relating to Islamic studies. However, key transliterated terms with diacritics are provided in the glossary in order to assist readers seeking further information and definitions in specialist sources. The general principles contained in the *Encyclopaedia of Islam: New Edition* (Leiden: E. J. Brill, 1960–) and associated systems have been adhered to, with the popular model featured in Ian Richard Netton's *A Popular Dictionary of Islam* (London: Curzon Press, 1991) also applied. Quotations from internet and textual sources retain their original transliterations; proper names maintain locally applied personal spellings and transliterations; and common anglicized spellings of Islamic terms are applied where possible in the text—that is, "mosque" for *masdjid*, "hajj" rather than *ḥadjdj*. Variants may be found in quotes and in the glossary. Where an Islamic term is contained in a quotation, I have given a general definition in parentheses.

Hashtag Islam

#Introduction

Entering Muslim Digital Worlds

The Sheikh Zayed Grand Mosque is an imposing landmark on the skyline of Abu Dhabi—an oasis of air-conditioning and minarets within the concrete heat and frenetic bustle of the United Arab Emirates. When I visited there in 2011, I was shown how it acts as a networking hub, integrating digital media in its precincts and streaming sermons and other religious materials to other mosques in the region. Many mosques and religious institutions can stream multimedia across platforms and services, a service now embedded in the expectations of their core users within Muslim digital worlds. Digital content has become a key part of expressions of contemporary Islam in many contexts, in terms of the ways in which faith, command, and control are manifest across complex systems of Muslim beliefs.

We live in a phase of sustained information technological development, where significant innovations in communications have combined with diverse Islamic agendas to create a significant shift in the ways in which command and control of Muslim contexts are driven. Muslims in many zones are attuned to the various ways in which the internet can be applied to fulfill religious and other objectives, demonstrating innovation and technological aptitude that can contradict some prevalent stereotypes of Islam and Muslims being "behind the times" or stuck in a "medieval" phase of development. While there may be much of merit associated with Islam and Muslims in medieval periods, it is clear that in many cases Islamic cyberspace is up to speed (or ahead) and delivering technologically adept objectives to a public for whom online systems are a natural adjunct to everyday life. Through the application of technology, some sectors of Muslim society have engineered elements of positive social change and activism in diverse political and cultural contexts. Other elements might be deemed "negative" in terms of technological application, such as the emergence of online "jihad" associated with the "Islamic State."

The diminished digital divide and increased web literacy across generations feed into forms of Islamic cyberspace that have a growing influence across diverse Muslim contexts—especially in relation to religious authority

1

issues. However, there are still major gaps in information literacy and training in a number of contexts, especially where education is at a premium and online services are restricted or unavailable to all. A 2017 report suggested that greater attention should be given to the economic factors affecting a widening inequality, where "the digital divide becomes a digital chasm."[1] Such factors have to be kept in mind within any discussion about contemporary Islamic discourse in cyberspace, as it cannot be assumed that technological improvements are consistent or universal.

Despite these economic considerations and disparities, those Muslim individuals, platforms, activists, and organizations that demonstrate adept awareness of the potential for digital media in furthering their multifarious religious objectives will have increasing influence in connected local and—potentially—global contexts. They project specific notions of Muslim digital identities, integrated with "real world" statements and agendas.

This book derives its title from the ubiquity of the hashtag (#) in social media, where it is used to flag specific themes and content across a variety of applications, which can then "trend" if they are circulated through networks in social media such as Twitter and Facebook. I have focused on ideas associated with faith, command, and control because these resonate within many contemporary agendas associated with Islam, including ideas about who has the power to interpret religion and how that power manifests itself in guiding (or forcing) individuals to follow certain parts and patterns of behavior. The terms "command" and "control" are relevant in this context but can also be found on computer keyboards and are part of programming language. For some of the chapter headings, I have also utilized various terminologies associated with computer-mediated communication in its various forms. I have endeavored not to be too jargon-centered in relation to technological ideas, or indeed religious ones, and appreciate that there may be scope for more detailed drilling down in relation to issues of software, programming, and applications within Islamic contexts.

When I refer to the internet, I am aware that this encompasses a multiplicity of communications and networking tools, protocols, and channels—although the term has become synonymous for some with the World Wide Web. The term has evolved in light of technological advances, and the internet itself is very different from its origins in the 1960s U.S. ARPANET. In line with contemporary usage in many quarters, I have chosen not to capitalize "internet" here, while recognizing that there is dialogue on the uppercase rendition of the term.

Hashtag Islam intends to take readers to the next level of the study of contemporary Islam, where technology has moved to the heart of religious teachings, mobilization, and networking. It incorporates the sustained gathering of data in diverse contexts, together with observation of key events, in order to synthesize an approach to a constantly evolving and dynamic field of study. Given the multidisciplinary and interdisciplinary nature of the field, the book encompasses a range of perspectives and approaches, which can intersect and help inform understandings. The intention here is to present an element of that diversity, in terms of how it affects and indicates developments within studies of Islam and the internet. The internet in its varied forms has been crucial in (and integrated into) the dissemination of diverse worldviews associated with Islam and Muslims.

Now more than ever, people are turning to the internet for advice and answers to important religious questions, are contacting authorities directly, or are exploring archives and databases of opinions based on a variety of interpretative models. Use of the internet is significant in the way it sometimes subverts traditional models of religious authority and offers alternative approaches and information. Some authorities have responded by investing time and resources into the digital mediation of fatwas and other information. While not a recent development, in internet terms, the immediacy of information circulation has intensified through the use of Twitter, Facebook, and other interfaces—offering real-time commentary, opinion, and advice to substantial and diverse ranges of followers. The result is the emergence of digitally literate religious scholars, whose influence and impact may go beyond traditional boundaries of imams, mullahs, and sheikhs. The significance of internet-driven religious authority has been amplified with the implementation of strategic digital media policies by the Islamic State in Syria and Iraq; these developments are discussed in *Hashtag Islam*, with a recognition of their continuity of trends established by al-Qaeda (in its multifarious forms) and other jihad-oriented platforms.

Hashtag Islam explores the ways in which, through the influence of the internet, a significant shift in forms and styles of Muslim religious discourse within global and local contexts affects issues of faith and authority. It examines the relationships between technological interfaces and Islam, within diverse contexts, and shows how digital advances have been embraced to fulfill spiritual, mystical, and legalistic agendas. The book reflects sustained observation and analysis across a pivotal period in the evolution of Muslim digital worlds.

Hashtag Islam provides an overview of developments within *cyber-Islamic environments* (CIEs) and presents theoretical approaches toward the interpretation of this complex subject matter. Advances in internet technology, especially the reduction in the digital divide and an opening up of technology access, have had dramatic implications in a number of Islamic contexts. Increased scrutiny of the ways in which diverse Muslim organizations and individuals have been applying the internet to present their concepts of religious identity and understanding, drawing on social media and internet networking, has resulted in some cases in a reconfiguration of understandings of models of religious authority and the dissemination of Islamic knowledge. This fast-moving sphere of activity is discussed in this book, based upon sustained monitoring and interpretation.

While there is linkage with my previous work, *Hashtag Islam* can also be read completely independently, although readers will recognize some of the themes and elements if they have explored any of my earlier output. It is appreciated that readers will approach this work in many ways, not just in a traditional reading from page 1 onward. From using the index, it may be possible to glean specific areas of interest. The book can also be searched via its e-book format. Readers may be using the internet to look at some of the sites that are under discussion or to locate hyperlinks in order to view some of the original source material; the book can also be read in conjunction with URL listings on my VirtuallyIslamic.com website. Some of the source material is now missing from the internet; there are certain areas of cyberspace, in particular in relation to jihad-oriented content, that should be visited only with caution, and it may be necessary to negotiate such access with content providers in institutions. It is not recommended to download this material or indeed travel with it copied onto devices or USB flash drives nationally or internationally, wherever you happen to be located.

Whatever way you intend to read this work, some indication of the traditional print structure may be relevant. Chapter 1 takes a look at perspectives on the subject matter and explores theoretical approaches from a range of sources in order that the book can be positioned within its disciplinary frameworks. Chapter 2 considers the interfaces of social media and technology in relation to specific elements of Muslim digital worlds. This then links into chapter 3, which explores particular dimensions of faith and their representation online. Chapter 4 discusses ideas associated with religious authority in its multifarious forms online, which plays a significant role within CIEs and is particularly influential within diverse Muslim contexts. Chapters

5 and 6 then look at the ideas associated with jihad within cyberspace, which might constitute only a small element within overall online activity but is dominant within many agendas associated with contemporary Islam.

I hope that this book will provide a springboard for further exploration and understanding, given that the multidisciplinary and interdisciplinary subject area has plenty of opportunities for further research and reading. Feedback can be sent to VirtuallyIslamic.com, which has resources and links to related content.

#ChapterOne

Perspectives on
Muslim Digital Worlds

PROCESS/RESEARCH PATHWAYS

Hashtag Islam was written in my university office in the heart of Wales, which in itself may seem an unusual location for the writer of a book about contemporary Islam. There is a mosque in the town, and I work with Muslim students, both here in Wales and internationally. I have experience of traveling within diverse Muslim contexts and living within Muslim communities in the UK. However, the essence of this book is virtual or digital content, which I have been researching for two decades.

While writing on religious authority and decision-making within Islamic contexts, I undertook fieldwork in Pakistan and Malaysia during the mid-1990s, where I picked up on how email and digital conversations were starting to have an impact on real-world issues and events. Scholars were exchanging ideas via this recently introduced entity (at least for public consumption) called the internet. Admittedly, their machines were usually deskbound, and they had to go into the universities in order to access the data. Nascent conversations were taking place via chat rooms, and various groups were setting themselves up in relation to specific campaigns and interests.

From my location on the smallest university campus in the UK, I locked into conversations about significant global issues associated with Islam and Muslims. The impact of these early digital dialogues went largely undocumented, and the conversations online had not reached a critical mass where they were necessarily going to be fully observed or recorded. I established that something important was going on. This became more relevant when I started my lecturing career and students brought material into classes about Islam that had been sourced online, often without attribution or understanding of where it was located geographically, culturally, academically, or indeed spiritually. To assist my students, I taught myself how to code and built the Islamic Pathways website to provide guidance on the background on various online resources in 1996. I drew on my activities prior to academia, including in broadcast and print media, and on my experience of using very early forms of computers.

The Islamic Pathways site acquired a wider international audience, alerting me of the potential interest for further analysis within this subject area. My interest manifested itself in my writing, which has combined my interests in religious authority and media. I introduced the term *cyber-Islamic environments* (CIEs) as an umbrella concept, utilized to cover a range of online activities, whether an online thesis from an Islamic scholar or a tweet from a social media activist. The term *Islamic* is used to refer to any view that describes itself as belonging to Islam, even if that view is not universally shared by all Muslims. The term CIE itself has evolved in line with developments in technology and digital literacy.

This book's primary focus is the 2009–17 period. Materials were observed and recorded from diverse contexts in relation to specific issues associated with Islam and the internet. The technological interplay and relationship with religious articulation and values are primary concerns, developed in line with technological innovations in numerous Muslim contexts. Although I operate as an outsider-observer, I am focused on themes, conversations, and events concerning contemporary Islam. *Hashtag Islam* discusses substantial materials from English-language sources, but reference is also made to other works in Arabic, Turkish, Malay, and other languages. This work seeks to encourage further studies on CIEs within these and other linguistic and cultural contexts.

In part, this book reflects my academic work in a university and a specific interest in teaching about and studying events affecting Muslims in Western contexts. Social media amplifies the events that were once distant to Muslims in Western contexts and has a profound impact on the intellectual, emotional, political, and religious relationships between Muslims in majority and minority contexts. Elements associated with information technology have featured in the Arab Spring, the development of "Islamic State," and the displacement of Iraqi and Syrian refugees.[1] These and other events have demanded monitoring and analysis of technological concerns, including their impact on CIEs.

UNDERSTANDING ISLAM AND THE INTERNET

My principal concern is how the immediacy and searchability of the internet (in particular, the World Wide Web) influences the development of Islamic religious authority online. Traditional authorities are challenged and usurped online by contenders whose authority is based as much on digital proficiency and online networks as on traditional training and values. The algorithms of Sheikh Google and re-tweets of Imam Hashtag mediate among the information overload of fatwas and religious opinions. When Islam is always on, does this aid or impede clarity and understanding of religious values by Muslims? How does social media affect notions of religious understanding?

These issues combine a contemporary focus with a resonance in traditional frameworks associated with Islamic history and religious development. Networks and micro-networks that have emerged in cyberspace reflect this combination in processes that inform their members (and also observers) about historical and contemporary influences on the interpretation of Islam. Generated and circulated with immediacy online, religious opinions and decisions have a basis in and continuity in traditional spheres of knowledge and religious engagement. In the constantly changing contexts of CIEs, awareness of information technology developments is a crucial adjunct to activities and agendas in the analog worlds of Islam and Muslims. In some cases, analog and digital cannot be separated.

Understanding technological interfaces is increasingly important in developing a comprehension of contemporary Islamic issues and their dissemination. The continual evolution of interfaces, software, and hardware must be accommodated within academic interpretations. Some are recent innovations, quickly adopted by users; consider the exponential growth of Facebook, YouTube, and Twitter in the first decade of the 2000s and the impact of enhanced forms of internet access through mobile devices such as smartphones and tablets. There is a tendency for publicity surrounding jihadi online zones to obscure dynamic and vital aspects of everyday online Islamic activities. Mundane religious practices, business, shopping, chat, and social networking do not make international headlines but are as equally significant as the jihadi sites that attract so much contemporary media coverage. A digital native generation, combined with increased net literacy and access, has had a profound impact on CIE development.

An overarching transformational effect on the practice of Islam can be observed, influencing the representation of Islam to the wider world and the ways Muslim societies perceive themselves and their peers. On one level, this affects practical performance of Islamic duties and rituals and the interpretation and understanding of the Qur'an. On another level, there is exposure to radical and new influences outside of traditional spheres of knowledge and authority, causing paradigmatic and seismic shifts at a grassroots level within societies. The emergence of social media, including Twitter and Facebook, has accelerated these changes.

For digital natives, expectations in terms of communications and content acquisition are markedly different and have evolved substantially, in line with a reduced digital divide. The physical act of using a deskbound computer in order to access the internet is anachronistic; mobile devices provide connectivity and access on the move. Interfaces heralded as game changers, such as Google Glass, have not been as successful as their developers intended. Wearable technologies, such as the Apple Watch, introduce new ethical issues and ritualistic responses. Options for internet access continue to increase: my gym has web-enabled machines, giving access to social media while I try to get fit, although it does not make me run any faster. This is part of an envisaged Internet of Things that may, in time, incorporate physical religious objects and symbols in a dynamic way.

There are different expectations and approaches to Islam, Muslims, and the internet. Impact may not be scientifically measurable. Proximity in terms of time makes it difficult to determine other patterns, until a greater amount of time elapses between the period of observation and the writing of any analysis. The impact may be subtle rather than overt, and it combines with numerous other factors. It is not the intention here to provide a quantifiable, scientific calibration of the transformative capacity or impact of computer-mediated communication on Islam, Muslims, or CIEs. Determining the measures would necessitate extensive international surveys and resources. This book seeks to steer future research in this area and act as a reflective guide within the processes associated with formulating methodologies and multidisciplinary approaches in the field.

The ways in which interpretations of Islam by pro-jihad platforms and organizations has captured public attention is reflected in this book. For some, Islam and the internet have become synonymous through the publication of online magazines and videos, including the emergence of post-al-Qaeda platforms associated with the Islamic State. Jihad-oriented campaigns by networks including al-Qaeda have been influenced by the internet, which has made a significant difference to the engendering of Islamic activism and radicalization. Jihadi networks and organizations have used the internet as a logistical and publicity tool for many years; after 9/11, attention and speculation focused on their internet presence. Adept application of the net, including free web space, encryption, and anonymizing tools, have allowed al-Qaeda and others to skillfully manipulate press agendas and promote their worldviews across the globe. For some, this represents Islam in its entirety on the internet. *Hashtag Islam* demonstrates that multifarious jihadi output *is* an important strand of Muslim expression, which requires focused attention and understanding, but it is not the full picture relating to Islam and cyberspace.

A variety of theoretical perspectives contribute to this dynamic and ever-expanding field. These determine this book's influences and contribute to other perspectives of CIEs.

THEORETICAL APPROACHES

Theoretical perspectives aid the exploration of communication and the internet. A brief survey of these sources follows, with emphasis on how they shape ideas of Islam and the internet. It places the book within the context of existing scholarship to determine the connections (if any) with significant ideas associated with communications, Islam, and cyberspace.

Perspectives on Media and Communications

An early study of media impact by John Dewey suggested that people were actors, not simply spectators, and that education presented a role in developing critical awareness. Dewey's significant early studies were a foundation for later works on media and interpretation of communication. For those with the appropriate impulse and disposition, Dewey stresses the importance of opportunity within education in relation to intellectual interest.[2] Notions of a passive audience have played out in many interpretations of Islam and the media. These negate the critical and engaged approaches utilized in responses to media projections about religious issues and are linked to educational issues in relation to critical thinking and its special relationship with received wisdom and acceptance (rather than challenging) of religious tradition. Within a contemporary context, such notions influence how information from the internet and other sources is received, filtered, and interpreted. In subsequent chapters, this book explores how some traditional religious contexts see a challenge to dominant interpretive formula as a subversive and dangerous activity.

In relation to the study of the media, reference is frequently made to Marshall McLuhan and his focus on the impact of the global village. Here, ideas and issues are shared beyond the traditional analog boundaries, including geography and nation-state barriers. McLuhan explored how communication is shaped by media technology, comparing different forms in relation to immediacy, sustainability, and transportability. The focus of analysis should be on the media being the message, according to McLuhan.[3] Media in various forms shape dialectical and communicative content.[4] This is relevant, as diverse types of media influence ideas about Islam and Muslim societies. The dynamics of the internet has led to an evolution (if not a revolution) of information flow and projection of authority, shaping contemporary understandings of religion when technology is accessible and available. Expression of Muslim religious values can change in line with the forms of communicative technologies presented. This may be a limitation, in terms of the character restrictions of a Tweet, but it may also be an opportunity, in terms of potential audiences and immediacy of impact.

The boundaries between reality and representation, as explored by Jean Baudrillard, suggest that mass media has had a profound impact that can define the world. Hyperreality, a form of discourse based on media forms, is a key element of postmodern world perceptions. In his discussion of the break from what Baudrillard saw as modernity, the concept of hyperreality suggests that perceptions are shaped through the synthesis of individual behavior and media content (the latter being based around other media content, which may lack a basis in "reality").[5] These technologically focused constructions affect forms of online religious expression generated within diverse Muslim digital worlds. This links into ideas on differentials between religion online and online religion.[6] Is the Islam presented online the same as the Islam experienced in analog dimensions, or should there be a separation between the two contexts?

These ideas can be connected to Michel Foucault's work, including discussion on knowledge construction and how its application controls groups and societies.[7] There are ramifications on the internet, as diverse interests generate, manipulate, and represent information about Islam and Muslims. The work of Roland Barthes is influential here, in his analysis of the structuring of images and signs to convey specific meanings within societies and cultures.[8] The explicit and implicit meaning of symbols within religious contexts has relevance online. Specific codes of etiquette and symbolic application are embedded within digital content. These notions are explored later in *Hashtag Islam*.

Jürgen Habermas has also played a distinct role within the development of theories associated with the impact of mass media on formulating public opinion. He discusses the "public sphere" (*Öffentlichkeit*) within the Enlightenment period, focusing on the salons of London and Paris in the seventeenth and eighteenth centuries. Their impact on generating specific dynamics of interface and debate between ruling classes and the bourgeoisie challenged hierarchies of power and authority during that period. There is a sense that, for Habermas, the public sphere engendered principles of democracy through a public discussion of shared concerns by individuals on an equal platform. Habermas describes how in the nineteenth century, the media interfaces that had been utilized to encourage debate were compromised and corrupted through the machinations of industry and state power, meaning that any democratic development was to an extent negated.[9]

This exploration of the mediation between state and society within the public sphere is important, especially concerning the ways in which information flows and how media institutions have an impact on issues of opinion and control. Habermas analyzes how communicative action can be divided into the elements of instrumental rationality, in which technology is applied to achieve specific goals, and communicative rationality, where the use of reasoning is applied to reach specific forms of understanding.[10]

A dynamic between publicity and public opinion, described by Habermas as "structural transformation," suggests that uncritical consumers can be manipulated by public opinion when mass media exert influences over reason. Through generation of specific forms of discussion, mass media can establish control of public policy, which affects the formulation of public opinion.[11] Media can pressurize authoritarian governments, but the role of media as articulated by Habermas is degraded in the light of government influence and commercial media concerns. The importance of media as a means of influencing opinion—in contrast to the public sphere letting that opinion evolve—has led to an erosion of critical perspectives.

Habermas's paradigms are challenged by critics who suggest that the salon culture related specifically to higher social classes and that the public sphere was exclusive in relation to issues that legitimized inequalities, including gender, class, and ethnicity. During the period of the salon culture, education and property ownership influenced access to the public sphere. The idealized bourgeois public sphere was not necessarily a reality. Critics have suggested that Habermas treats people as passive recipients of media.[12] Habermas reassessed his ideas in later work, being more optimistic with regard to the participatory elements of modern media and how the public sphere is constituted.[13]

Can the notion of the public sphere be relevant today, in a society that is no longer bound by print, given that Habermas originally wrote in a pre-digital context? Dynamic changes in information access and availability have challenged our notion of the public sphere.[14] Ideas about passive consumption of media are still relevant, along with media construction, but the impact of social media and public forums have led to new dimensions of participatory opinion formation, including within CIEs.

Can elements of Habermas and the related critiques be brought into our understanding of Islam and the internet, raising issues of globalization and parity in relation to some of the conceptual frameworks? There is certainly a distance of culture, time, and geography between the seventeenth-century London and Paris salon cultures and Islamic contemporary contexts. Habermas held a specific Eurocentric perspective in relation to the media, one not necessarily relevant when looking at the dynamics of participation, authority, and religious understanding within Islamic frameworks. However, aspects such as the passive consumption of information and knowledge, together with the control and influence of the media, are clearly relevant within some Muslim frameworks. The Muslim public digital sphere(s) vary from cyber-location to cyberlocation, often without a physical equivalent, being located more within Baudrillard's hyperreality. Key players attempt to use technology to promote the goals of religion, including faith perspectives, ideological and political influence, and adherence to specific worldviews.

As will be seen in *Hashtag Islam*, technology elements such as apps are used to develop what is defined as "instrumental rationality" by Habermas. They draw on specific key Islamic sources and influences to develop communicative rationality, with particular forms of reasoning applied to reach religious and spiritual understandings. Different dimensions of objective and factual information in relation to core religious values are found in Islamic public spheres. They feature aspects of specific subjective interpretive approaches, which guide normative perspectives of religion. Depending on the context, an individual consumer of this online information may not have had a choice in terms of challenging these perspectives. The internet is used to challenge many normative ideas about Islam, from outside and within CIEs, including the ways different opinions about critical topics are addressed and how traditional authorities and other globalized or regional players present challenges on Islamic issues.

Conflicting ideas about religious understanding play out within the public sphere online. Traditional approaches toward religious understanding and identities can be shaped by the media in a way that Anthony Giddens describes as "self-reflexive."[15] There is flexibility, in the sense that the shaping is dependent on issues of media access and censorship, in which the freedom to present a narrative or identity is contingent on location and digital literacy. Giddens suggests that social media does not affect identity formation within this self-reflexive process.[16] This notion is contradicted, however, by the evidence of participants in CIEs whose religious and other identities are formed directly through online interaction and by those individual digital natives who feel compelled to consistently articulate and document their lives through social media.[17] Such expression can include their religious identity and affiliation, alongside a multiplicity of other identities in complex online interactions. Giddens disputes Baudrillard's notion of hyperreality, however, while recognizing that media open users to wider world views.[18]

Specific theoretical perspectives on networks and virtual communities are significant within *Hashtag Islam,* such as the ideas of virtual communities and internet connectivity explored by Howard Rheingold in discussions on the prototype Whole Earth 'Lectronic Link (The WELL) community of 1980s San Francisco. Viewed through the prism of our current digital connectivity, ideas contained within this period can seem somewhat idealistic. The potential negative elements associated with computer-mediated communication were flagged by Rheingold.[19] The internet rapidly became a commercial entity, with associated issues of control and surveillance countering the positive aspects of sociability. However, as I noted in 2000, Rheingold's projections associated with interconnectivity had a resonance within CIEs.[20]

Manuel Castells has focused on networking to address connectivity and the alignment of patterns of social communication. He provides a conceptual framework for the understanding of an informational economy in which components and networks of interaction feature.[21] This framework was within a business economics context, but I have previously suggested that this model of networking and interaction also has relevance within CIEs. Castells also critiqued existing research on the internet in what he described in 2001 as the "rather sterile debate" in the early phase of the internet and an "absence of a substantial body of reliable empirical research on the actual uses of the Internet."[22]

The challenges of a networked world have been significant for Castells. He presents awareness of issues surrounding monopolization by political and commercial interests of network infrastructures and has articulated concern about the ways in which individuals can be excluded from significant areas of communication.[23] These are factors that are particularly important when exploring ideas about CIEs today, where elements of control can feature strongly within certain frameworks. Such control can be at a state level, through censorship and filtering, but can equally result from cultural restrictions on internet usage, even in an age of increased digital literacy and networking access. There are indicators that internet access restrictions continue for some individuals and communities within CIEs.

When viewing works on contemporary religion, the impact of the internet is often underrepresented or absent from the otherwise credible output of academics. However, the use of the internet for religious purposes is a growing area of study and publication, including general works associated with religion and the internet and religion and media. These have helped establish fields of study, which have gone through significant changes in line with shifts in media forms and usage. It is relevant to survey some of these sources here.

Discussions on religion and the media include formative works by Stewart M. Hoover and Lynn Schofield Clark (together and separately), which engage in important methodological concerns associated with studies of religions and media, including responses to satellite television.[24] Specifically, in relation to religion and the internet, Jeffrey K. Hadden and Douglas E. Cowan's edited publication in 2000 introduced approaches to the subject area, including cutting-edge theoretical material and contributions from early theorists in this developing field.[25] Significant edited collections of associated studies have refined approaches, two emerging from international academic conferences.[26] This is important, given that the subject was receiving more academic attention and credibility where there had previously been resistance.

A greater granulation of content emerged within the variety of studies that contribute to the understandings about religion and the internet, including guides to online resources associated with religions and cyberspace.[27] An early overview of issues related to computer-mediated religion was provided by Gwilym Beckerlegge, who explored methodological concerns as a basis for further study.[28] Approaches to the significance of sacred time and virtual pilgrimage were provided by Brenda E. Brasher, who provided a phenomenological analysis of religious online content.[29] The University of Heidelberg commenced the production of the *Journal of Religions on the Internet* in 2005, featuring significant works by scholars on different religious perspectives.[30] Detailed studies of specific religions and the diversity of sacred (and other) online phenomena within them include Heidi Campbell's study of Christian communities online, Christopher Helland's studies of Buddhism, and Douglas Cowan's analysis of cyberpaganism.[31]

A dynamic relationship exists between works associated with the study of diverse religions online and the study of Islam in cyberspace. I have found it beneficial to operate to an extent in both areas. A great deal in the way of shared practice and approaches can be gleaned from sources such as those discussed above, which contribute significantly to understandings of contemporary religions in general. There are also some specific disciplinary and methodological variations in relation to the study of Islam in cyberspace.

Perspectives on Islam, Muslims, and the Internet

The intention here is to provide an overview of the contributions made by scholars influential in developing approaches to the study of Islam and Muslims in cyberspace. It has been a dynamic period regarding approaches to contemporary Islam in general and in relation to the internet in particular. Specific focal points of studies are increasingly granulated. However, it is difficult to build a perspective when CIE issues are taking place contemporaneously with the writing of books and chapters. This immediacy of content is a personal issue for myself, as I have occasionally drawn on the news of the day during the writing process.

My own output presents snapshots of specific time periods and phases, from the emergence of Islam on the internet onward. The formative phase was covered by *Virtually Islamic*, post-9/11 contexts are explored in *Islam in the Digital Age*, and the emergence of forms of social media ("Web 2.0") and their implications feature in *iMuslims*. Other work explores aspects of online discourse and activity in depth.[32] Approaches to methodological concerns have evolved, including the recording and observation of online materials. One consistent element has been rooting the work in the intersected zone of religious studies and Islamic studies. These works reflect changes in technology and the interface dynamics, which have shifted substantially from the early days of discussing CIEs.

Specialists within the study of Islam have made contributions to the field, reflecting diverse disciplinary perspectives and interests. The work of Bruce B. Lawrence and miriam cooke (together and separately) demonstrates a conscious academic approach toward the internet's impact on forms of Muslim discourse.[33] Important studies have emerged, referring to the interactions between the media, Muslims, and society. These works recognize the internet as a significant channel for diverse forms of Muslim communication, integrated into other forms of dialogue and interaction.[34]

Academic recognition of the significance of the internet as a tool for Islamic discourse takes numerous forms. Studies on the media, including the internet, explore their influence on the Middle East.[35] Some scholars use fieldwork to interpret notions of political liberalization in Arabic-speaking contexts.[36] Work on religion and spirituality in networking includes analysis of how anonymity is applied for Islamic purposes.[37] The emergence of entrepreneurial CIE elements shows the development of apps facilitating prayer, Islamic finance, and marriage.[38] As part of a wider gaming spectrum, online games feature Islam-related products and project educational and proselytization strategies for organizations and commercial concerns, alongside other forms of digital communication.[39]

Gender issues are an important zone of CIE research, open to further development given the potential multiplicity of themes within different and currently underrepresented religious and cultural contexts. Useful work has emerged, including the role of cyberspace in Islamic dress discussions and a consideration of how gender-specific approaches affect interpretation issues within online discussions.[40] Studies include explorations of how computer-mediated communication creates a sense of place and belonging for young Muslim women in Denmark, the United States, and the UK.[41] Such studies relate to concepts of female self-representation in CIEs and the development of female online subcultures.[42] Through social media, Muslim women develop relationships in ways very different from the ways they do so in the analog world.[43]

The range of research on Islam and the internet encompasses surprisingly diverse subject areas: a study of Islamic emoticons goes beyond traditional scholarship of Islam in showing how the digital Muslim symbols influence computer-mediated human interaction.[44] Ideas of religiosity are approached in methodologically innovative ways, such as the examination of search engine logs, providing a highly technical key to CIE research.[45] General studies on religion and social media have also included chapters or content relating to Islam and the internet.[46] Substantial scholarship is emerging from younger generations of academics who have applied some of the work mentioned above to build their own theses.

One cannot assume that the internet is such a significant game changer in every context, and care has to be taken with any underlying assumptions as to its efficacy and impact.[47] Political elements relating to online activities have held a particular significance, however, given complex shifts in contemporary Muslim contexts. Numerous works seek to increase understanding of the real-world impact of online activities, reflecting ongoing and intensive fieldwork, together with regional specialisms.[48] In zones with high-tech connectivity levels, the dynamics affecting change in the Arabic world are substantial.[49] Internet change agents influenced Muslim political contexts and related social movements such as the Arab Spring and its aftermath.[50] Such developments became the focus of analysis on relationships between social media technologies and revolutionary movements.[51]

Understanding of CIEs in general, and specific regional situations in particular, has been enhanced by academic projects that provide benchmarks for research, analysis, and models of good practice. The Berkman Klein Center for Internet and Society at Harvard University produced a detailed and informed analysis of the blogosphere, visualizing 6,000 Arabic blogs from a baseline of 35,000 blogs. This captured a significant snapshot of blogging activity in a formative period of Arab internet development.[52] Numerous studies relate to civil engagement within Muslim social media.[53] Studies on youth, religiosity, and family values in relation to the internet emerged from Muslim contexts.[54]

Radicalization and its relationship to the internet has become a growing issue for governments, committees, and advisers. Controversial efforts have been made by some parties to stereotype and profile Muslim communities in a homogeneous manner, especially in relation to approaches to internet radicalization. Such actions can feature in official publications. In the United States, the Republican chair of the House Committee on Homeland Security was condemned as racist during 2011 hearings on radical Muslims.[55] Some academic perspectives on terrorism have been criticized for support of American policy.[56]

Studies on jihad-oriented online activities can counter the sensationalist media and print journalism that has fed the frenzy of speculation about changing forms of jihad online.[57] Research on counterterrorism has focused on semantic approaches to locate those with shared perspectives.[58] Valuable works have concentrated on particular regions, with a subtext of how the internet is informing and stimulating e-jihad developments.[59] As will be seen in the chapters on jihad, studies within the field represent specific challenges and face a number of barriers that may not be found within conventional academic studies.

CONCLUSION

Hashtag Islam reflects the complex and expanding field emerging in response to religious, social, and technological changes in Muslim contexts and shows how work in this multidisciplinary and interdisciplinary subject continues to develop. The next chapter explores ideas associated with interfaces utilized in accessing CIEs, including social media and specific forms of technology. There is a direct relationship between these elements and contemporary understandings of CIEs, so it is appropriate to consider how they function.

Changing Digital Spaces

Islam, Technology, and Social Media

It is hard to imagine the world these days without social media, found in so many virtual and analog contexts and spaces. The phenomenon of people status-checking as they walk is as common within Muslim contexts as it is in any other. The reduced digital divide and access improvements have rapidly made social media a global phenomenon, through tools such as Twitter, Facebook, Snapchat, WhatsApp, and Instagram.

Increased mobile phone access to the internet, rather than through desk-bound devices, and the concept of true mobility of access have meant an exponential increase, across languages, cultures, and contexts, of channels disseminating information about Islam. Connections made between and within networks have evolved so that even groups and channels adverse to technology recognize the need to step up to the challenges of social media. To make an online impact, this means developing a constant, regularly updated online presence.

Earlier cyber-Islamic environment phases saw contention of digital space between existing and new authorities, where technical literacy and creativity led to a greater market share than that held by more staid, technologically adverse players. This pattern has extended into social media, with the sophisticated use of content development stimulating emergence of new Islamic voices and influences. New Islamic identities based around social media constructs have emerged.

The importance of a viral hashtag rapidly reaching an extended audience is as much about good marketing as it is about the content; Marshall McLuhan's aphorism of the media being the message is as appropriate within CIEs as anywhere else in the ways that personalities and groups present understandings of religious interpretation to global or regional audiences via social media. Internet-literate and digital-native audiences draw on online Islamic content in much the same way that they do on other areas of life; yet while there is a greater dissemination of specific messages and the ability to tap into particular authorities or individuals, there is also greater competition for increasingly finite attention spans on social media. Muslim social networking is not restricted to issues of religion: "It is . . . where Muslims discuss cooking skills, relationship problems, political views, economic concerns and even meet their long-lost High School crush."[1]

Islam may continue to be always "on," but the babble of content and distractions means that strategic approaches must be made so that messages reach intended audiences. Like among other demographic groups, the projection of individuals and groups as being media savvy, with hip tech abilities and professionally presented content, influences social media within Muslim contexts. Some parties capitalize on this, to draw in and maintain online audiences, developing brand loyalty in the process. The sense of connection, albeit through a mobile device, combines with other channels and within virtual and analog contexts. Social media offers an entry point into content transcending the original 140-character limits of a tweet and into more developed and refined materials. It is a competitive business, with popular social media suffering the effects of competition from alternative dissemination and content production models: Telegram and Snapchat have eroded usages of channels such as Twitter and Facebook. For some, Twitter has become passé, with other tools being used to access material and activate peer-group discussion. Having said that, relatively long-standing channels have maintained significant audience shares, including within Islamic contexts.

UNDERSTANDING ISLAMIC SOCIAL MEDIA SPHERES

Given that it is the rule, rather than the exception, for key players to have high levels of technical literacy awareness within their organization, can we still discuss any form of discourse within political and religious spheres in Muslim contexts without reference to the internet—and in particular to social media?

Consideration of social media in Muslim contexts suggests it is a significant game changer in relation to articulation of religious values and concepts. The extent to which this has become a cliché is open to question. There can be a simplification of paradigms that ignore the bigger picture. Attention has focused on social media application in prominent events such as the 2009 Iranian Green Revolution and the Arab Spring and its sequential aftermath. These distract from more mundane social media applications and other events played out online away from media glare. Developments in the Middle East in 2010–11 and the Arab Spring were referred to as the Facebook

Islam, Technology, and Social Media

Revolution or Twitter Revolution, but these terms were open to question. Overemphasis of digital activism negates factors associated with economics, politics, human rights, and poverty, which themselves are change agents. Aspects of the Arab Spring played out in diverse locations and contexts via the internet. This facilitated and publicized elements of protest, even though in retrospect the optimism articulated during this formative phase was dissipated by a grim and negative reality for many participants, especially in Egypt, Yemen, and Syria.

During the Arab Spring, relatively small protests received rapid coverage through domestic and satellite television broadcasts, repurposing cell phone clips and reports posted online. In Tunisia and Egypt, Facebook and Twitter were applied through use of hashtags, which helped users follow events. Campaigns were not Islamic in orientation, although some key participants had Muslim identities (on a number of levels). Some Muslim platforms did not engage fully in demonstrations, such as Egypt's Ikhwan al-Muslimin (Muslim Brotherhood).

Protests continued in various forms in Libya, Bahrain, Syria, and Yemen. At each stage, events were accompanied by extensive online activities via Twitter feeds and reportage from the public sphere, including religious invocations, symbols, and language. Organization and promotion of protests drew on online resources, with every stage digitally documented and disseminated. Parties previously reluctant to use social media acquired technological literacy to capitalize on the increasingly youthful and digitally literate participant demographic.

INFORMATION BREAKDOWN: SOCIAL MEDIA USAGE

By 2010, social media users were in the ascendancy in the Middle East, although traditional media forms still played a role. The *Arab News* noted that "as of May 2010, Facebook has more than 15 million users in the Middle East and North Africa, easily surpassing for the first time the region's newspaper sales of just under 14 million."[2] A 2015 study by Northwestern University in Qatar, based on research in Egypt, Lebanon, Qatar, Saudi Arabia, Tunisia, and the United Arab Emirates, suggested that, overall, there were subtle declines in use of Twitter (from 48 percent in 2014 to 40 percent in 2015) and Facebook (from 89 percent to 83 percent) in these areas, while the Facebook-owned photo app Instagram had substantial growth (from 6 percent in 2013 to 28 percent in 2015). A 2016 survey suggested that younger users of Twitter (ages eighteen to thirty-five) used the platform from two to six hours a day, while older users (ages thirty-six to fifty-five) were on Twitter from thirty minutes to two hours a day.[3] Messaging tool WhatsApp held a 77 percent (and rising) share of the social media platform usage table, topped only by Facebook (at 83 percent).[4] While not indicative of the entire Muslim sector, this report shows competitive factors within platform provision and demonstrates that different interest groups utilize forms of social media to circumnavigate censorship (in some cases). It should be emphasized that religious concerns form a small but significant component or subtext of online conversations through these media forms.

Technological business developments mean that some players have developed a greater influence in relation to social media content and distribution within Muslim contexts. For example, Jordanian servers hosted substantial amounts of Arabic content, due to a technological boom that was enhanced during the Arab Spring. The International Telecommunication Union noted that by 2015, Jordan was hosting around three-quarters of Arabic content on the internet.[5] This is a lucrative and potentially influential sphere, which can go beyond traditional geopolitical borders.

ACCESSING THE INTERNET

Shifts in technology hold significant implications for CIEs, which evolve in line with minor and major adjustments in software, hardware, and interfaces. Increased content became available in diverse "Muslim" languages and scripts. For example, Arabic content grew substantially online, ranking eighth globally in usage and expansion.[6] Such growth led to sustained increases in technological developments within Muslim contexts, including content creation for commercial and other purposes.

Availability of non-Latin-character web domains became a further innovative element, enhancing access to online content and further reducing the digital divide.[7] Arabic top-level domains emerged in 2010, allowing functional websites with suffixes such as .arab, .emarat, and .qatar (in Arabic).[8] Arabic was the fastest growing language on Twitter in 2011, with demand rising exponentially across platforms and devices.[9]

Concerns were expressed that the internet would damage Arabic language use, through hybridized Arabizi (English and Arabic).[10] A counter to this was the emergence of Arabic-friendly social media, including Twitter, which offered input in Arabic.[11] Tools such as the Microsoft Maren app provided Arabic and other language transliteration, useful in a variety of web contexts.[12] Arabic language markets became economically significant for key players such as Google, which intensified development of Arabic search and advertising products.[13]

The digital divide continues between and within Muslim societies, and basic internet access remains a core concern. While an educated elite may have access, at a grassroots level there are still major gaps, which represent an element of control by authorities. Innovative measures have been introduced to overcome these barriers. Profound technological shifts have an impact on reducing the digital divide in creative ways. In Bangladesh, this was because of a combination of old and new technology: "Amina Begum had never seen a computer until a few years ago, but now she's on Skype regularly with her husband. A woman on a bicycle brings the Internet to her."[14] Solar power has been considered as an option to enhance accessibility.[15]

This type of innovation does not necessarily mean that religion is a key content driver. Rather, it is recognition that even basic internet access offers potential social, cultural, and economic benefits, whether this is simply mobile phone access or something more developed. The International Telecommunications Union noted in 2015 that "of the 940 million people living in the least developed countries . . . , only 89 million use the Internet, corresponding to a 9.5 percent penetration rate."[16] The same report noted that, even in developing countries, four billion people (two-thirds of the population) were still offline.[17] These least developed and developing countries include substantial Muslim populations, affecting the assessment of CIEs. Therefore, one would not wish to be too idealistic in terms of the transformative elements of the internet in Muslim contexts.

There are zones, though, where it has cut across boundaries and provided a real voice for marginalized groups and individuals. Social media is applied to tackle long-standing, controversial issues, including concerns about gender issues and issues of gender. Blogger Dalia Ziada used her online channels to criticize al-Azhar's tacit support of the face veil and suggested that the internet was having a positive impact for women activists.[18] The fusion of social media and activism has given voice to individuals and groups; for example, emojis featuring women in different styles of hijabs have emerged for use on social media.[19]

Assessing internet access is reliant on diverse factors; whereas in the past, computer access was the paramount issue, now mobile telephone and tablet access are key drivers in developing internet markets. Mirroring concerns in other societal contexts, some religious authorities have felt that internet penetration can lead to developments detrimental to societal and Islamic interests, including a perceived negative impact on morality.[20] For example, it was reported that pornography is a key component within usage statistics in Muslim-majority (and other) contexts. The filtering of pornography offers legitimacy to imposition of control within other internet zones. [21] As with other elements of the World Wide Web, care should be taken when determining the amount of pornography in cyberspace. Some suggest figures are sensationalized, being based on data quantities rather than on individual usage clicks on sites. Researchers exploring the proportion of pornography on the internet determined that "in 2010, out of the million most popular (most trafficked) websites in the world, 42,337 were sex-related sites. That's about 4 percent of sites."[22] This statement came from one of the writers of detailed academic research on pornography use.[23] While the figures are still substantial, it does suggest an element of proportionality in relation to such online activities, although a zero-tolerance attitude may be prevalent in many Muslim contexts. Conversely, there have been online opinions selectively approving some forms of pornography within traditional relationship settings.

Similar concerns were expressed in other contexts, where control was sought for religious and political reasons. In Malaysia, the Islamic Development Department (Jakim) suggested in a sermon that there should be specific Islamic parameters for internet use.[24] Censorship takes many forms. Along with several other countries, at the time of the Arab Spring Saudi Arabia suspended specific systems of communication deemed dangerous to the state. This included the BlackBerry phone system, which effectively was beyond censorship at that time. The United Arab Emirates followed a similar path, banning email, web access, and messaging.[25] This ban restricted confidential messaging, with implications for the personal lives of users as well as for potential political and religious impact. In Pakistan, frequent blocking of social media for reasons of religion also helped prevent the antigovernmental use of the internet. The blocking of services such as YouTube was not popular publicly, but censorship could be mitigated by providing a religious edge to the justification.[26]

CONTROL AND SOCIAL MEDIA

Cheaper, more accessible information technology is not a panacea for societal ills. It is significant, however, for religious content distribution, alongside more mundane content. Access to material can be restricted by societal and cultural barriers. Production of material deemed subversive, challenging, or threatening to societal norms is subject to restriction or censorship. There can be restrictions or punishments for posting "inappropriate" content online in relation to Islam.[27]

Within and between diverse Muslim contexts, contrasting reasons have emerged associated with demands for internet control. It can be linked with efforts to prevent various forms of activism, such as during the Arab Spring, where assorted techniques were utilized to avoid censorship.[28] In Muslim contexts, examples emerged where bloggers received substantial jail sentences for online activities. In 2010, pioneer Iranian-Canadian blogger Hossein Derakhshan received a considerable sentence in Iran for online campaigns but was released in 2014.[29] Threats to online activists also came in the form of personal attacks, with four secular bloggers being killed in Bangladesh in 2015, allegedly by religious activists.[30] In Pakistan, social media personality Qandeel Baloch was killed in 2016, allegedly by her brother in an "honor killing" after she posted challenges to societal gender norms in diverse media.[31] Other examples later in this chapter highlight that, while a significant potential driver for social and religious change, internet utilization was not without its dangers or difficulties for online commentators, whose profiles rose in line with technological innovations and a reduced digital divide.

Monitoring and controlling information has a long history predating the internet, with a continuity of themes. Specific morality concerns, associated with sex and sexuality, also influenced web-control advocates. These issues, of course, were not Muslim-specific, reflecting wider discussions. Technological fixes linked to generic internet controls were universally applied with culturally and religiously oriented filters. In Kuwait, it was denied that state authorities were monitoring Twitter posts and referring "offenders" for prosecution.[32] Turkey introduced a content filtering system that blocked not just pornography but also sites referring to evolution and Charles Darwin.[33] The Turkey-Google relationship was fraught, with access to specific Google sites being limited or shut off; YouTube was banned for hosting videos allegedly insulting Mustafa Kemal Atatürk.[34] Coup attempts and subsequent prosecution of Fethullah Gülen supporters led to sustained internet filtering.[35]

In many Muslim-majority contexts, religion is a key factor associated with censorship.[36] Even locations with relatively low internet access levels, such as Afghanistan, have banned forms of online content seen to conflict with Islam.[37] But using antifiltering software and other tools, technologically literate individuals often find ways around censorship. Technology from Western companies have facilitated different forms of censorship, including during the Arab Spring, leading to criticism for aiding (directly or otherwise) filtering and censorship.[38] Conversely, several agencies have offered advice on evading censorship: Access Now provided information on protecting online activities for users in a range of contexts.[39] In some cases, advice led users to the Dark Web through interfaces such as the Tor browser.[40] When issues associated with religion were paramount, censorship was seen by some as a positive action, even by digital natives. In Afghanistan, positive reactions were expressed in support of censoring YouTube even among younger demographics when concerns about religious representation emerged.[41]

Pakistan is an additional zone where internet censorship is significant. The Islamic Republic's relationship with technology has fluctuated, in line with political and religious shifts. Around 2010, access to popular sites and services was frequently restricted, but religious content often escaped the censors and "religious hate material" was easily obtained online.[42] Whether deliberately overlooked or not, that situation did not continue when the Pakistan Telecommunications Authority blocked internet services.[43] Critics expressed concerns that forms of censorship stifled discussion about religious values in Pakistani society.[44] In 2012, Pakistan authorities blocked Twitter for offensive images that insulted the Prophet Muhammad. Complaints were made to Interpol after authorities failed to convince Twitter to remove the offensive tweets.[45] In 2013, the government realized that it was politically expedient to develop a more nuanced approach to censoring content deemed blasphemous.[46]

In India, FatwaOnline.in religious scholar Mufti Aijaz Arshad Qasmi engaged internet content providers in a legal action to determine what they had done to block content described as against Islamic precepts. This case reflected wider issues of what is deemed offensive and blasphemous and how that should be judged in local, regional, and global contexts. He was successful in his action, in which the court determined that defamatory material had been posted by the defendants.[47] After the case emerged in 2011, Qasmi's website was defaced by hackers.

Internet companies were reluctantly embroiled in religious issues, especially at times of crisis. When a film perceived to be anti-Islamic was produced in the United States and hosted online in 2012, Google blocked access to it for internet users in Jordan.[48] Developing appropriate responses to social media became problematic for several governments. Religiously motivated censorship was utilized in some cases as smoke and mirrors to deal with more secular content issues, including political satire.[49]

Motivations for demands to control and censor were complex, reflecting contrasting concerns about religious discussions on social media, from legalistic issues to spiritual dimensions. In a Nigerian dialogue on sharia punishments, Ustaz Safiyan Abukarar of the Association of Muslim Brotherhood of Nigeria noted, "Facebook and Twitter are unholy place[s] to talk about Sharia, doing that is an intimidation and undermining of the teachings of Islam."[50] Spiritual dimensions of social media were viewed with suspicion, especially in relation to forms of popular religion. In Malaysia, concerns emerged that the posting of photos online could lead to them being used for witchcraft, with one authority in Kelantan stating that "djin (spirits) are able to 'connect' with humans through the Internet, including Facebook."[51]

Within some CIEs, concerns about popular religion and spirituality indicate another dimension (in every way) associated with complex censorship and control demands. The concept of a djinn in the machine is not necessarily controllable with conventional software(!). Such notions challenge conventional and traditional religious authorities, especially online, where proponents have a sustained presence. These are real elements and concerns for many Muslims, when understanding of Islam goes beyond legalistic models into realms associated with popular, complex, and diverse concepts of spirituality—a zone of angels, djinn, and ethereal beings.

COMPLETE CONTROL? SAUDI ARABIA
AND IRAN IN PERSPECTIVE

Saudi Arabia

Notions of the public sphere in Saudi Arabia are affected by religious and cultural considerations, by the use of the internet in general, and by social media in particular. Saudi Arabia had 18 percent Facebook penetration in 2014 and 1.9 million active Twitter users. The kingdom had the most Twitter users in the Middle East region, while it lagged behind the United Arab Emirates (41.66 percent), Jordan (31.9 percent), Lebanon, Qatar, Tunisia, Kuwait, and Bahrain with regard to Facebook users.[52] By 2016, Saudi Arabia had 25 percent Facebook penetration (7.96 million users) and 20 percent Twitter penetration (6.37 million users). Messaging was dominated by WhatsApp (8.59 million users) and Facebook Messenger (6.37 million users).[53] In 2012, Riyadh was deemed the most active Twitter city in the Middle East; the most active Muslim-majority population city overall on Twitter was Jakarta, Indonesia.[54] In Saudi Arabia, YouTube offered alternatives to state content and influence—and citizens became "the world's most avid watchers of YouTube."[55]

Control of Arabic content presents religious, economic, and political implications. It can be lucrative and influential to regulate technology in general and social media in particular. Control is contested in Muslim-majority contexts and markets, as have been opinions about the presence of social media within some regions. This has played out in Saudi Arabia, with its strong Middle East and Muslim business connections with social media, especially in zones of high influence and authority: Saudi Prince Alwaleed bin Talal owned a 4.9 percent passive stake in Twitter in 2017.[56] Paradoxically, perhaps, Grand Mufti Sheikh Abdul-Aziz Al-Sheikh of Saudi Arabia attacked the microblogging site, "calling it 'a council for jokesters' and a place for unjust, incorrect messages."[57] This did not stop anonymous government members from using Twitter, who were criticized for not posting photos or providing personal information. In line with the generic image provided for those not posting their photo online, they were described as "egg people."[58]

The relationship between improved access and cultural shifts in Saudi Arabia can be felt on all sides, with a variety of perspectives benefiting from access to internet media. This is demonstrated in the ways in which traditionally oriented authorities utilize social media: "Being increasingly wired, however, will not necessarily bring Western-style liberalization. Religious conservatives use social media as adeptly as liberals, and many young Saudis remain committed to and proud of their culture. Even those who want change say it must come gradually."[59]

Saudi Arabia has seen numerous contestations on the application of the internet. Previously reluctant parties have engaged with the media and its processes, under pressure from alternative perspectives emerging online. Facebook has become a forum for varied outlooks on religious issues and reacting to pressures of everyday life, including the questioning of long-standing religious traditions and values.[60] Social media is a natural zone for interaction and discussion, on serious as well as more mundane issues. There has been a suggestion that more males than females were active in social media,[61] and in Saudi Arabia, concerns arose that internet growth would lead to more intermingling between the sexes and the erosion of attendant cultural and religious values.[62] The internet certainly became a place for self-expression and exploration of values.[63]

Posting on social media has led to detentions and prosecutions. Saudi Arabian law professor Mohammed Abdallah Al-Abdulkarim was detained in 2010 for writing online about splits in the royal family, resulting in sustained criticism, locally and internationally, questioning the legality of his arrest. Supportive pages and feeds in social media emerged, although according to critics, local media were avoiding the issue.[64]

By 2011, Saudi Arabia had introduced legal measures to restrict certain forms of online content, including that deemed as disobeying Islamic law.[65] Despite this, numerous official viewpoints recognized the need to present themselves online, including the Facebook Committee for the Promotion of Virtue and the Prevention of Vice or "religious police" (Hayaa). In Damman in 2013, the Hayaa were a target of vitriol when a woman shopper protested against their closure of a shopping center's dinosaur model exhibition.[66] Reactions to this were tweeted in real time; social media had become a platform for everyday issues, often with a religious subtext.

Authorities and activists in Saudi Arabia and the Gulf have promoted "positive" attributes associated with social media, including its role in women's education.[67] Activism in Saudi Arabia circumnavigated censorship in a 2010 YouTube campaign promoting female driving. It featured a "No Woman, No Drive" video based on Bob Marley's song "No Woman, No Cry." Social media played a significant role in showing participation in the protests. Women driving in defiance of the ban used a hashtag to represent the day of protest: "I will drive on #Oct26, even if I have to run over every bearded man in my way," said Fatima al-Faloul, a thirty-one-year-old Saudi mother of three. "I have two young daughters, I will not allow them to face the same frustrations I have faced."[68] The campaign's central figure was Manal al-Sharif, who eventually was forced to leave Saudi Arabia, ending up in Australia (where she continued her campaigning).[69] In the same period, ironically, a Saudi Girls Revolution app was released that allowed Saudi women to drive—but only virtually.[70] In September 2017, a royal decree announced that Saudi women would be permitted to drive.

Filtering and censorship took a variety of forms: in 2010, Facebook was blocked and temporarily closed in Saudi Arabia in response to the emergence of pages deemed anti-Islamic.[71] In 2011, censorship in Saudi Arabia was deemed as growing in intensity.[72] By 2012, the kingdom was considering legal approaches concerning online blasphemy. The 2014 *Penal Law for Crimes of Terrorism and Financing* permitted criminalization of free expression and was followed by a royal decree and a separate set of Interior Ministry regulations that defined any critical expression of the government as "terrorism." This included Article 1: "Calling for atheist thought in any form, or calling into question the fundamentals of the Islamic religion on which this country is based."[73] Subsequent court cases convicted individuals of incitement for social media comments against religious and other authorities in Saudi Arabia.

Saudi expectations for online content production included that writers of electronic newspapers were government-registered Saudi citizens, at least twenty years old.[74] However, barriers previously inhibiting knowledge development dissolved in line with increases in digital access, especially social media use. Concerns about social media included how it might be applied in the kingdom to mobilize different forms of activism, such as the 2011 Day of Rage protests promoting democracy.[75]

Activities on social media, in particular with religiously themed content, have led some individuals to prosecution. A Saudi journalist was accused of being an apostate after tweeting about the Prophet Muhammad, having been previously deported from Malaysia for the same offense.[76] In a separate case, blogger Raif Badawi was publicly lashed for comments about Islam presented on the Saudi Free Liberals Forum.[77] Despite international protests, the first fifty lashes were meted out in 2015, although ill health delayed further punishment.[78] Badawi was the subject of the international campaign #JeSuisRaif.

Contestation for internet influence and authority in Saudi Arabia was tempered with realization that economic benefits were to be had with the acquisition of international Muslim audiences online. Such concerns were not unique to Saudi Arabia, however, and are reflected in other contexts as well, as discussed below.

Islamic Republic of Iran

In a reflection of analog life, while there is a contestation of online influence between Iran and Saudi Arabia, there are issues of commonality in approaches to the quest for internet control. But some Iranian technological approaches have been different when filtering and managing online activities.

With a projected population of over 79 million in 2017, Iran had a substantial potential user base for social media (although data acquisition of figures of social media use are limited, due to restrictions on Twitter and filtering on Facebook). A 2012 survey indicated that 58 percent of the population used Facebook.[79] In 2016, it was suggested that Telegram—a messaging app with high levels of end-to-end encryption, which means that it can evade some forms of censorship[80]—was the most popular social media application, followed by WhatsApp and Instagram.[81]

Iran sought to develop a country-specific internet infrastructure immune to external influences, indicative of international political and strategic developments and reflecting societal concerns that went beyond the internet.[82] The intention was for the network to be substantially faster than previously but also easier to control.[83] Iranian platforms (official and other) promoted a variety of activities, including hacking; the Iranian Cyber Army launched high-profile hacks against political-religious opponents of the government and generic targets such as Twitter.[84] In addition, Iranian authorities censored websites associated with ayatollahs whose views did not match those of the government.[85] In 2011, an Iranian cyberpolice unit was established, focusing on the online conflict between Iran and the United States.[86] Still, Iranian internet infrastructures were affected by the Stuxnet worm in 2011.[87]

Iranian censorship led to some retribution by other governments, reflecting the complex equation between religious-cultural values and technology.[88] The Iranian government suggested that internet companies could operate unhindered in Iran if they followed "cultural rules."[89] Yet Iranian authorities recognized that forms of censorship were ineffective and difficult to police. Ali Jannati, President Hassan Rouhani's culture minister, said that if the "Qur'an was not sent from God, Iranian censors would have rejected it." In a recent speech, he admitted that Iran's policy of filtering the internet or blocking satellite channels had proved futile. "It's like blocking the entire highway for the violation of a few cars," he said. "The best way to control public opinion is to go with it not to fight it."[90] Elsewhere, President Rouhani challenged claims from some religious factions, including Ayatollah Ali Khamenei, about the "immorality" and "un-Islamic" nature of the internet.[91] Khamenei's office maintained a Twitter account from 2009 and provided a regularly updated personal website.

By 2016, plans were announced for the first phase of the Iran National Data Network, based on fiber-optic cables substantially faster than the existing network, albeit under specific forms of religiously influenced control.[92] Concerns regarding control extend to the social media apps available on mobile networks, with Telegram drawing on 40 percent of available bandwidth in 2016 and the Cyber Police being unable to access its servers: the authorities sought the development of locally sourced equivalent apps, which could be more easily controlled.[93] The relative anonymity of apps such as Telegram and WhatsApp offer Iranians opportunities for discussion outside of the observation and control of authorities. The contention between religious authority and digital control, which started in the early days of the internet, continues to play a role in Iran.

ISLAMIC SOCIAL MEDIA ALTERNATIVES

Concerns about the nature of Islamic content online led to development of Islamically focused alternatives. Social media platforms MillatFacebook in Pakistan and more globally oriented Salam World had limited impact despite substantial launch publicity.[94] In 2015, Muslim Face was announced:

"Adopting the slogan 'by Muslims, through Muslims, to the world,' the unique social network aims to bring Muslims closer together through its smart features, fresh trends and spiritual inspiration."[95] Muslim Face promised Qur'an quotes, prayer times, and a FindSpouse feature that included *mahram* (chaperone) filters to ensure appropriate contact between genders.[96] Other social networking products have also emerged, including Ummaland, Salamyou, and Masjidway.[97] The "Islamic State" announced its own short-lived social network in 2015, 5elafabook.com.[98]

In 2010, the Muslim Brotherhood in Egypt launched its IkhwanBook social media outlet.[99] The pages promoted the Brotherhood agenda, organizing members and supporters as part of a proactive media strategy, which was curtailed only after Muhammad Morsi's fall in 2013. In Egypt, further social networks emerged, such as Naqeshny, which could be logged into via Facebook. This was advertised as an arena for debates, in which parties could be linked with others of similar interests (denoted by colors).[100] None of these products made a substantial impact or change in Muslim social networking usage away from "generic" products, such as Facebook.

In Iran, social networking was also presented with an Iranian edge, in the form of Velayatmardan (meaning followers of the *velayat*, or supreme leader). The site included photos of Ayatollah Khamenei and cartoons against political protests but did not supersede Facebook, Twitter, and other forms of social media in Iran.[101]

External influences, from Muslim and other sources, influenced conversations about religion in a variety of contexts. Indonesia, the country with the highest world Muslim population, was particularly attuned to these developments.[102] Indonesian internet users had a strong focus on social media: "With even cheap cell phones in Indonesia sold already bundled with Facebook applications, for many, 'Fesbuk'—as it is written in the national Bahasa language—simply is the Internet."[103] Despite an urban/rural digital divide, engagement with Twitter and Facebook became a national preoccupation in Indonesia.[104] In 2016, it was estimated that there were over 80 million social media users, focused in Jakarta.[105]

Attempts at launching social media spaces with a Muslim focus continue, although levels of success so far are limited despite the potential markets. So far, no platform has been able to achieve sufficient momentum or market capture to challenge mainstream players. Public preference has been to remain with popular sites such as Facebook and Twitter. This is in contrast to the development of apps, discussed below, a further potential channel of knowledge, information, influence, and control.

As with Islamic social media platform development, there are numerous examples of attempts to develop interfaces with an Islamic emphasis. Alongside the plethora of web interfaces, Islamic apps provide additional options with mobility and utility in mind. Technological developments do not pay attention to ethical-religious considerations. A response has been the evolution of diverse tools and complex options for information access, integrating technology with traditional approaches to Islamic knowledge and religious legal interpretation. The result is an array of apps that can affect everyday religiosity, observation of precepts, and expression of Islamic identity—from relationships to eating habits.

According to industry analysts in 2015, specific online services for Muslim markets were at a critical juncture.[106] The Islamic knowledge economy featured numerous Islamic apps, with encouragement given to their development through practical events; this included an app-building Haqqathon in the United Arab Emirates that sought to "create viable ways of fusing technology and faith to bridge the gap between Islamic scholars and young people."[107]

App-development has been a significant adjunct to online discourse and understanding of Islam. A multitude of products on Android and Apple iOS platforms have functionality for hajj, Ramadan, prayer, Qur'an recitation, and zakat collection.[108] In 2017, Google introduced Qiblafinder, part of its wider RamadanHub, as a means to locate prayer direction toward Mecca.[109] Further apps have emerged in line with market shifts, data growth, and technological developments.

Inevitably, concerns have been raised on how apps are or should be utilized in sacred spaces such as Mecca. Apps also link to other forms of internet media, providing essential guidance and reminders on core religious issues. Social media is a location where Islamic sources find new audiences. For example, the divine revelation of the Qur'an, received by the Prophet Muhammad from God via the angel Gabriel, can be found in the Twittersphere. Apps are discussed in more detail in the next chapter.

As well as the apps and software loaded onto phones, social adaptations toward technological use require reconsideration of conventions and approaches to information dissemination. There is recognition of a nuanced perspective on social media in CIEs, influencing specific sectors more than others.

CONCLUSION

The expectations that major international technology and internet corporations will necessarily comply with the demands of religious authorities and scholars are unrealistic unless there is an economic bottom line and impact. Integration of multimedia and globalized religious discourse into online frameworks, through constantly streaming channels of information and knowledge pumping out data to rapidly increasing audiences, has dramatically altered paradigms of religious authority—even in zones where internet access remains relatively low. One key element here is the changes in mobile concepts, from desk-based origins to always-on cell phone usage focused on social media, in which CIEs can be part of surfing habits for many people.

Social media has become a key driver in many Muslim contexts, associated with diverse issues, including those directly linked to Islam. Rather than being a novelty, it is embedded into the thoughts, actions, and activities of key individuals and groups with diverse interpretative and political agendas. It can be integrated with apps or multiplatform perspectives on Islam and Muslim issues. Technology is a subtext to the conflicts, religious issues, and intimate personal data that jostle for attention on social media, assimilated into many forms of Muslim digital conversations.

Status Update

Islamic Dimensions of Faith in Cyberspace

DIGITALLY INTEGRATED MUSLIMS

This chapter explores how the internet became digitally integrated into dynamics of Islamic religious issues and faith, often with a seamless divide between offline and online components. Digital concerns are a subject for analysis and discussion by religious authorities. In fully wired zones inhabited by digital natives, fewer conversations emerge on how these issues are innovative or unique; there is a natural acceptance that digital interfaces are of specific importance for religious performance and ritual. The concept of Islam being not just spiritually but digitally always on is significant. Reactions to particular issues and circumstances are streamed and articulated through digital formats, discussed and circulated rapidly for consumption within and between different networks.

The permutation of digital content into numerous aspects of religious expression may not be to everybody's tastes. Some say Islam should be a digital-free zone unencumbered by technology. Another perspective is that technology facilitates many aspects of religious knowledge and experience. Without these interfaces, opportunities to fulfill religious precepts and demands could not be taken. It is open to question whether there is now an obligation to go online every time new Islamic circumstances and issues emerge.

Similarly, to solve a particular religious question, should the approach be to search a digital text, read a printed source, or consult a scholar locally or via the internet? This may seem a strange quandary in an era where requirements of prayer come through mobile phones, fatwas are delivered by Twitter, and religious discussions are observed online in real time or revisited through numerous archives. Every pronouncement and opinion is recorded. Opportunity for contemplation of an issue or a gradual dissemination of information may be lost in the immediacy of digital media and their audiences' expectations.

Not all readers and users of an online resource demand daily updates, let alone minute-by-minute tweets; in fact, these may be intrusive. It can be difficult or impossible to achieve a balance between online religious activities and other forms of digital life. Even in mosques, sermons are now filmed, tweeted, and streamed to international audiences. One is reminded of when Muhammad requested fifty daily prayers and was talked down to five daily prayers by Moses during the Night Journey.[1] A separation of space may be desired between constant streaming of religious information and other everyday activities. While it may be seen as commendable to interlace conversations with religious phrases, so that one is constantly reminded of religious duties, it may now be the case, when digital media are on 24/7, that such things are a form of dysfunctional bombardment. Having said this, there is evidence that the use of Islamic apps assists individuals with busy working lives in reminding them of religious duties.

Those unable to reach religious buildings or interact with authorities due to distance, work, health, or cultural or religious barriers (including gender-specific obstacles) are helped online. Exposure to scholars and other shades of opinion is granulated. New forms of knowledge can be acquired outside of traditional cultural and religious contexts. What "traditional" precisely means is open to scrutiny: intergenerational differences exist between ideas on religion and its place within society, along with distinctions between and within communities at all levels. Whether or not internet technology makes the individual a better Muslim is in the eye of the beholder (or a Higher Power). Taking an iPad to the mosque and studying religious digital content can be as commendable and spiritually valid as studying more conventional printed media; listening to recitation online provides spiritual merit to individuals if its content and context is appropriate.

Digital devices are utilized to broaden religious horizons, for example through exploring various manuscripts and collections or debating influences with peer groups in different locations. Does it matter whether an individual uses electronic interfaces to study the Qur'an? If intent is sincere and the objectives are met, there may be much to commend this action. Searchability of the digital Qur'an can answer questions with greater precision. The option to follow Qur'anic recitation online and learn its meaning and pronunciation rules enhances prayer.

The balance of religious online activity with other daily internet interaction can be significant: to what extent does it form a major or minor proportion of overall surfing activities? Shopping, chat, entertainment, and some of the more dubious elements within the internet such as gambling or pornography can play a part of an individual's personal online habits. Can these interests be segregated from purely religious aspects of online activity?

Every element of life may be permeated by religion. Nuanced apps and sites offer answers to significant contemporary questions within Islam. A further important question is this: Who monitors this material or provides the page content? With the right tools and knowledge, setting up an internet presence is straightforward. There are many examples of Twitter feeds being created by individuals purporting to be particular personalities. Inputting of text can be prone to mistakes (deliberate or otherwise). To what extent is it possible to monitor the authenticity of Islamic materials? Is this necessary?

It can be difficult to maintain focus on what is going on in cyber-Islamic environments, given the petabytes of data that have appeared in relation to Islamic religious questions. Censorship attempts are problematic. Authorities cannot always control adherents' online activities. Immersive 24/7 online content has intensified as part of the overall demands of religious identity and activity. When censorship can be facilitated, for example at the state level, this can channel and manipulate audiences toward specific endorsed perspectives. To an extent, this might reflect notions of consumer manipulation and erosion of critical perspectives, as explored by Jürgen Habermas. Censorship can also be linked to prosecution, in some cases negating the impact of virtual public spaces' ability to challenge power and authority. These spaces become regulated and controlled, a reflection of their analog equivalents.

For some groups and communities, it is imperative that followers using online tools are able to keep up to date with activities. This perpetual reminder, bordering on the obsessive, affects ideas about religion and identity. Reacting to user demands for online content and in an attempt to broaden online influence CIE service providers have developed nuanced ideas of audiences and their stratification. There may be user and service provider expectations based on notoriously inconsistent elements of web access levels and internet surfing habits. One significant change agent has been increased opportunities for digital interaction. Has the potential for inserting religion into everyday life increased?

Anecdotally, there is some evidence of this increase in religious online products having an impact on individuals: people use apps to facilitate prayers or to generate calls to prayer when no muezzin is available. Individuals point out that there are profound moments where religious actions have been made possible. Apps can also facilitate religious activity and extend notions of sacred

Android Store results for "Koran" search, https://play
.google.com/store/search?q=koran&c=apps&hl=en.

space into virtual zones. It was noted in Indonesia that during Ramadan and
Eid al-Adha, apps were essential to fulfill religious obligations.[2]

Issues relating to the pros and cons of internet use have emerged. For instance, the *Los Angeles Times* reported that "an influential Iranian ayatollah is
telling his students to spend more time praying and less time clicking through cyberspace,"[3] but there are contrasting perspectives associated with the popularity
of specific religious leaders in this regard. In the context of Iran, opinions relating
to the internet can vary substantially. In 2014 President Hassan Rouhani stated,
"We ought to see (the Internet) as an opportunity. We must recognize our citizens' right to connect to the World Wide Web."[4] Rouhani suggested that modern
means were available to face any "onslaught" that the internet might engender.

A counterargument to fears of digital distraction can be found in the
commercial edge to Islamic online products and services. Tariq Ramadan has
suggested that "in a hi-tech age, with its instantaneous processing of information and global competition, Islam is profitable. No doubt about it: Islam
makes money, plenty of money. Caught between ideological manipulation
and the logic of capitalism, Islam—and with it the fate of Muslims—finds
itself in a negative, not to say oppressive, dynamic."[5]

Islamic Dimensions of Faith in Cyberspace

Conflicts between being spiritual and being capitalist may not exist. There are many Islamic business models providing a halal approach to commerce. Muhammad's wife Khadija was a successful trader who encouraged her husband into business. Could the Prophet's approach to business ethics be reflected online? The Prophet does not negate profit. The following section shows ways in which the dimensions of faith are marketed online.

DIGITAL MEDIATION OF THE QUR'AN

The digital mediation of the Qur'an is the latest phase in the history of what is, according to tradition, a divine revelation revealed to the Prophet Muhammad via the angel Gabriel between 610 and 632 CE. From its original memorization by Muhammad and subsequently by his early followers to the recording of fragments on bone and parchment and the recension of the text into a definitive edition, the Qur'an has been recited, read, memorized, and copied over time in every location in which Islam has spread. It has also been disseminated through diverse media, taking advantage of technological developments along the way, from paper to print to broadcast media to the internet.[6]

Numerous websites featuring the Qur'an in various editions and forms have emerged. While there is consistency in terms of the Arabic text content, creative digital interfaces can reflect design innovation and technological aptitude. Often integrated into sites with a broad Islamic focus, Qur'anic content includes entry points into commentaries, sermons, advice, resources, multimedia recitations, and religious opinions or edicts). Qur'anic material is frequently associated with specific Muslim worldviews or ideologues. Political portals and activist platforms promote agendas through Qur'anic text. Qur'anic context is integrated into social media, such as Twitter, Facebook, and Tumblr. Organizations and individuals utilize YouTube and other media channels to present recitation, with reciters ranging from professional exponents of the art of *tajweed* (recitation) to those appearing on home videos, even children. Ownership of the Qur'an is represented in a number of ways online, although some organizations and individuals seek to monopolize control over audiences.

A site intended for an academic scholar familiar with classical Arabic will be different from a site intended for newcomers to Arabic and Islam, containing translations of the meaning of the Qur'an and related commentaries. Points between these two poles demonstrate creativity, financial investment, and diverse approaches toward the Qur'an in its many forms. It is a revelation that has to be listened to, read, recited, and reproduced with an accuracy and consistency of pronunciation and printing. A change of one Arabic diacritic point can have an impact on the meaning of a word. Within these parameters, websites provide a multiplicity of approaches to this divine source, including opportunities to learn the text phrase by phrase with meanings attached in translation; there are also variations in translation, which can alter the subtleties.

An immersive Qur'an experience can draw upon the multiplicity of recitations uploaded online. This is not a new phenomenon. With technological developments, interfaces have evolved from simple MP3 audio files of short extracts to fully interactive and visual recitation models. The use of apps provides Qur'an access in an interpersonal and highly accessible portable format across a range of platforms. Resources utilize prayer time finding (via GPS), sources such as prayers and sayings (*ahadith*) of the Prophet Muhammad, and adherent networking opportunities.

Integration of Islamic sources in social media tools ranges from daily tweets of Qur'an verses to utilization of hashtags to promote specific interpretations, translations, and worldviews. Twitter's @quran and @dailyquran lend themselves to the character limitations of the format, given the length of *'āyat* (or verses) within the Qur'an.[7] Social network channels provide the Qur'an to audiences ranging from the curious to the academic; for some, it is the only way to access the Qur'an, whether through text, recitation, or translation. Digital interfaces assist audiences unable to interact with other formats; deaf Muslims, for example, campaigned for translated sign language versions of the Qur'an.[8] The internet provides ways to study the Qur'an at every level; for example, university databases make Qur'an resources accessible for research. Initiatives have included digitization of rare Qur'an manuscripts, bringing together dispersed and fragile manuscripts online.[9]

Accessing the Qur'an and other sources online has been endorsed and supported by Muslim authorities. The Ifta (fatwa issuing) center of the Abu Dhabi General Authority of Islamic Affairs and Endowments issued a fatwa permitting access to the Qur'an on smartphones and other interfaces, drawing on the Qur'an to justify the decision: "Reciting a verse from the *Al Muzzammil* chapter in the Quran, the fatwa says: 'Read you, therefore, of the Quran as much as may be easy for you' (20:73)."[10]

The dissemination of the message of the Qur'an can be conducted through media channels and devices with a commercial and competitive edge, necessary to support research and development. As with apps in other sectors, Qur'an materials for mobile devices require software updates in response to technological and user demands. The ways in which materials are approached via search engines is significant: the placing of a Qur'an site or service within a Google ranking, for example, can be dictated by complex factors associated with metadata and linkages, and its position influences the amount of site traffic it receives. Once a surfer is on a site or viewing a product, the amount of time spent using the source is significant, being contingent on content and design issues.

As with other software, free editions and enhanced editions requiring payment are available: the Guided Ways website offers multiformat Qur'an tools and downloads and a searchable Qur'an and hadith database. Its iQuran was available across platforms.[11] iPray featured automatic *adhan* or call to prayer alerts, enabling precise prayer timing and *qibla* (direction), and an Apple Watch app.[12] Obtaining the precise time to pray is an important ritualistic element in Islam, based on scientific calculations. A number of websites (also accessible via mobile devices) provide nuanced calculations based on more precise locations, given that there are subtle differences even within a time zone.

Numerous Qur'an apps have emerged on the market, offering levels of interactivity, including note recording and sharing capacity. Apps feature specific reciters, language translations, and tools for teaching children to read and recite.[13] Other Qur'an products included *al-Mushaf*, a reproduction of the Qur'an in Arabic by Egyptian company iPhoneIslam. There was a sense of familiarity of layout, typeface, and ornamentation in the digital copy, echoing traditional Qur'an manuscripts.[14]

Whether such sources are appropriate or necessary within a mosque setting is debatable. Some copies of the Qur'an come with exegesis (*tafsir*), and apps incorporating such commentaries and interpretations are popular. The meaning of the Qur'an has been translated from Arabic into many languages. Familiar printed editions are found in official and unofficial online versions; for example, English-language versions predominate by the classic orientalist A. J. Arberry, as well as by Abdullah Yusuf Ali, Marmaduke Pickthall, and Muhammad Asad. Elsewhere, the Qur'an is available for e-book download.[15]

THE QUR'AN IN DIGITAL FOCUS

Numerous online products present interfaces through which to encounter Islam's core values through the Qur'an in translation. It is problematic to select one or two, as sites appear and disappear with alarming regularity. When my research on Islam and the internet commenced in the 1990s, there were only a few Qur'an-related sites. Now there are thousands. Some key players have disappeared over time or merged into other sites, as site maintainers went on to other things (especially student developers of online databases). Technological innovation has brought in new content providers as well. For example, the music streaming service Spotify features numerous reciters and styles.[16]

The website IslamAwakened.com emerged in 2003, encompassing apps and social media. Each verse in the database has an Arabic page accompanied by all relevant English translations available (according to the site organizer). Discussions on moral commandments, etiquette, and Muhammad and Jesus are provided, alongside links to an online Qur'anic Arabic pronunciation course and a curious juxtaposition of Qur'an extracts and Google ads. Over fifty different Qur'an versions in English are listed, each linked to Amazon book pages. Translations can be compared line by line, with audio files, transliteration, and the opportunity to donate to PayPal. Extra levels of content include a verse of the day and an Android app with forty-one Qur'an translations.[17]

IslamAwakened can be compared with Tanzil.net, with its focus on multilingual Qur'an translations, from Albanian to Uzbek. Within the listing of more than 115 translations, the greatest proportion (16) are in English, available to download or browse in an encoded format (UTF-8). Visitors to the site can mouse over translations, and each sura is browsable, with twenty-six Arabic recitation recordings and translation audio in Azerbaijani, English, and Persian. Prior knowledge of the text is necessary to take full advantage of the site.[18]

More complex online services have emerged, offering different recitation options. For instance, on Assabile.com, a page associated with Saudi imam Abu Bakr Al Shatri offers portions of the Qur'an sorted by traditional order, chronological order, numbers of verses, place of revelation, and the most listened to categories. A biography of Al Shatri and feedback from various users of the page are also featured. This is one example of a series of recitations available via the Assabile website, downloadable for free on MP3 and with user feedback options. In total, the multilingual site includes 18,622 recitations, along with sermons, over 500 Islamic songs, and more than 5,500 lessons. Famous reciters appear in video clips from various occasions. For example, Abdul Rahman al-Sudais's page includes four recitation videos in Mecca and photographs of him with various personalities and in performance.[19]

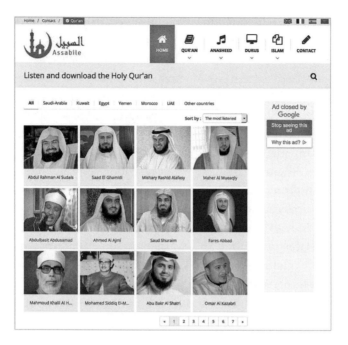

Home page of Assabile, http://assabile.com.

Content produced in Egypt demonstrates concerns and issues associated with the digital Qur'an. In the 1990s, after initially dismissing internet technology, al-Azhar University in Cairo was propelled into providing an internet site as a reaction to the SuraLikeIt site that was producing fabricated verses purportedly in the style of the Qur'an.[20] The university's later projects to bring manuscripts online was not deemed successful, leading to other groups and platforms seizing the opportunities to exert religious influence online.[21]

Concerns arose as to who was providing certain elements of online advice and interpretation. Some parents were worried that radical individuals were inculcating from a distance.[22] In Pakistan, online instruction in reading and recitation of the Qur'an became big business internationally, and delivery platforms blended aspects of social media into their formats. Providers struggled to recruit suitably qualified scholars to provide Skype lessons, and demand increased, especially from parents seeking to negate the online influence of the "Islamic State," which led to increased scrutiny of materials available through the internet.[23]

Qur'anic (and other) multimedia contributed to the CIE array, including within Shi'a Islam. A prominent example is the website Al-Islam, established by the Ahlul Bayt Digital Islamic Library Project in 1998. It licensed the Arabic Qur'an from Tanzil.net and provides translations from Marmaduke Pickthall and Abdullah Yusuf Ali; in addition, the site features two Shi'a-oriented versions from M. H. Shakir, and Agha Pooya Yazdi and S. V. Mir Ahmed Ali, which place emphasis on Ali ibn Abi Talib and the imamate.[24] Al-Islam also provides information on Qur'anic sciences, and the Online Ahlulbayt Quran Center offers distance-learning Qur'anic recitation courses.[25]

Contentions regarding the successors to the Prophet Muhammad, reflected historically in the split between Sunni and Shi'a Islam, also play out in cyberspace. As with other aspects of the perceived differences and intrafaith dialogues between Sunni and Shi'a Muslims in some contexts, issues of recitation can be mired in controversy. Numerous sectors of Shi'a cyberspace contain aspects of recitation. From sound files to video clips, they represent diverse locations where Shi'ism is found. Recitations from the Imam Ali Shrine in Najaf and Imam Husayn Mosque in Karbala circulate on social media.[26]

The ways in which the Qur'an is mediated online has presented a shift in reading styles and perspectives. Digital content offers more sociable reading opportunities, including discussions on "authentic knowledge."[27] Searching for key terms and concepts is a significant aspect of this equation. Depending on search parameters and device reliability, instantaneous responses to specific questions are available. This can mean that the complexity and subtlety of the Qur'an are lost to online readers, if they do not approach the text in its entirety and read or absorb it through traditional methods. Similar arguments might have been presented in the transition period between aural mediation and the production of the written (and codified) Qur'an, or indeed in the time between written and mass-printed texts.

Some initiatives have achieved impact, in terms of providing either academic resources or focused material for specific communities. The development of translated Qur'ans is a key part of propagation efforts. Provision of the Qur'an in multilingual translations has been a core element of online activities in CIEs. It represents technological innovation and flexibility in response to shifting patterns of digital consumption. Not all languages are fully represented online, although information marketplace gaps are continually being filled and updated. These will form the technological and religious foundations for future Muslim digital worlds and versions of Islamic life online.

Islamic Dimensions of Faith in Cyberspace

The hajj was an early feature of pioneer CIEs. Over time, text-only descriptions on initial websites were augmented with photographs, film clips, graphics, and interactive features. Social networking material discussing the hajj then linked to film clips and personal accounts. Some experimental content represented contemporary manifestations of the pilgrimage guides, which have roots in the early days of Islam.

A broad range of products has been introduced for the use of pilgrims during hajj. Utilized on cell phones and tablets as software became more sophisticated and the digital divide reduced, the number of hajj apps and related content has increased. Hajj has a commercial edge in the online marketing of hajj travel packages, bookable via the internet. Multilingual pilgrimage advice is featured on official Saudi Arabian websites. Specific religious interpretations aid in pilgrimage preparation and organization. Effective pilgrimage through mapping apps, drawing on GPS tools and technology, facilitates successful fulfillment of hajj objectives. For those with digital access, the internet and mobile phone access are natural channels for acquiring advice and information about the pilgrimage.

However, mobile phones could impede the spiritual dimensions of the hajj and *umrah* (minor pilgrimage), according to critics. A prohibition of filming near the Ka'bah has not been strictly followed by pilgrims, although use of phones for hajj selfies and tweets is discouraged.[28] Not all parties necessarily appreciate the presence of mobile technology in the precincts of the Ka'bah, suggesting religious reasons for this, as in the *Arab News*:

> "How can you focus on circling the Kaaba or concentrate on prayers when the guy in front of you is talking to his wife on his cell phone?" said pilgrim Imran Zahid.
>
> "There can definitely be a disturbance. This is a spiritual journey, a journey to develop ourselves from within. All that Internet stuff can wait."[29]

Despite this, the Saudi Arabian authorities made IT access improvements in the sacred precincts.[30] There were practical and logistical reasons for pilgrims being connected. When disaster struck prior to and during the 2015 hajj, social media (official and other) provided reportage and advice to the victims and their families. The sacred precinct of Mecca, known as the Haram, became Wi-Fi-enabled, while compulsory GPS-enabled wristbands were introduced to track pilgrims, control footfall, and advise on prayer direction and ritual practice.[31] Guides and satellite-linked apps taking pilgrims through every stage of pilgrimage implied mobile phone use in sync with participation, offering tutorials, ritualistic assistance, and an emergency assistance button.[32] Wearable technology embedded within digital content may acquire specific symbolism itself over time, as tools within religious processes, attaining meaning that might reflect Roland Barthes's ideas of explicit and implicit religious symbols.

The digital hajj benefits nonparticipants, who can view every pilgrimage station online. The internet can play a part in such rituals as Eid al-Adha, where the sacrifice of animals in celebration of Ibrahim's sacrifice is facilitated online; at one time, this sacrifice had to be undertaken by the pilgrims themselves.[33] Individuals also sell specialist and unique hajj products, including prized animals.[34] The extent to which the ritual slaughter of animals for Eid has simply become another online product or app is open to discussion, where apps smooth the processing and decision-making while fulfilling religious obligations.[35]

To add to the social media presence of the hajj, in 2017 tweets emerged from an account describing itself as @HolyKaaba. This page, in Arabic and English, provided short media clips and quotations from the Qur'an relating to ritual performance. A distinctive logo of the Ka'bah was used for each tweet. Although the account was registered in March 2017, its tweets started to emerge around the time of Eid al-Adha. These included a Periscope video showing the changing of the kiswa, the embroidered covering of the Ka'bah that is changed annually. By the conclusion of the 2017 hajj, the account had 35,000 followers for its seventy-six tweets.[36] It was significant that the pivotal focal point within Muslim worship and ritual now had a distinctive social media voice and identity.

Technology, health and safety, mass meat processing, and the rise in pilgrim numbers led to a hajj modernization process. The pilgrimage itself became open to wider scrutiny, from Muslims and other interested parties, through media coverage, including satellite television, conventional print media, and internet coverage—formal and informal, official and unofficial. This was evident in 2015, following the two major accidents in Mecca (one in the week prior to the hajj, one during events). Reactions were immediately conveyed by social media, including requests for disaster coordination, support for victims, and event actuality.[37] Comments played out on numerous hashtags, including #hajj2015, which continued to report on the victims in the days following the conclusion of the hajj.

Online expression extends to concepts surrounding the spirituality of places and spaces outside of the hajj. These include sites associated with the Prophet Muhammad, such as Medina and Jerusalem. Within Shi'a Islam, significant locations connected with the imamate and other key religious figures

Islamic Dimensions of Faith in Cyberspace

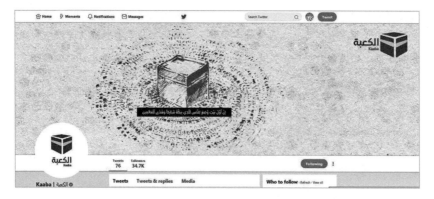

Twitter page of @HolyKaaba, https://twitter.com/holykaaba.

have acquired specific status for religious activity and pilgrimage. The tombs of Sufi saints have also taken on (for their followers) a special role. Add to these locations the importance of regional and culturally focused religious buildings and institutions, from city mosques to village shines, and one finds a wealth of places and spaces associated with Islamic expression.[38] Many of these are themselves becoming wired.

Traditional physical religious and sacred spaces have a virtual presence. Integration of online sources and hardware into traditional sacred space is an essential part of mosque development, supported by religious scholars and governments. In the United Arab Emirates, such integration includes sermons in languages other than Arabic.[39] The use of streaming media as a delivery method helps resolve problems of access to religious sites, rituals, and festivals.

The presence of digital technology in sacred spaces has raised issues associated with netiquette, ethics, and appropriate behavior—including cases where people have been using their phones during sermons.[40] There may be positives and negatives associated with high levels of mosque connectivity and with finite attention spans competing with alternative mundane and religious digital distractions.

CELEBRATING MUSLIM LIFE ONLINE

Technology is integrated into many facets of everyday Muslim religious life, including significant events and festivals. Ramadan increasingly features technological input from commercial and religious sectors. From a commercial perspective this is a lucrative market. Telecommunication companies launch products in Muslim-majority contexts during Ramadan or devise promotional activities at a time when mobile phone use reaches a significant peak and household spending and gift buying hit yearly highs. The month of fasting is also a focus for major international technological players: Google launched the Makkah Live YouTube streaming service from Mecca during Ramadan in 2011, in conjunction with the Saudi government.[41] Ramadan apps made an impact, with live Mecca feeds, Qur'an recitations, and special Ramadan online events.[42] Google additionally introduced a one-stop platform, incorporating links to recipes, Ramadan television, location-based prayer information, and interactivity options.[43]

Ramadan is significant for the launching of numerous television specials, also represented online. More significant, perhaps, is the issue of moon sighting within Ramadan. Accurate moon timing has long been an issue that has generated dialogue over the years. It affects prayer timing, festival dates, and fasting periods and reflects religious authority issues in diverse communities and contexts. Muslim organizations across international contexts appoint moon-sighting committees of experts to ensure accuracy, with opinions and timings circulated online. Established in 1993, Moonsighting.com has been a long-standing source, presenting international moon timings and calculations.[44] The resources of the Islamic Crescents' Observation Project also enable calculation of phases.[45] Crowdsourcing of data, in which the public send in their own moon sightings, further contributes. One organizer noted, "This can lead to some mistakes. . . . If people want to see it [the moon] then they will."[46]

A multiplicity of Ramadan apps and online material has led to calls for "detoxification" from the internet during that month. Despite this, technology is integrated into the contemporary Ramadan experience.[47]

FINDING ISLAM ONLINE

Online conversion has become a significant issue in CIEs, with opportunities for proselytization. This is, of course, not a new phenomenon, as it emerged in the early stages of cyber-Islamic discourse. The difference is that, through apps and interfaces such as Skype, there are more opportunities for personal contact and interaction, as noted in this excerpt appearing on OnIslam.net:

> Maryam, formerly known as Molly, was certain of her belief in Islam, and converted when she was only 17 years old. She still lived at home with her parents in the state of Arkansas. The nearest masjid [mosque] was over 100 miles away, and she had never met another Muslim face-to-face.

Islamic Dimensions of Faith in Cyberspace

Her only support was from Muslims she met online. While she gained some emotional support from them, she received very little else. The little she learned about Islam was from YouTube videos and Facebook groups.[48]

OnIslam.net advised that in some contexts, secrecy should be utilized for new Muslims; the internet could play a positive role in this regard.[49] In China, it was noted that through internet use, converts acquired knowledge of religious practices before setting foot in a mosque, through copying rituals on the internet.[50] Online conversion processes were also applied to negative effect in the jihadi sphere. Islamic State used technology to encourage conversion to (its version of) Islam and toward radicalization causes. This reflected the organization's strategic advice, based on similar al-Qaeda policies and influences.[51]

A consistent feature of CIEs is the stress on the internet being a cost-efficient tool for propagation of Islam, which has extended to social media, such as Twitter and Facebook. The engagement of interested parties in online conversations in order to encourage involvement and adherence extends across global Islamic contexts. Audiences include Muslims from different perspectives and those whose religiosity levels have lapsed. Amid sustained cyberchatter of celebrity and gossip, tweets and hashtags point surfers toward digital inspiration.

ISLAM, RELATIONSHIPS, AND THE INTERNET

Islam, gender, and sexuality issues dominate discussions about religious authority on the internet.[52] Relationships are constructed online but can also be damaged and destroyed. The internet is a significant element in relationship building, for those inside and outside of Islamic norms. Online marriage (if not dating) is an important component for communities and can present a commercial edge.

Searchable websites, with numerous filters based on religious values and cultural backgrounds, are big business.[53] The site SingleMuslim claimed over a million members in 2014 and four marriages a day.[54] HalfOurDeen.com seeks to maintain the privacy of its clients but keeps a tally of the matches achieved by its service.[55] Religiously charged opinion has emerged in relation to online marriage agencies.[56] In Nigeria, there was speculation that the sites wasted time: "In most cases it involves giving false impression about oneself just to win the heart of the man or woman. It also involves wasting our precious time in writing polished e-mails and exchanging worthless chats."[57] In Iran, however, the Islamic Development Organization launched an Islamic matchmaking site endorsed by the Supreme Leader.[58] An Islamic app styled after the Tinder dating app was also released, allowing users to post details without providing a photo. Other apps for single Muslims have been appeared in various markets.[59] The Muzmatch app includes a granulated questionnaire in order that precise details of prospective partners can be ascertained, demonstrating the needs and commitment of its customer base.[60] Although apps have become an important element for building relationships in Muslim contexts, resistance in some quarters has led to one developer providing a more traditional online component to its product, including the ability to check on the families and friends and the personal details of a prospective partner.[61] A website for men seeking second wives and for women seeking to enter a polygamous relationship has also emerged online.[62]

CIEs additionally feature long-term discussions on whether internet divorce is religiously permissible. This issue relates specifically to the articulation of the term *talaq* (I divorce you), the number of times the statement is made, and whether it is spoken face-to-face or transmitted through other means. The articulation of divorce through SMS, WhatsApp, Skype, internet chat, and other digital interfaces has been explored by scholars, with differing opinions emerging, from legitimacy to the suggestion that it mocks processes of law and authority.[63] Relationships are formed and broken on electronic media—and a spectrum of opinions can be found in favor of or against such activities.[64] Pronouncing *talaq* three times online was sufficient in one case for a man to divorce his wife, even when an "error" was made.[65]

The internet has been seen as a cause of divorce through encouraging "inappropriate" relationships and mixing between the sexes. In Malaysia, it was seen as a factor in rising divorce rates among Muslim couples.[66] CIE halal netiquette development has been increasingly necessary for authorities and individuals, leading to a multiplicity of responses.

Internet technology can be blamed for perceived personal and social transgressions, and parties go online seeking resolution to issues.[67] "Cyber-infidelity" has become a common issue for discussion in Muslim (as in other) contexts, with suggestions that it is the cause of increased divorce rates.[68]

Online expressions of lesbian, gay, bisexual, and transgender Muslim relationships date back to the early days of CIEs and have become technically more refined through social media.[69] Muslim religious campaigning

Islamic Dimensions of Faith in Cyberspace

Screenshot from Muzmatch, https://muzmatch.com/.

associated with gay marriage has also been represented online.[70] Additionally, the internet has been utilized as a means of entrapment in Muslim-majority contexts where such relationships are socially stigmatized or illegal, making online anonymity a critical factor.[71]

GENDER ISSUES AND ISLAM

Gender issues play out online. Muslim women discuss and explore religious interpretation and authority issues in relative online safety,[72] but use of the internet has been challenged by some (male) scholars and authorities.[73] The acceptability (or not) of online dialogues between the sexes has become a frequent theme online over the years. The development of specific netiquette has challenged authorities and scholars, as well as chat room and forum contributors. Some have suggested that online conversations should retain the same parameters as other forms of communication and dialogue.[74]

In Saudi Arabia, Sheikh Saad El-Ghamdi indicated that women could not log onto the internet without a guardian.[75] Opponents countered that there were many advantages of internet access for Muslim women, even when at times the result was inappropriate responses or trolling.[76] For instance, Saudi women used the internet to demand driving rights;[77] following prosecution of women wearing nail polish, protests were filmed and posted online;[78] and when a woman being flogged went online, dozens were arrested in subsequent protests.[79] Women-only internet cafés provide a safe space for online activities, including in Afghanistan.[80] Women can coordinate online to discuss and coordinate regarding their rights, especially in contexts where for religious and cultural reasons other forms of dialogue may be problematic.[81]

The ubiquitous selfie became the subject of online pronouncements, with Indonesian cleric Felix Siauw suggesting that the technology challenged the "purity" of women.[82] This resulted in the cleric being attacked online by women posting selfies.[83] Others authorities issued opinions on selfie-culture, including Dar al-Ifta in Egypt.[84] Egyptian activist Aliaa Magda Elmahdy protested the treatment of women by posting a naked selfie on her blog; #NudePhotoRevolutionary boosted the publicity. Predictably, this resulted in sustained protests and attacks on Elmahdy from various religious and political perspectives, and she sought asylum on the basis of death threats received.[85] She continued to blog and tweet about associated issues when out of Egypt.[86]

Ideas and attitudes regarding gender and religious values can be shaped through popular cultural expression, including fusion of musical styles. Examples abound: Syrian American rapper and poet Mona Haydar released two videos in 2017 that went viral with a focus on dress code issues, "Islamophobia," and empowerment. The first video, "Hijabi (Wrap My Hijab)," received nearly two million views on YouTube and featured Haydar (who was pregnant), surrounded by women with different hijab styles, proclaiming that she "Keep swaggin my hijabis, / Swag-swaggin my hijabis." Haydar's second video, "Dog," comments on being harassed through "DM" (private direct messaging though social media) by "sheikhs" and other nefarious religious figures.[87]

The notion of choice in dress code is also featured in Deen Squad's "Cover Girl (Rockin' That Hijab)." This track, performed by two Canadian male rappers, received over two million views in its representation of women in diverse locations wearing a hijab (and stressing their choice in this), including U.S. Olympic fencer Ibtihaj Muhammad.[88] Deen Squad member Karter Zaher also released the music video "Hijabi Queen," which was intended to link to a relating clothing brand. Deen Squad utilized its website and social media to promote products, mixtapes, and streaming media outlets, including those with different perspectives on gender issues.[89]

The fusion of dress codes and fashion feature widely on the internet, tapping into the substantial market for modest clothing and the wider halal marketplaces.[90] Muslim vloggers (video bloggers) have linked with fashion magazine Elle to present their approach to dress codes.[91] So called "hijabistas" present their style to tens of thousands of readers via social media. On Instagram, Dina Tokio has been reaching 1.3 million followers for her views, describing herself (tongue-in-cheek) as "A Modest Fashion Know-It-All."[92]

Mariam Moufid's @hijabmuslim Instagram page had over 880,000 followers in 2017, with fashion-oriented photos set against the backdrop of mosques and souks. From her base in Sweden, Moufid also blogs on hijab-oriented fashion, linking to various products.[93] A number of hijabistas synchronize their Instagram output with products from their own companies and lines, reaching substantial regional and international markets.[94]

The net has become a significant zone for Muslim women for religious, social, and cultural reasons, having relevance as much in terms of activism as in social relations. Traditional gender divides in some Muslim societies may be negated online, but a reflection of "real world" gender issues and disparities remains.

Internet e-fatwas (discussed in the next chapter) also cover subjects in which there are other forms of substantial taboos, such as advice and opinions in the fields of medical ethics.[95] Numerous fatwas online have caused confusion and, in some cases, complaint. These include opinions about banning multimedia devices, which transcend diverse interpretive frameworks of Islam. Such opinions hit hard on those who are constantly online and technologically literate. There can be a generational divide between those issuing the opinions and the audiences for them, which can lead to disenchantment and in some cases ridicule.

The Islamic school Darul Uloom Deoband attempted to ban camera phones on its campus because of misuse. This opened up questions of how electronic devices could be deployed appropriately for educational purposes without profane distractions.[96] In Iran, a fatwa (according to Shi'a principles) was issued against 3G internet phones and video communication. "The decadence and corruption associated with [RighTel's] use outweighs its benefits," decreed Grand Ayatollah Makarem-Shirazi. "It will cause new deviances in our society, which is unfortunately already plagued with deviances." Ayatollah Alavi Gorghani said that the video-call service would "jeopardize the public chastity" and "inflicts numerous damages" on Iran's religion and political system.[97] Despite these opinions, 3G+ services have increased exponentially in Iran within a lively digital economy.

ISLAMIC SPIRITUALITY AND RELIGIOUS FIGURES ONLINE

In addition to being a resource on spiritual places, the internet is a space where data on religious figures—including Muhammad, earlier prophets of Islam, members of the Prophet's family, followers, saints, ideologues, and other key figures—may be found. Substantial materials are available in academic databases and online libraries. More general and less specialized content is located through a variety of channels. The internet is a micro-area for grouping specialisms together in the "long tail" of market forces and knowledge demands.[98] The information ranges from the *sira* (biography) of the Prophet to esoteric details on religious figures beyond the mainstream.[99]

Veracity of religious data is an important consideration when exploring religious figures online. Open-source materials such as Wikipedia contain detailed biographical information on religious figures, with attendant issues relating to accuracy and authenticity. Commercial online academic encyclopedias specializing in Islamic subjects can offer greater degrees of academic integrity. Acquisition of primary knowledge about religious figures from blogs, social networking sites, and unofficial channels can be problematic in contested spaces where followers, analysts, and detractors post information and opinions online.

Hagiographic accounts of Muslim saints are presented through websites of organizations and followers.[100] These are often linked to other sites representing sacred places associated with pilgrimages and shrine locations. The pages are focused around community and follower expectations, although some present their beliefs to a wider audience. The Naqshbandi-Haqqani order is a good example of how a Sufi order has utilized a range of social networking sites and resources to present the worldview of its leader, Mawlana Shaykh Nazim Adil Al-Haqqani. From a base in Northern Cyprus, the group networks with adherents across continents, streaming media and capturing religious activities. Alongside the sermons and thoughts of its spiritual guides, recordings of followers are distributed, such as a rap track recorded in a Michigan mosque.[101]

The Qadiri Sufi Order's online activities are an element within worldwide networks and movements based on principles established by the twelfth-century scholar Abdul Qader Jeelani. Spirituality and religious experience are evoked in a YouTube video of the *dhikr*. This ritual invocation of Allah's names, Qur'an verses, and other recitations has a performative element. Ten followers are positioned in a circle around their leader, filmed from an overhead camera.[102]

The Tidjaniya Sufi Order holds a presence in western and northern Africa and is linked to its diaspora communities and networks through online materials: the website Tidjaniya Way highlights the order's founder, Sidī 'Ahmad al-Tidjani, through biography accompanied by an audio reading.[103] Sacred spaces and shrines in Senegal are depicted through video, photos, and plans of religious sites. Ritual group *dhikr* and *hadra* invocations take the viewer into a shrine at the *zaouiya* (school) of Sidi Abdel Moutalib Tidjani Dakar, Senegal.[104] Different *Zaouiya* also use social networks: Fez Zaouiya has a Facebook page.[105] Key teachers of the order, such as El-Hadji Malick, have busy Facebook pages linking to video, information, and networks.[106] Sufism takes many forms online, representing different shades of esoteric and at times political emphases.

SHI'A BELIEFS ONLINE

Shi'a historical and contemporary figures present a strong presence in cyberspace. Members of the Prophet's family (the *ahl al-bayt*) and their descendants, as represented in the lives of the imamate, are depicted in detail. Shi'a branches manifested online include those linked to Zaydi, Ismaili, and Ithna 'Ashari Shi'a identities; political-religious leaderships from Iran, Iraq, Lebanon, and Bahrain are also wired, while relatively minor branches present intertwined online activity hubs.

Figures are represented in terms of events, spaces, and rituals surrounding them. Annual commemorations of Husayn ibn Ali's 680 CE martyrdom in Karbala attract thousands of people across the world and are filmed and archived online.[107] Other imams in Shi'a history are represented in literary form, with libraries reproducing and translating significant texts; the Maaref Foundation has published extracts from biographical volumes covering a breadth of Shi'a historical sources.[108]

Key figures find representation on social networking sites, with Facebook pages for many. Hazrat Ali Ibne Abi Talib (A.S.)—The Commander of [the] Faithful quotes from Ali's sayings, linking to videos of Shi'a activities and discussions on religious issues.[109] Long-standing historical enmity between some elements of the Islamic spectrum means that detractors of Shi'ism inevitably also find a place online: Why I Am Not a Shia is a prominent example of this, with multimedia statements indicating "evidence" of the "schismatic" nature of Shi'a beliefs.[110] UK-based English language station AhlulBayt TV draws on social media to stream its religious programming, including children's shows, sermons, and broadcasts from mosques. Programming also includes streaming Q&A sessions from Ahlulbayt TV and videos of Sayed Muhammad al-Mousawi's responses to questions.[111]

Imam Ali Foundation–London is a gateway to a more traditional library of Shi'a materials. The foundation links to the office of Ayatollah Ali Husayni al-Sistani, including photos of the influential Iraq-based Shi'a leader.[112] Al-Sistani's pages connect to content associated with the Aalulbayt Global Information Center, including regional sites, affiliates, and supporter chat rooms. They reflect special interests, such as Qur'an study, political activism, poetry recital, and religious art. The Specialist Studies Centre of al-Imam al-Mahdi archives cultural-religious activities in a gallery of paintings showing religious figures, scenes of battle, and iconography demonstrating dynamic core themes of Shi'a beliefs.[113] Many sites also offer audio-video lectures from contemporary religious figures.

A significant amount of online content regarding key Shi'a figures emanates from Iran; the Islamic Republic was quick to realize the potential of online materials in presenting detailed sites on the life and scholarly output of Ayatollah Ruhollah Khomeini, drawing on multimedia content. Original

Sun's House pages from the 1990s remain online, containing documentary film clips and archive materials.[114] Numerous Facebook pages center on the ayatollah, providing a forum for opinions to be expressed (on all sides) relating to Khomeini.[115] Khomeini's grandson Seyyed Hasan Khomeini has a Facebook site, showing his activities as a cleric in Iran. Even on more recent social media, Khomeini has been represented, such as the @Emamkhomeini Instagram account—temporarily suspended in 2015 before re-emerging.[116]

Facebook has been controversial in Iran; attempts to ban the social networking site have been made there. Despite this, religious and clerical figures in government and elsewhere are represented on Facebook. The Supreme Leader Ali Khamenei's "Speeches and Quotes" are archived on the site. The Facebook group Waiting for the Reappearance of Imam Mehdi draws together supporters of Shi'a networks, with extensive quotes from Khomeini and his followers.[117] In 2012, former president Akbar Hashemi Rafsanjani described Facebook as a "blessing," particularly as a mobilizing tool that bypasses conventional media restrictions.[118] Iran was developing a national internet system, designed to restrict internet access for Iranian citizens, and was prosecuting and imprisoning bloggers and cyberactivists who were deemed to go against national interests.[119] In 2009, Facebook was blocked (and subsequently unblocked) in Iran. Negative statements were made by clerics regarding Facebook, but political parties and senior clerics continued to keep a presence there. Opposition leader Mir Hossein Mousavi's supporters maintain a regularly updated Facebook site, which coordinates activism and records protest activities.[120] Qom University, one of the primary centers of Shi'a Islamic learning, has Facebook pages.[121]

Iran has recognized the importance of social media with its military propaganda, including a 2017 rap track recorded by Amir Tataloo on a naval vessel in the Persian Gulf, proclaiming Iran's rights to defend its territorial waters. With music soundtracks combining metal and more traditional music, together with the aesthetics of computer games, Hamed Zamani's 2016 video "The Shield" highlighted Iran-backed fighters against the "Islamic State" in Syria and their motivation for defending Shi'a shrines.[122]

Shi'ism is not just an Iranian phenomenon. Shi'a networks are represented in diverse contexts. The extent to which this is a reflection of spirituality is open to question. Many sites include political activism and elements that could be seen to be outside the religious sphere. Shi'a Muslims in Pakistan use Facebook to coordinate responses to being targeted and attacked, and the Husayni Centre has promoted protest meetings and videos of activities.[123] Members of the Warriors of Imam Mahdi Facebook group have presented

Screenshot from Amir Tataloo's music video "Energy Hasteei" on YouTube, https://youtu.be/koN9ARqkuFU.

quotes from imams as well as the Qur'an on their Facebook page, which also suggests that Facebook is a tool for procrastination. Despite this, the writers continue their Facebook activities.[124]

Evidence of regional variations in beliefs and practices are found through social networking sites. An audio recording was posted of the Zanzibar- or Mombasa-style mourning ritual Saff Matam Nauha, which commemorates the death of Husayn and can in different contexts involve recitation, processions, ritual movements, self-flagellation, and chest beating. Videos of *mourning* in Karbala appear on YouTube, while recordings from numerous other locations are represented on additional websites.[125] A cell phone clip of bloodied participants provided a visceral edge to proceedings in its perspective from within the mass of flagellants.[126] Recordings of other Shi'ism performative ritualistic religious practices are widely distributed online: the Sina Zani in Afghanistan archives recordings of these made in Afghanistan, Iran, and Australia.[127]

Many Shi'a communities draw on the internet to network with their members worldwide. With communities having origins in Yemen, a base in India, and members worldwide, the Dawoodi Bohra have utilized the internet to network internationally.[128] Their websites integrate news of religious leaders on their pages with targeted advertisements for community-related products.[129] Social activities are recorded through a blog. Multimedia of ritual activities are uploaded regularly, with substantial minutiae of detail—whether from Texas, Kuwait, or Mumbai—blended together to form a single online community.[130]

The Dawoodi Bohra are an offshoot of Ismaili Shi'ism, which itself is well represented online. Channels range from the offices of the Ismaili spiritual leader, the Aga Khan, to the academic channels of the Aga Khan University

Islamic Dimensions of Faith in Cyberspace

and to the online forums and gateways associated with Ismaili Shi'ism. Ismaili. net is a long-standing hub for the communities, with archives on religious matters, education, and Ismaili issues. Through this one-stop shop, one can enter into deep areas of spiritual interest. Those seeking to listen to *waez* (sermons) commemorating significant Shi'a occasions can locate audio versions online in Gujarati, Urdu, Hindi, and English. However, the element of mourning is different within Ismaili Shi'ism, given that the "light" of the imamate is not seen to have been extinguished but has a presence in the Aga Khan; this is reflected upon in the sermons and is amplified through the internet. It is also a subject of conjecture and debate in wider online Shi'a spheres.[131]

The diffuse nature of Ismaili communities worldwide lends itself to internet communication. While there is an Ismaili official site, there are numerous local and unofficial channels that provide entry points into Ismaili values, beliefs, and spirituality, including details of ritualistic practices, Qur'anic interpretations, and sacred spaces. Pragmatic information such as prayer times, mosque locations, and matrimonial sites is also given through these channels.[132] The Ismaili Social Network was created but struggled to compete with Facebook and other generic media, whose Ismaili sites had more subscribers and featured the Aga Khan's family. These official pages are regularly updated with news and information, although not by the Aga Khan personally.[133] This spiritual head's philanthropic and business activities are recorded for posterity through video, audio, and photo streams. More esoteric material relating to Ismaili beliefs can be encountered through audio recordings of prayers, invocations, recitations, religious music, and speeches.[134]

This pattern is replicated within other Shi'a contexts. Similarly dispersed Shi'a communities have long-standing internet hubs. The Khoja Shi'a Ithna Ashari communities, which have roots in Ismaili Shi'ism, have utilized the internet to network communities in Afghanistan, Pakistan, United Arab Emirates, and Yemen and across North America, Australia, Europe, and Africa. The networks coordinate humanitarian activities and educational courses and seeks to present a range of internal and external *tableegh* (proclamation of Islam) in multimedia format.[135] The pages present religious experiences of students: one pilgrim from Tanzania provides an account of her visit to Qom, Mashhad, and Nishapur, explaining its emotional and religious significance and encouraging others to participate in future visits.[136]

Diversity is represented in the use of social networking sites, such as Facebook. The Babulilm Network has numerous nodes within cyberspace: in Pakistan, its Facebook page has been used extensively to bring together its communities. A 2012 conference on the Qur'an was archived and photographed, and the site linked to political commentary and discussions on the status of Shi'a Muslims in Pakistan. The commentary included a focus on festivals and religious performance, promoting the network's Pakistan identity was emphasized through the use of flags and empathy with political-religious views against a "US agenda."[137]

This may have been politically and religiously expedient in the Pakistan context, but other nodes within the community are located in North America and promote *their* local identity. The Babul Ilm Islamic Center in Southern California has brought together its local community and archived religious activities through photos and sermon recordings.[138] The Bab ul-Ilm Bani Hashim Society in Mississauga, Ontario, quotes Gandhi and Charles Dickens on its front page and includes an online form through which the resident imam can be sent questions. An archive of religious sermons and streaming "live shows" of recitation and sermons provide a multimedia experience, which is shared with other Ithna 'Ashari sites in Canada.[139]

ALTERNATIVE SECTORS

Alternative sectors of Islamic belief, not always recognized by others, function effectively online. The Ahmadiyya Muslim Community follows a messianic understanding of Islam focused on the nineteenth century Indian religious figure Mirza Ghulam Ahmad, deemed by followers as a "second coming" of Jesus, with its "jihad of the pen." The movement has been persecuted in particular by Pakistan Sunni Muslim authorities for its perceived challenge to the status of the Prophet Muhammad.[140] With headquarters in London and an international network of mosques, the Ahmadiyya movement has utilized the internet to promote its interpretation of Islam—and seeks to demonstrate its relationship with core Islamic beliefs.[141] The movement's current leader, Mirza Masroor Ahmad, has a website and Twitter presence, which are updated with his pronouncements and activities; sermons are available via YouTube, translated into eleven languages. Qur'an translations and commentaries from the Ahmadiyya Muslim perspective are available online in over fifty languages.[142] This online presence provides some cohesion for a Muslim perspective that is not always acknowledged as belonging to the mainstream.

ISLAM 3.0—DIGITAL TRANSFORMATION OF MUSLIM SOCIETIES

From the above brief survey, it is possible to determine that Islamic expression is represented online by diverse networks and nodes, drawing on diffuse understandings of interpretation and cultural-religious knowledge. The technologies applied may be generic, but their application has a sacred dimension, as cutting-edge as other utilizations of the internet in more profane zones.

The transformational impact of the internet on Muslim societies has had a substantial impact, in line with a shrinking digital divide, reduced internet access costs, and new digital interfaces. This impact has been felt in many ways across different Muslim societies. It can be measured by the interplay and reactions associated with netiquette, ideas of religiosity, and the ways in which some parties have sought to implement restrictions on internet use in line with notions of religious knowledge, censorship, and morality. There is a diversity of opinion within and between various Muslim contexts/communities, and Islam is not homogeneous, but some issues may be shared or comparable.

The power of digital media to inflict damage on religious sensitivities reached one peak with the 2012 emergence of a short film on YouTube, *Innocence of Muslims*. This led to internet filtering in Malaysia, Pakistan, and India. Global protests occurred in response to this film that critics believed deliberately portrayed the Prophet Muhammad in a negative light.[143] Demonstrations made outside of embassies and Google's London headquarters influenced anti-American protests in Yemen, Egypt, and Libya. On September 12, 2012, U.S. ambassador J. Christopher Stevens was killed in a missile attack on the U.S. consulate in Benghazi, ostensibly during a demonstration against the film (this was not proven).[144]

In the aftermath, there was discussion about the types of responses to online content that could be made. The aims of the film's makers may have been achieved, through protesters spreading images from it via the internet.[145] In Lebanon, Hezbollah's Sayyed Hassan Nasrallah demonstrated against the film's continued circulation.[146] While the protests galvanized in September 2012, the content had been available for a substantial period before then; Bruce B. Lawrence suggested the motivations for the protests were not strictly religious: "What makes the current saga surreal is the seamless manner in which a hackneyed 14-month-old movie becomes the flashpoint for violence against American officialdom in the Arab Muslim world, and that it came both on the anniversary of 9/11 and during an intense presidential election."[147]

The relationship between the online and offline worlds, in which digital content can inspire analog protest, is a significant one. Sensitivities can be inflamed through the production of media and become an appropriate cause around which dissent can be manufactured. This became particularly apparent during the 2005 cartoons crisis. Danish newspaper *Jyllands-Posten* published controversial images claiming to depict the "Prophet Muhammed," which circulated globally online. This resulted in the newspaper and its staff being targeted by jihad-oriented individuals. Subsequent reproduction of these images in the French satirical magazine *Charlie Hebdo*, along with related cartoons produced by the magazine, led to the magazine's Paris office being firebombed in November 2011. In January 2015, *Charlie Hebdo*'s office was attacked by gunmen, leading to the deaths of twelve magazine staff and security personnel.

Without the internet, it is unlikely that the audiences for the cartoons would have extended beyond traditional print borders. The speed with which campaigns can be mounted and become viral is significant. Questions about freedom of speech, the boundaries of acceptable criticism, and concepts of blasphemy have been highlighted through controversies associated with online content. Of course, these issues predate the internet. The 1988 print publication of Salman Rushdie's *Satanic Verses* and subsequent protests that spread from the United Kingdom to various international contexts resulted in a fatwa from Ayatollah Khomeini. This was mediated through pre-internet media, including the fax machine.

Shifts in dissemination patterns of religious authority, from print to phone to fax to internet (and points in between), are significant when evaluating contemporary Islamic developments from numerous spheres—in particular in relation to religious authority. This transformation and transition of paradigms will be explored in the next chapter.

Fatwa Machine

Command and Control in Muslim Digital Worlds

Religious authority is a key driver within cyber-Islamic environments. How has a spectrum of organizations, institutions, and individuals utilized the developing media form to promote specific worldviews of Islam? What responses have been provided to the significant issues sent to religious authorities?[1] To address these questions, this chapter includes snapshot case studies of key online religious authorities to demonstrate their diverse approaches and concerns.

THE AUTHORITY ALGORITHM

The authority algorithm continues to evolve in a combination of divine revelation, human programming, and machine-driven fatwas. A website's encoding will influence how readers search and locate religious advice and knowledge. Whether computer-recommended advice will supersede the role of human expertise is open to question, but there is a symbiotic relationship between analog and digital interfaces that is apparent within this CIE zone.

By going online, new notions of Muslim authority and identity transcend traditional cultural and religious frameworks. Does the internet represent a transformation in the transmission of Islamic knowledge? This electronic authority can influence political networking and activism by mobilizing the immediacy of the internet to promote specific worldviews and agendas.

Requesting advice on religious matters has been a central concern for Muslims. Answers have traditionally been sought from a scholar or an individual best qualified (if not academically qualified) to interpret and provide an opinion, based on a synthesis of Islamic sources. This is, of course, a pre-internet phenomenon. I recall seeing queues of people outside a madrassa in Lahore, Pakistan, in the 1990s. They were seeking a religiously sanctioned option on (what were invariably) family matters. Prominent concerns were marriage, divorce, and property. Face-to-face communication remains a common method of seeking advice, but there is now a digital intermediary available for net-literate and net-enabled Muslims.

Interfaces have evolved, part of the exponential growth in options via websites, social media, and multimedia platforms. An extensive market for the more conventional question-and-answer websites/forums remains. These feature searchable archives of questions and answers and capture other dialogues with scholars. Transcending international boundaries, this CIE zone provides a "glue" for religious networks to stick together with shared values and outlooks. Religious opinions also galvanize a spectrum of conjecture and controversy.

While in certain zones there is the uncritical consumption of CIE content (reflecting Jürgen Habermas's theory), there are also places where the participatory elements of social media engender substantial challenges to passive consumption of media content, in particular in relation to religious norms and concepts. The early ideas of Habermas are confronted by the rapid spread and utilization of accessible online media within CIEs, developing a series of virtual public spaces or information marketplaces in which critiques of interpretative models predominate. The immediacy of internet media, difficult or impossible for religious powers and authorities to control, has let loose voices that contradict and in some cases violate the traditional power dynamic models between authorities and individual believers. The relationship is between a digitally mediated interface and a person, which negates the need for face-to-face etiquette demanded in an analog context, such as a mosque, while also extending the public space beyond traditional political, religious, or geographical borders. Issues of anonymity and security affect the dynamics of social and personal interaction online in CIEs for consumers while also providing some content providers with similar options in the distribution and promotion of religious ideas.

For net-literate generations, an expectation of instant gratification from 24/7 electronic media outlets makes them the choice for delivery and circulation of religious opinions (which may or may not be followed). Media-savvy organizations and platforms have a developed awareness that an opinion can have an immediate impact and response, negating the effect of more traditional communication channels of authority and the gradual release of information. Such developments are not without their negative elements: periods of reflection, learning, review, and editing of views that occurred over time are lost in favor of rapidly produced and promulgated opinions. There is no clawback of digital media. Information is immediately circulated to supporters (and opponents).

In an avalanche of opinion and information overload, audiences are gained or lost with a single tweet or are diminished by social media trends. Readers may perceive religious opinions as simply another element of their social media feeds and not necessarily spend time reflecting or acting on the information received. Data is lost in the constant stream of updates and feeds. For those whose digital media interfaces are always on, while more information about religious opinions and knowledge is available, this does not necessarily result in a greater depth of analysis or interpretation. Within a competitive media marketplace, nuanced readership expectations mean that religious authority channels have developed brand awareness, accessible presentation standards, and a vision that brings together diverse media forms and outlets. Those using media-aware specialists to present content have a better opportunity of reaching specific audiences.

The key is to draw readers into content. In marketing language, this is Islamic clickbait, with stories and information designed to lure casual visitors into a site. The objective is to get readers to sign up for, subscribe to, or like specific channels. Investment of time, money, and expertise can yield results in terms of reader numbers, networking opportunities, and market share growth. The principles are similar whether it is a state-led or state-linked religious authority in a traditional sphere or a nonaffiliated global actor constructing religious authority networks across borders.

Individuals or small groups with technical ability have constructed global audiences for their perspectives on Islam, which can run counter to state or traditional interpretations. Into the mix go notions of religious identity and exploration of knowledge, with an expectation of guidance and a sense of utilizing authority gleaned from scholarship, tradition, political frameworks, or other forms of expertise. The role of charisma, a sense of divine leadership, and affinity with authority based on personal experience cannot be underestimated. Within a multimedia framework, the power of personality can be expressed across the internet and other channels, drawing in new audiences through a combination of inspiration, media techniques, and internet awareness. The utilization of colloquial language and a recognition of specific identities (for example, based on region, age group, social class, political perspectives, or religious identity) mean that nuanced interfaces have developed in order to reach out to specific audiences perhaps unserved by conventional expressions of Islam.

The increasing role of internet-mediated religious authority places further emphasis on who is qualified to deliver religious opinions in relation to everyday issues and opinions. This can be explored by looking at the significant interpretive ideologues in Muslim histories. Exposure to traditional and modern approaches of knowledge and interpretation is closely linked to evolving technological interfaces over time. New personalities have emerged within authority paradigms, while traditional scholars have adapted to new media, including satellite television and the internet.[2]

DEFINING RELIGIOUS AUTHORITY ONLINE

When establishing the qualifications of Muslim religious authorities in cyberspace, as with any product or opinion on the internet, verification of authenticity is a significant concern. Popularity, comments, feedback, and audience ratings are influential elements reflected between and within diverse Sunni and Shi'a interpretations of Islam. The extent to which site users exercise criticism and caution is question. Critical questions emerge: What kind of Islamic opinions are sought, and by whom? What are the qualities of an online fatwa? How does it differ from "conventional" authority and sources?

CIEs can be linked to an organization or platform but potentially can be equally effective (in terms of audience reach) when produced by an individual seeking to present his or her worldview. The substantial financial investment in the internet by various Islamic organizations and platforms represents an attempt to secure online ideological advantages. Theoretically, an individual's home page or Twitter feed on Islam can carry the same weight and interest to a neutral surfer. This is particularly apparent when approaching issues relating to decision-making and interpretation of Islam and the qualifications (if any, and if relevant) of those making pronouncements and providing online advice to Muslims (and others). It may be difficult to determine the credentials of an online Islamic authority, which raises a significant contemporary issue relating to Islam.

Muslim activists, scholars, and individuals have introduced online Islamic approaches to a variety of concerns. The search for Islamic remedies in the Qur'an or in other sources goes beyond the preserve of traditionally trained Muslim scholars. Others from outside of these paradigms believe they are qualified to interpret sources according to their own abilities, without recourse to conventional authorities, which some perceive as being out of touch with contemporary concerns.

These issues have implications not just for Islamic contexts but also for individuals and institutions (insiders and outsiders) engaging with Muslims in the local, national, and global spheres. The application of Islamic sources within decision-making processes in different CIEs has had an impact on the nature of Muslim societies. Understanding authority within Islamic contexts informs approaches toward decision-making processes in such areas as ethics, personal law, economics, technology, education, and medicine. Knowledge of the diversity of Islamic values enhances the potential to see beyond the homogenized perspectives presented in some media and academic sources relating to Islam. An interest in human interaction and intellectual thought is informed by an awareness of how Muslims reconcile the dynamics of varied Islamic beliefs and interpretations with life in secularizing or modernizing societies. Extra-Islamic sociopolitical and religious interests also have an impact on decision-making processes. Exploring CIEs has incorporated a subtext on interpretations of Islam. One underlying theme is the frequently articulated understanding that solutions for all issues can be located in the Qur'an: "And no question do they bring to thee but We reveal to thee the truth and the best explanation (thereof)."[3]

The multiplicity of themes that emerged from my early studies of Islam in cyberspace still have resonance today: What are the questions being brought for "the best explanation" within CIEs? How do online Islamic authorities approach new issues of practical concern to Muslims? Who is qualified to make a decision or provide an opinion, based upon interpretation of Islamic sources? Can these sources be utilized to tackle the different pressures on contemporary Islamic societies?

A key to examining processes associated with religious authority has been developing an understanding of *ijtihad*. This goes back to formative discussions on the nature of authority and law in Islam. The term is often (but not exclusively) utilized in Sunni contexts as a striving for the pragmatic interpretation of Islamic primary sources in the light of contemporary conditions.[4] It is synonymous with renewal and reform within certain Islamic contexts, although reevaluation and realignment may be appropriate alternatives. *Ijtihad* is defined as "exerting oneself to the utmost degree to understand *shariah* through disciplined judgement," sharia being seen as divine law as articulated in the Qur'an and interpreted by human beings to contribute to Islamic law or jurisprudence (*fiqh*).[5] It was while I was researching contemporary *ijtihad* in analog contexts in the mid-1990s that I became increasingly aware of the digital exchanges taking place between scholars across contexts and continents via the nascent internet.[6]

These concepts entered Muslim discourses in several languages but are often referred to within dialogues without explanation and, depending on context, can have several levels of meaning and relevance. The term *ijtihad* has been defined and used in many ways, and a number of these different shades of opinion relating to the definition emerge on the internet.

Within Sunni contexts, in particular, these opinions can be linked to concerns associated with the formulation of fatwas or legal opinions produced by religious scholars and authorities.[7] In Shiʿa contexts, authorities have also strategically invested time and resources to present their own online conceptual approaches toward interpretation to a global audience. Significant materials exist in Shiʿa and Sufi CIEs, although I am not suggesting that there is a polarity between these sectors or that one sector has priority over others. When exploring Sunni models, there is a need to determine the types of issues deemed significant and to consider whether they constitute part of the traditional and contemporary manifestations of *ijtihad* and associated interpretative decision-making processes.

Sunni Islam represents an umbrella term for a variety of cultural, historical, political, legalistic, religious, and sociological perspectives, not always in agreement with one another. The focus is the notion that religious authority and interpretation emanate from the Prophet Muhammad and his *followers* (including, for some perspective, elected caliphs). They are contained in an array of sources, including assorted legal interpretations and (in varying degrees, depending on the perspective) collections of Muhammad's sayings and actions.

Shiʿa Islam is an umbrella term for separate but interrelated cultural, historical, political, legalistic, religious, and sociological perspectives. In contrast to Sunni Islam, these focus on the concept that religious authority and interpretation emanate from the Prophet Muhammad and his *descendants*, including the various lines of spiritual leaders or imams.

There are varied understandings of who is entitled to apply *ijtihad*, including whether an appropriately qualified *mujtahid* is required and whether his decision is binding on individuals, a community, or the Islamic world. A *mujtahid* is a person (invariably male) who is properly eligible to exercise judgment on issues of interpretation, utilizing authoritative sources (which can vary according to the individual's perspective but are likely to include the Qur'an). This opinion may be articulated in the form of a fatwa. This term, which historically reflects a legalistic statement, opinion, or edict, possesses an inherent flexibility in Islamic discourse—especially on the internet—referring to a variety of authoritative statements and declarations. A fatwa does not need to incorporate contemporary *ijtihad* by an interpreter in order to be effective or relevant, especially if an authority is drawing on the opinions of earlier scholars and sources.

The issue of too many questions emerging on religious issues is not just a contemporary concern; it predates the internet. In fact, there is reference to this issue in the Qur'an: "You who believe, do not ask about matters which, if made known to you, might make things difficult for you—if you ask about them while the Qur'an is being revealed, they will be made known to you—for God has kept silent about them: God is most forgiving and forbearing. Before you, some people asked about things, then ignored [the answers]."[8]

This portion from the Qur'an has been used to support the view that too much *ijtihad* causes difficulty, and it could have been applied to support the alleged closure of the gates of *ijtihad,* as mentioned in a hadith: "The most sinful person among the Muslims is the one who asked about something which had not been prohibited, but was prohibited because of his asking."[9]

Muhammad's concern regarding the number of questions that his followers asked had an impact upon them. There is a stress throughout the body of *hadith* on avoiding an excess of questions: "Avoid that which I forbid you to do and do that which I command you to do to the best of your capacity. Verily the people before you went to their doom because they had put too many questions to their Prophets and then disagreed with their teachings."[10] A further hadith noted, "A person asked about a thing from Allah's Apostle (may peace be upon him) and he indulged in hair-splitting."[11] Muhammad stressed that his personal decision-making had limitations and that there was potential for error.[12]

Despite this tendency toward hair-splitting and potential for error, various CIEs have been preoccupied with issues of religious questions, qualification, and authority. Muslim reformers have presented their own views on the qualities for such interpretation, seeking to take authority away from traditional scholars and sources of understanding in order to construct new paradigms for contemporary societies. With the emergence of substantial opinions online, this means that the term *ijtihad* itself has acquired a new currency amid discussions as to whether the "doors of interpretation" closed during the period of classical Muslim scholarship.[13]

Within such considerations, perhaps it should also be noted that not all Muslims necessarily followed the complex quasi-legalistic discourse. This group included those whose focus on Islamic spirituality possessed a more esoteric edge, although some legal scholars were also Sufis and legalistic interpretations additionally pervade esoteric dimensions of Shi'a discourse. Such textured and textual disputation was primarily a concern of an educated male elite rather than of the average person in the marketplace, in the field, in seclusion, or in the mosque.

"Reforms" have been articulated in oral, written, printed, broadcast, and now electronic formats. These may be seen as a threat by other authorities or imposed upon an unwilling population. There may or may not be an element of consensus. The reasoning behind reforms can disguise ulterior political agendas, not necessarily equating with sincerely held Muslim beliefs (depending on the level of cynicism of an observer). There is no single reform paradigm; it ranges from ultraconservative Sunni "orthodox" to modernizing reforms integrating Islamic thought with elements considered by others as secular or un-Islamic. Mystical interpretations have sought to bring new (not always welcome) perspectives to Islamic understandings, which have in turn been linked to reform-centered influences and endeavors.

Some Muslims see this "reform" as a challenge to their model of how pragmatic and viable the Qur'an is in all situations. They may well ask why there should be any reliance on subsequent texts and new interpretations of Islam when Muhammad was understood to be the Final Prophet and everything can be learned from the Qur'an. Some suggest that it was Muhammad's practice, and its articulation in his Companions and Successors' communities, that was to give clarity of Qur'anic understanding, especially to those aspects that were not fully articulated in the Qur'an's chapters. From within Shi'a contexts, others place additional emphasis on Muhammad's successors as represented in different lines of infallible and divinely inspired imams.

It has been suggested that critics emphasize the disunity rather than any unity of Islam. However, the pragmatic recognition of difference has been a feature of Islamic interpretations from the time of the first Medina community in 622 CE. Critics often attack Islam and Muslims for something that was never sought and attempt to squeeze Islam into confines that Muslims themselves feel are narrow and restrictive, what certain interpreters would describe as "fundamentalist." It is possible to conclude that the mechanisms within Islam, revealed and interpreted esoterically and exoterically, were intended to accommodate a basic flexibility of viewpoints in certain matters.

If the sayings and actions of Muhammad, recorded in hadith and sunna sources (and compiled many years after his death), are brought into the equation, then we have a body of material drawn together through diverse sources and channels. The dependence on the exactitude of the sources is reflected in the provision, on occasion, of several different versions of an event or saying, whereas the Qur'an provides one definitive Divinely Revealed text. However, depending on the verse, several different commentaries (not necessarily complementary) may be applied, drawing on different interpretational

Command and Control in Muslim Digital Worlds

techniques and dependent on the personal situation, background, and qualifications of the interpreter(s).

This variation plays a significant role in creating the basis of "reform-centered" movements, as when the layers of understanding are believed to obscure the text's "true" meaning. There can be a dichotomy between the literal and implied readings of the Qur'an, which may lead to a conflict of interests. This is part of an ongoing conversation about Islam that dates back to the foundation of schools of law within different traditional frameworks, including the four principal Sunni schools (Hanafi, Hanbali, Maliki, Shafi'i) and their offshoots. This can also be associated with the collection of *hadith*, which traditionally in the classical period of Islam were sought by students literally traveling to sit at the feet of scholars. There, they would learn about the authenticity of traditions, including which sources were most reliable and had the best *isnad*, or chain of transmission.

The journeys to the scholars can now be undertaken digitally, and chains of transmission traverse cybernetworks and internet service providers in search of authenticity. Early conversations defining Islam can be digitally linked with contemporary discourse on social media. There is now a relationship between the nature of religious authority, the application of *ijtihad*, and the complexities and issues introduced with developments in information technology. As technology has evolved, shifted, and adapted, these issues become a constant subtext, whether expressed on a webpage, in a YouTube video, on a Facebook page, or on Snapchat or Twitter. The essence of traditional knowledge transmission across the centuries, from oral to written to print to digital, reflects to its advocates continuity with the message received by Muhammad from God via the angel Gabriel. However, Islamic authority is now live-streaming, instantaneous, and virtual.

THE DIGITAL AUTHORITY CONNECTION

Given the reduced digital divide and increased digital literacy, online media have become important drivers for projecting religious ideals and concerns to different sectors and audiences. New databases have emerged to collect religious opinions.[14] Traditional authority paradigms have reconfigured to respond to emerging online culture. Expectations from digitally literate audiences mean that they expect to access forms of authority—sermons, fatwas, and prayers—via the internet.[15] In an echo of Marshall McLuhan, the notion of authority is being shaped by the applications it utilizes, and the message of Islam is converted accordingly—whether into a tweet, a meme, or a video clip. This fashions different and contrasting expectations for digitally literate generations in terms of how religion *can* be presented and consumed while also reflecting evolving and shifting attention spans, multitasking, and the potential to receive such content on multiple devices anywhere there is an uncensored internet service. The challenges these constantly changing consumption patterns create have led to dynamic responses by technology-literate authorities and platforms, while those more driven by analog dissemination patterns lose out within digital knowledge marketplaces.

Authorities have sought to build platforms based on net technology and traditional authority patterns in a variety of contexts, utilizing different approaches. In Kazakhstan, workshops for mullahs were introduced to expand digital literacy in the religious sector, recognizing that audiences for religious knowledge had altered within online contexts. One imam noted, "Nobody wants to bother to listen to mosque sermons. . . . Young people prefer to get answers to their questions [about religion] without leaving their homes. That's why imams should be proactive on social networks."[16] Access to mosques can also be limited in some minority contexts, resulting in the seeking of knowledge online.[17] Opinion is divided as to the legitimacy of using the internet for religious purposes. Zakir Naik, a controversial Indian preacher who has used the internet to develop his own high profile, noted: "If we use Internet for good purposes it is a blessing for us but if the same Internet is used for wrong things it can create lot of problems. May Allah . . . help everyone in making correct use of Internet."[18]

The emergence of celebrity religious figures has challenged norms, through development of profiles beyond traditional concepts of authority into the realms of fandom: "The celebrity Shaykh has become enthroned on a pedestal, the pedestal of unimpeachable piety and character, the pedestal of 'see no wrong, do no wrong,' in which we, the adoring students, have cast this very fallible human being as larger than life."[19] The internet has also become a place where scholars gather to discuss and disseminate their opinions. Creating connections between micro-networks and organizations is a particular development of CIEs, with imams establishing personal websites to showcase sermons and interpretations.[20] Websites also offer real-world and creative interactions with authorities: in Tatarstan, users can order religious services online via iMulla, and apps are being developed for conducting online rituals and ceremonies.[21]

Popular internet media personalities have also been introduced into trouble spots. Within the post–Arab Spring context of Yemen, Egyptian preacher Amr Khaled was brought in to respond to Islamic teaching issues through podcasts and a team of scholars.[22] This did not necessarily have a positive impact on subsequent developments in Yemen, however. The rise in status of new media-savvy preachers was in marked contrast to more traditional centers, whose influence and popularity was eroded in part by new media. Egypt's al-Azhar University faced specific problems in this regard, with a slow emergence online and a contestation of space with media imams on satellite television and the internet.[23]

Those operating within traditional frameworks have, at times, presented a more pragmatic approach toward technological innovation. Qatar-based Egyptian scholar and media personality Yusuf al-Qaradawi is significant because of his influential Al Jazeera satellite broadcasts, which are not always well received in the contested fields of Islamic religious authority.[24] Al-Qaradawi was an unlikely advocate of independent media when they matched with his own worldview.[25] He utilized the internet to promulgate his own fatwas and opinions on aspects of world affairs, especially within the Middle East, including a fatwa against Libya's Muammar Gaddafi.[26] Al-Qaradawi is a prominent example of how a scholar with an effective media-aware organization behind him can dominate mixed-media conversations about religious authority within Islamic contexts. He held a significant role in the development of the website IslamOnline (discussed below). During the Arab Spring, he reflected opinions of the key players within the Muslim Brotherhood: "He is a hypermarket of dogma, dispensing advice on subjects ranging from mother's milk to suicide bombing. . . . This man is a word machine, a one-man talk show that leaves no subject unexamined."[27] As a result of a dispute between Qatar and other regional powers, al-Qaradawi was "blacklisted" in 2017 by authorities in Saudi Arabia, Bahrain, United Arab Emirates, and Egypt for alleged links to terrorism, but his media activities have continued.[28]

Internet mobility means that an authority figure does not have to be located within an institution or official premises in order to present religious messages. A degree of influence and authority can be acquired through internet technology, such as the use of video conferencing in order to present live lectures. Internet technology offers the opportunity for in-depth discussions on controversial issues and questions. Conversations range from microissues of interpretation to complex and emotive explorations of radicalization.[29] The application of the internet in order to transcend physical boundaries and engage in real-life discussions is a significant game-changer within controversial and sensitive subject areas.

Ideas about contemporary Islamic thought have naturally entered the information marketplace, where key ideologues and organizations are able to articulate their understandings of Islam and politics in cyberspace. They are able to reach substantial educated audiences with high degrees of information literacy, which go beyond the traditional audiences for these materials. In some cases, they are able to circumnavigate censorship, especially if they are exiled from their places of origin. Through the internet, these ideologues and organizations are able to have dynamic presence and influence that can affect societies at domestic and regional levels. Contemporary political discourse naturally includes content via social media, including speeches, comments on the news, and other ways of engendering different forms of loyalty online.

Audiences for political content have also been extended for deceased yet still influential individuals whose supporters are able to examine content online. There is a blurring between religious and political content in many contexts, and this has been shown throughout the development of the internet, where organizations and platforms were proactive within the early phases of websites and chat rooms. The market for this content was identified, and it became a cost-effective means for political or religious figures to present their ideas about Islam as part of wider media strategies, including television broadcasts by satellite and more basic forms of dissemination, such as audiocassette tapes.[30] There has been a shift from the early days of internet content, where it was an adjunct to other forms of political dissemination, such as print media, so that now it is central to many platforms' strategies. In addition to organizations utilizing the internet—in particular the World Wide Web—to present their perspectives on religious and political issues, the rise of the individual perspective through social media, together with the emergence of new platforms and organizations online, has influenced traditional discourse. This is well represented in the context of the Arab Spring and its aftermath, where online content has had a specific impact.[31]

A number of significant political figures have presented themselves online, and it would be onerous to list them all here, given that they have featured in a number of different linguistic, cultural, and religious contexts. In relation to ideas about modernity and Islam, some have demonstrated the centrality of the internet as a means of communicating their notions of "reform." They are simply the latest in a line of political communicators who have drawn upon available media sources in order to disseminate their points of view, from the earliest days of the printing press to today's social media use.

They approach significant issues associated with aspects and interpretations of Islamic law to explore particular concepts associated with the dynamics and diversity of Islamic "reform."

Anwar Ibrahim promoted the idea of *reformasi* or Islamic reform in Malaysia as part of his long-standing political activities, which have been punctuated by periods of imprisonment.[32] Despite this, he and his supporters have been proactive online within a variety of internet contexts, including blogging and social media. From behind prison bars, on contested allegations of sodomy, Ibrahim has maintained a proactive media presence, with commentary on regional and international concerns, including a #freeanwar campaign, which Ibrahim's critics have also used to voice their opposition to Ibrahim and his release.[33] Wan Azizah, Ibrahim's wife, has also maintained a proactive presence promoting his release and the agenda of their Parti Keadilan Rakyat (People's Justice Party), which she leads in opposition to the Malaysian government.[34]

The application of the internet as a means of promoting specific interpretive aspects of politics and religion can be seen in the output of the Iranian thinker Abdolkarim Soroush, whose Persian- and English-language website and YouTube channel discuss his approaches to religious knowledge (which is seen as changeable) and the consistency of an eternal religion.[35] Soroush's perspective draws attention to his belief that religious clerics should not monopolize interpretations or insist on the implementation of a single religious-political perspective.[36] Other critical voices on Iran have utilized the internet consistently to present their perspectives on religion and politics, both from within and outside of the borders of the Islamic Republic.[37] Duke University academic Mohsen Kadivar supported the Green Revolution in 2009 and seeks separation of religious and civil law. He draws on the internet to facilitate this discussion, with his home page publishing e-books in Persian and other materials in English.[38] Hasan Yousefi Eshkevari, who was imprisoned in Iran between 2002 and 2005, uses the internet for a sustained commentary on Iranian issues from his base in Germany.[39]

Key figures who are located in minority contexts also utilize the internet to express their views on important aspects of political discourse. The writer and academic Tariq Ramadan is a good example; his online outputs in Arabic, French, and English from his Oxford base form part of his body of work and enable him to reach a wider global audience for his interpretation of notions of reform.[40] His social media output includes content showing his activities in a variety of contexts, including (on Twitter) use of the Periscope app, which presents and archives his lectures.[41]

The contestation for political and religious influence extends into areas of gender and the multiplicity of interpretations associated with, in particular, organizations and individuals articulating specific agendas associated with promoting women's political participation in Islamic contexts. These are complex and dynamic issues within many Muslim population zones.[42] The utilization of the internet became an important element in networking for women, where connections could be made that had sustained impact even in the early days of the World Wide Web.[43] The types of online discourse on aspects of politics and religion can range from grassroots activists to those who hold a degree of power. American academic Amina Wadud draws on the internet to promote her interpretive approaches toward the Qur'an and other sources, using social media as a campaigning tool in American and international contexts.[44]

Toronto-based scholar Farhat Hashmi left her native Pakistan to pursue academic studies in Scotland, returning with a PhD to teach at the International Islamic University in Islamabad. Hashmi now promotes her worldview via satellite television and the internet, focusing on family and gender issues designed primarily for a female audience, with a basis in traditional interpretations based on the Qur'an and hadith.[45] Hashmi's presentations evoke a specific religious perspective, as she wears a full veil and is often seated at a desk with a laptop and a set of Islamic texts. Her website offers a series of apps, including one called Quran in Hand, incorporating commentaries on the Qur'an with related audio content.[46] The app Al-Huda offers distance learning options on different aspects of translation and interpretation, based on internet lectures. In these presentations, Hashmi presents a strong focus on parenting and marriage. Al-Huda has been the focus of controversy and criticism because of Hashmi's perceived anti-Shi'a stance, influenced by certain Saudi Arabian and Pakistani religious scholars.[47] Hashmi's output and online presence are noteworthy examples of how issues of gender can combine with pious religious tradition and modern media.

Organizations including Women Living under Muslim Laws provide an online platform for global networking and regional activities while chronicling significant news stories and developments in seven languages. Cross-translation allows campaigns to compare approaches within different contexts and levels of advocacy on law and reform issues.[48] The notion of political advocacy is a significant one within local contexts as well: for example, in the UK, the Bradford Muslim Women's Council seeks to present advocacy as a nongovernmental organization in order to focus on a number of issues pertinent within local and global contexts.[49] French campaigning organization Lallab uses social media to combat gender specific issues as well as wider themes including "Islamophobia."[50]

There is an interplay between the religious and political dimensions of modern Islamic thought, although these elements are not always complementary. It can incorporate activists commenting on more traditionally religious pronouncements and vice versa. These elements inform twenty-first-century conversations about what Islam is and who Muslims are, and as such social media and internet-driven content are embedded within the dynamics of contemporary religious identities and activities.

CUT-AND-PASTE ISLAM

Utilization of the internet in support of religious purposes is not without complications. The net is no guarantee that sources developed for online consumption will be applied in an "Islamically correct" manner, even by those supposedly proficient in Islamic sciences or trained as religious authorities. A "cut-and-paste" culture has arisen, where source materials are drawn from the internet and other sites and utilized with or without attribution in sermons. Additionally, accusations of copying, pasting, and reading sermons without understanding their contents have occurred.[51] Such actions may suggest that a level of training should be required in terms of how information is processed and transmitted.

Tedious and potentially plagiarized sermons are simply a further online challenge for religious authorities. It is an issue that predates the internet. Challenges to core religious values and beliefs and the impact of esoteric dimensions associated with religiosity are two pervading themes affecting traditional religious authorities. In areas where there are more orthodox approaches to interpretation, these challenges can be deemed innovative and un-Islamic. Saudi Arabia has been wrestling with the issue of "authenticity" in Islam for many years. Decision-making and interpretation are big business, with Saudi authorities being particularly critical of media channels providing "false and dangerous advice" within dream interpretation services.[52]

Alternative approaches to religious interpretation outside orthodox boundaries have a stronghold within CIE zones. Just how Islamic these activities are is clearly within the eye of the beholder. It is not the purpose here to suggest that they somehow fall outside of Islam. But while popular religious-cultural expressions have a significant place online, the Saudi Arabian government launched a series of initiatives on internet policy in 2011, in part to counter influences deemed innovative or extremist.[53] It focused on propagation efforts and countering radicalization agendas, and support for the application of information technology to promote "positive" interpretations of Islam reached an all-time high. Sheikh Abdul Rahman al-Sudais (imam of Masjid-al-Haram in Mecca) made an analogy between information technology and the foundation of Islam: "The Imam said the followers of Islam should use advances in technology to take the message of the religion across the world. 'If the Sahabah (companions of Prophet Muhammad) had not gone about spreading the Prophet's message, Islam would not have grown. The followers of Islam should, therefore, use the Internet and electronic media to spread the religion in the modern times,' he said."[54]

Senior clerics have adopted social media to present opinions, including those that fall outside of the parameters of Saudi Arabia's own values. Popular religious figures have acquired substantial social media followings that match those of prominent Western show business personalities.[55] Use of social media to discredit the Saudi royal family members in 2012 could have been linked to attempts by religious authorities to censure Twitter.[56] Saudi religious figures distributing online religious opinions and "e-fatwas" featured highly in Twitter ratings around the same time. High-profile clerics including Saleh al-Fawzan and Abdul Rahman al-Sudais were sanctioned by authorities, but unsanctioned cleric Salman al-Odah was also prominent on social media.[57] Mohamad al-Arefe had over nineteen million followers in 2017 for his (primarily) Arabic Twitter feed, which included commentaries on news stories as well as international issues.[58] In September 2017, al-Odah was one of several Saudi clerics arrested as part of a crackdown on critical religious voices in the kingdom, with suggestions he had not supported policies against Qatar during a time of regional dispute.[59]

Such clerical profiles are replicated across Muslim contexts worldwide. Indonesia, the most populous Muslim country, has a high level of digital interaction in relation to religion. Several clerics have created and developed substantial online profiles, promoting opinions that counter "extremist" arguments.[60]

FATWA TORRENT

In 2010, Saudi Arabia sought to restrict the publication of religious opinions outside of a select group, closing websites that violated its decree.[61] This action opened up an audience for unregulated fatwa channels outside of the control of the Kingdom of Saudi Arabia. Setting regulative parameters is predicated on a specific worldview; in the case of Saudi Arabia, that

Twitter page of Mohamad Alarefe, http://twitter.com/MohamadAlarefe.

worldview is associated with a Wahhabi interpretation of Islam. While other interpretations of Islam are available, this perspective dominates media perception of Islam when notions of orthodoxy combine with a desire to control extremism.

Elsewhere in 2010, Facebook was blamed for a rise in divorce and marital infidelity. An Egyptian cleric issued a fatwa stating that Muslims using such sites were acting in a sinful manner, developing relationships that run counter to Islamic law.[62] These claims were quickly refuted by al-Azhar University, which denied issuing fatwas itself against Facebook and suggested that its fatwa committee had not even received inquiries on the subject.[63] It is unclear where the cleric was obtaining his data regarding the internet's influence on marital infidelity. But questions about social media's religious legitimacy did not prevent al-Azhar from supporting its El-Hatef El-Islami Islamic Hotline. Enquiries in a variety of languages could be sent electronically to al-Azhar experts for a small fee, but by 2017 the service was unavailable.[64]

Detractors of the internet continue to emerge, often on the internet itself, denouncing it in emotive statements. In 2012 Sheikh Muhammad Hussein Yaqob called the internet "haram" or forbidden.[65] This was despite the fact that Yaqob's supporters had extensive internet activity, including a website and social media outlets. Yaqob's site focused on attacking Egyptian institutions such as al-Azhar. It presented sermons online and contained archived Ask the Shaykh Question and Answers.[66]

Determining the identity and authenticity of religious authorities has become a significant issue online. The proliferation of opinions amplifies authority concerns. The internet offers an alternative perspective to what is perceived in some quarters as a domination of Islamic discourse by orthodox religious figures.[67] Islamic perspectives maintain an internet presence through the use of professional staff and systems, managing and regulating multilingual content that is regularly refreshed. Controlling the flow of questions is a key issue when sites are inundated with questions ranging from the trivial to life-changing topics.

The goal of organizations and groups to develop Islam-friendly portals, websites, and social media was in part to distance readers from the more profane areas of the internet. From text to video clips, notions of religious authority and advice have emerged in a complex array of forms. There have been attempts to lock into the digital zeitgeist and attention spans of users. But according to analysts, attention spans have reduced in line with increased social media opportunities.[68] In a multimedia age, varying content formats make a difference. Islamic online initiatives have gone beyond simply filming sermons and posting them online. For example, StreetDawa.com brings together YouTube clips in an accessible and easy-to-navigate format, with Q&A interpretations on specific issues and guides on Islamic principles.[69] British organization Radical Middle Way published seventy-eight *iKhutbah* video sermons between 2009 and 2011.[70] The presentation of cross-platform online content has brought alternative audiences for religious opinions and sermons outside of traditional boundaries.[71] Religious authority and spirituality is also a commercial opportunity, including unofficial sources. In 2010, for instance, Iranian online prayer sellers offered intercession for a fee.[72] There is perhaps a paradox, in the opinion of some commentators, in modern media being used to convey traditional and at times anachronistic interpretations of Islam.[73]

AUTHORITY IN FOCUS

An online audience has emerged not just for traditional articulations of religious values and understandings but also for alternative Islamic opinions and interpretations. The extent to which knowledge acquired in cyberspace regarding Islam is applied is difficult to quantify, as the newspaper fatwas that archives placed online, based on columns written by scholars, transitioned to the introduction of specially created online fatwa resources.

Advice on a key issue can be solicited from different sources, through searching database archives of fatwas, edicts, opinions, questions, and answers or by contacting a religious authority with a question (for example via Facebook, Twitter, SMS, or email). One advantage for petitioners and the curious is that internet use can be anonymous. While this factor has perhaps been overemphasized in cyberstudies in general, in relation to CIEs anonymity raises some specific and unique issues. These include whether an online opinion is binding and the moral implications on the person making the petition or asking the question. Should an opinion solicited by email be followed? Are the moral and ethical dimensions of receiving an opinion from a scholar the same in a digital context as in a nondigital context? In trying to catch up with rapid developments in social media and the internet, authorities are refining approaches toward these religious and legalistic issues. In this information-rich marketplace, some are more proactive than others, where guidance on how to mediate with online authority and content is also required.

Studying online decision-making resources, which have emerged as indicators of contemporary needs of sectors of Muslim communities, can be beneficial. Digital resources provide insights into the concerns of individuals and provide a symbolic focus of Muslim authority in cyberspace. Indicators of language, sources, and methodological approaches of fatwa-issuing bodies can be found in CIEs. One proviso is that an online resource can look official and Islamic and can contain substantial content while not being representative of a majority opinion.

Self-proclaimed alternative authorities who appear online have their critics, but in terms of academic analysis they do give insight into contemporary Islamic diversity and represent opinions that may be difficult to locate within other source materials. They discuss important new issues, with no immediate basis in traditional sources. Their opinions can be disseminated rapidly but are not necessarily observed or followed. Readers may visit another website to locate an opinion more in line with their personal views. This reflects a consistent pattern I observed in real-world fieldwork exploring decision-making concerns and notions of religious authority in the 1990s, when scholars noted that petitioners would "shop around" for opinions that matched their expectations.

CIEs have presented fatwas in searchable databases, such as Fatwa-Online, Ask-Imam, and Islam Q&A. Opinions are often integrated into sermon content, prevalent in Sunni cyberspace. Those living in environments hostile to their religious worldview find comfort, advice, and inspiration through the content of online sources, while others might appreciate perspectives from other interpretative dimensions. The influence of scholars and others giving advice based on their interpretation of Islamic principles can extend from their own (micro-)communities to a global audience.

Authorities in various Shi'a and Sufi contexts have strategically invested time and resources to present their own online interpretative approaches to global audiences. Theoretically, an individual's home page on Islam can carry the same weight and interest to a neutral web surfer as one from a major player. This is apparent when approaching the qualifications (if any, and if relevant) of those making pronouncements and providing online advice to Muslims (and others). Determining the credentials of an online Islamic authority can be difficult. Within a Sunni context, this difficulty is reflected in concerns associated with the formulation of fatwas or legal opinions produced by religious scholars and authorities.

Issues considered dangerous or embarrassing to raise within a domestic framework can be anonymously presented to an online authority. This authority may be located in a local or global context or indeed from a different cultural-religious outlook. However, information overload, especially on controversial issues, is a significant matter in a saturated information marketplace. One Muslim gave this opinion: "I think many young people have lost their way when it comes to making choices. Those who have questions do not know where to turn. Now there's the Internet, but many young people cannot identify with the answers they get. They are too strict, they are not general enough or they do not relate to reality. Young people joke: 'Go to Sheikh Google, type something in and all kinds of stuff comes out.'"[74]

In Morocco, fatwa production became the subject of satirical "Fatwa Show" YouTube clips.[75] They featured "Sheikh Muslim Jiddan" ("good Muslim") and "his faithful disciple" dressed in traditional clothing. Jiddan articulated a fatwa reproduced from an original source and drew on ornate Arabic language in order to make his opinion known, seeking support from his companion. At the end of each clip was a slapstick element, which demonstrated the fatwa in detail. All the videos were based on real source material, linked on the website. One referred to an opinion about women wearing high heels, drawn from a statement by Sheikh Mohamed bin Saleh Al Othaimeen from the Council of Senior Scholars in Saudi Arabia. After pronouncing on this fatwa, the video duo went about sawing off the heels from a pair of shoes. Another clip used the same scholarly source to discuss the merits of contact lenses making people's eyes resemble those of animals, based on a fatwa produced by Al Othaimeen. The show also satirized a fatwa

Command and Control in Muslim Digital Worlds

by Sheikh Abdelbari Zemzami of Morocco that stated, "Women can lawfully use carrots or similar fruits or vegetables in order to ease their sexual frustration in a way that safeguards the honour and keeps them away from adultery and debauchery."[76]

These opinions influence areas of CIEs seeking to provide serious services, which is problematic given the infinite range of authoritative opinions that have emerged online. The website Muslim Matters addressed this issue head-on in 2012: "The age-old rule still stands true—that wherever there are Muslims hanging around, there are bound to be Muslims arguing over ridiculous things. Not surprisingly, the Internet is now the boxing ring for our new generation of *Shaykh* Googles and *Mufti* Wikipedias to profess their scholarly expertise and argue with one another with far more advanced tools of divisiveness, or as they say nowadays according to modern cyber *tajwīd*: 'trolling.'"[77]

Internet materials on Islamic issues have been described elsewhere as a form of entertainment, which trivializes significant issues and takes away a reliance on traditional methods of interpretation and knowledge. According to the website Muslimology, "The Internet does create a beguiling sense of 'know-it-all' when really, most Muslims online can rarely quote a hadith precisely and on the spot, which of course is what counts. We forget, all that information can be deleted instantly off the Internet, forever gone."[78] Disenchantment with online fatwas suggests that, rather than having purely Islamic values, their production has become competitive business. Saudi writer Abdullah Manna introduced the term "Takeaway Fatwas" to describe this process.[79]

Another argument is that fatwa (over)production stimulates debate and encourages critical interpretation of some religious opinions. In an era of prominent discussions on internet authenticity and "fake news," there could be some positives in this preponderance of opinions: "In the same way that the Internet is gradually teaching people they shouldn't believe everything they read on screen or in print, crazy fatwas serve a useful purpose. They demonstrate that there is no such thing as a single 'correct' interpretation of scripture, and force people who have never been accustomed to doing so to start sorting the wheat from the chaff."[80] This declaration assumes that one's critical faculties are available and that one has an option to exercise opinion, which is not necessarily always the case, especially when, as will be seen in the case studies, issues of allegiance and authority are extensively interwoven into the online dialogues, fatwas, and opinions presented in CIEs.[81]

This section explores examples of online authorities to determine their responses to technological shifts and changes in readership requirements. Some sites present a form of electronic *ijtihad*, with pragmatic responses to contemporary issues. With increases in digital literacy and access has come increased choice, a widening of online services and perspectives, and a resultant intensification for readers seeking knowledge, advice, information, and (in some cases) entertainment. In a rolling marketplace of knowledge transmission and production, or information souk, the sites presented here compose a snapshot rather than a scientific survey of the "Fatwa Machine."

OnIslam.net

OnIslam.net emerged in 2010 from the demise of the prominent resource IslamOnline. The formula developed by IslamOnline continued on the OnIslam brand, especially in its Arabic and English content, which extended to news and commentary. Egyptian scholar Yusuf al-Qaradawi endorsed both sites. OnIslam's main site disappeared from the internet in 2016, with some of its fatwa formats being absorbed by AboutIslam.net.

OnIslam.net offered content in English and Arabic, available via the main website as well as on Facebook, Twitter, Google+, YouTube, and Tumblr. In August 2015, the Facebook group OnIslam English claimed 1,143,000 "likes." OnIslam English's Twitter feed had 13,200 followers and had posted over 63,600 tweets since 2010.

Questions could be directed to particular sections of the OnIslam site; these included Ask the Scholar, Ask the Counsellor, Q&A Fatwas, and Ask about Parenting. The site provided real-time Live Fatwa sessions, allowing users to pose questions to specific authorities and receive an immediate reply. As with some IslamOnline pages, the questions were sensitive and highly personal. Some responses dated from 2003, ported from previous sites, but substantial questions were answered on a daily basis. Questioners had to complete a form, which noted that not all answers were published. Due to the sensitivity of the content as much as editorial control, some answers were emailed privately to individuals if they were not featured on the website itself.

In August 2015, the archive of previous questions was substantial, with over 5,300 articles. These were divided into subcategories and further subsections. "Family" was one of the most popular sections, holding over 850 articles dating back to August 2004. The marriage section held 180 articles; the marital relationships section contained 120 articles; and the intimate relations and divorce sections each held over 90 articles.

Live Fatwa sections brought expertise into an interactive format, allowing for immediate response. Some were general live sessions, whereas others specialized on topics such as finance, food, and personal relationships. Answers were couched in religious language with appropriate salutations. They referenced particular conceptual frameworks associated with Islam, although they were presented in a conversational way, without the depth of referencing and analysis found on other areas of the site.

Questions and responses followed a typical and standard format. Some questions were exhaustively detailed and could be highly personal, as was the case in the intimate relations section. The parameters of Islamic etiquette framed the responses, including opinions from the OnIslam team and other scholarly sources. Some provocative subjects emerged, including the permissibility of "Skype sex," pornography use, diverse sexual practices, and "marital intimacy in the open air." The marriage section included responses to questions on marrying non-Muslims, polygamy, civil marriage accreditation, convert marriage, adultery, and Sunni marriage to Shi'a Muslims (so-called Sushi marriage).

The divorce section included responses to questions about pronouncements of divorce in anger, qualifications for divorce, and the use of SMS to divorce a person. This long-standing issue about handling divorces with technology, ongoing since the emergence of the telephone and computers, retains a currency in contemporary contexts. The issue of pronouncing divorce traditionally requires the pronouncement of "*talaq*" ("I divorce you") three times by the male; the key question in this case is whether this has to be face-to-face or whether it can be facilitated online. This introduces the issue of analogy in relation to religious opinions and how precedent associated with writing (with a pen) an intent to divorce can be transferred to digital contexts. A key aspect is an intention to divorce and the need for witnesses.[82]

OnIslam featured different perspectives on particular issues. Critical questions, along with articles and related materials (thus multipurposing content), were hyperlinked and highlighted. A good example was the section "What Is It Like to Be in a Polygamous Marriage?," which was produced by the Family Editorial Board. The section included "True Stories," in which people reflected on personal experience with polygamy, and articles for and against such marriages. The format of this content suggested an easy-to-navigate, accessible, and user-friendly magazine approach.[83]

Index page on website AboutIslam, http://aboutislam.net.

In the Ask the Counselor series, questions were put out to readers and also posted on Facebook and other social media. Readers could complete a form and send back their advice. The topic "I Hate the Look of My Fat Husband" elicited substantial correspondence and opinion related directly to religious ideas and lifestyle choices.[84]

OnIslam hosted videos on general religious issues and opinions from scholars, with discussions on religious authority and the outsourcing of religious opinions. As a whole, OnIslam was self-reflective, presenting a range of views within Sunni religious authority paradigms.[85] The site had high visibility, given the numbers of hits received in different forms. OnIslam also included awareness of issues associated with the internet and Islam, with discussions on virtual relationships, use of technology, and its impact on religious practice.[86]

Some scholars from OnIslam are now featured on AboutIslam.net, which has similar sections for scholarly advice and questions. Although its contributors are international, the domain is registered in Egypt. The database provides a high degree of searchability and clarity, although it does not extend back earlier than 2015—meaning that the opinions from OnIslam were unavailable. It is significant that each page of opinions can be distributed via a range of social media, including Facebook Messenger and WhatsApp,

Screenshot of Muhammad Saalih al-Munajjid discussing religious issues on YouTube, https://youtu.be/Pi8BGr1w_DE.

---

and that forms of social media contact are embedded into the site at every level. Live sessions are also being delivered (and archived). It will be interesting to see how AboutIslam.net responds to further online competition.

IslamQA.info

IslamQA was founded in 1997 by Syrian-born Sheikh Muhammad Saalih al-Munajjid in Saudi Arabia, which in internet terms makes it one of the longest running fatwa/question sites in a web format. According to Alexa.com, in September 2016 IslamQA.info held the highest profile for an Islam-related website.[87]

The site's content has evolved since its inception to include material in sixteen languages (in 2016) presented in web format and the use of diverse social media tools including WhatsApp.[88] It has been regularly updated since its launch, and the database is fully searchable. Questions can be emailed to the site. In August 2015, the English-language Twitter feed had 29,500 followers and had produced 3,900 tweets since 2009. The Arabic feed for IslamQA had only 94 followers for 704 tweets.[89] However, al-Munajjid's personal Arabic Twitter feed indicated over 964,000 followers and nearly 32,000 tweets; a personal English-language feed had 8,738 tweets and 5,462 followers (from August 2011).[90]

Al-Munajjid, who retains an extensive personal website as a hub for social media and other content, takes advantage of multimedia, using Twitter, Facebook, YouTube, and Google+ to present videos from his broadcasts (live-streamed and recorded). These include question-and-answer phone-in sessions and general discussions, where he has a laptop or tablet prominently placed on his desk as he speaks.[91] During the programs, IslamQA.info is peppered with slick animated infomercials, showing online channels promoting the website's services in various languages and utilizing Qur'anic recitation.[92] The videos demonstrate the centrality of the internet to al-Munajjid's IslamQA mission.

Al-Munajjid was trained by Shaykh 'Abd al-'Azeez ibn 'Abd-Allaah ibn Baaz, the influential Saudi Arabian theologian and scholar to whom al-Munajjid attributes his knowledge of fatwas. As with many traditional scholars, al-Munajjid presents full details of his educational bona fides, including his teachers. He provides information on where he was taught and particulars of the courses, offering a comprehensive picture of the types of influences that inform IslamQA. He gives less emphasis on his previous role as a diplomat in the Saudi Embassy in Washington, D.C.

Shaykh al-Munajjid came into conflict with authorities in Saudi Arabia, as only organizations directly linked to the kingdom were permitted to produce religious opinions. Despite this he has a high profile, even though the IslamQA site was blocked in Saudi Arabia in 2010.[93] Al-Munajjid attracted international publicity for banning snowmen and condemning Mickey Mouse—although it is possible in both cases something was lost in translation. Indeed, al-Munajjid issued a YouTube rebuttal in English on the subject.[94]

An article from Al Jazeera described al-Munajjid as a leading Salafi, allegedly influencing the activities of al-Qaeda and ISIS ("Islamic State").[95] The term *Salafi* has been used as shorthand for a complex myriad of positions and definitions of Islam, not necessarily mutually complementary. It has associations with reform-centered movements and also fundamentalism. The Islamic practices of the "pious ancestors" (*al-salaf as-salih*), the generation after Muhammad, are also described as Salafi. *Ahl al-Sunnah wa'l Jam'aa* can refer to "the People of Custom and Community," a traditional name for people adhering to the practices of the Prophet Muhammad. Groups using these terms are not necessarily affiliated or associated within an organizational hierarchy. Al-Munajjid has been criticized by other Muslim websites, including those that define themselves as "pure Salafi," and negatively associated with the Egyptian reformer and Muslim Brotherhood ideologue Sayyid Qutb.[96]

Command and Control in Muslim Digital Worlds

While reflecting technological and software shifts, IslamQA retains many of the categories from its earlier incarnations, with emphasis on personal law, basic tenets of belief, family law, jurisprudence, and Islamic sources. These and other categories are subdivided within the searchable database. All questions contained within the database have answers incorporating very detailed rulings and references to Islamic sources. There are numerous responses to technological issues within the site, demonstrating that IslamQA is aware of the potential problems that new technologies bring in relation to interpretive issues. The site includes a significant article on the "challenges" of rumors on the internet and the ways in which they influence attitudes toward religious beliefs.[97] One petitioner requested advice on whether he should give up the internet because it was leading him into sin. The response was as follows: "Yes, you may find in the Internet things that you will not find in the other sources mentioned, but what we are talking about here is the basis for your committing sin and blocking one means will not prevent a person from committing sin."[98]

The shift away from computers to mobile devices is reflected in the direction of IslamQA's content design. On the back of his website, al-Munajjid and his followers built an integrated media organization for his opinions and interpretations, with multilingual material outside of the core website, including e-books. All points integrate effectively with each other across technological platforms, and IslamQA has been quick to adopt the latest apps and multimedia forms.

Darul Ifta Deoband

Established in nineteenth-century India, the Deobandi movement traces its scholarly lineage back to the time of the Prophet Muhammad. The Darul Ifta (Fatwa Council, often referred to as the Department of Fatwa Research and Training) was founded in Deoband, India, and its founders, having unsuccessfully fought the British in the 1857 rebellion, chose to focus on religious practice and identity through the foundation of the Darul Uloom ("House of Knowledge"). This included a shift away from so-called innovative religious practices, although there was an element of Sufi influence.[99]

This core Darul Ifta website is based in the center of the city of Deoband, Uttar Pradesh, India. Developed in 2007, the database includes Urdu and English opinions from a team of muftis, operating with a dedicated internet department that translates, composes, and uploads the opinions.[100] In addition to the readership in the Indian subcontinent is a network of worldwide

Deobandi followers. Numerous other websites are associated with the Deobandi perspectives, which place great emphasis on scholarly precedent and authority, although they do not all claim to have official endorsement by Darul Ifta.[101] The production of these fatwas do not mean that they are binding but can be seen as potentially influential for followers guided by a particular scholar. Concerns have been generated regarding some of the opinions offered in Deoband, particularly associated with gender roles.[102]

The Darul Ifta's emphasis on internet materials has required a substantial investment of time and people in order to develop, maintain, and facilitate the website. This can be seen in the amount of content that is presented: in August 2015, for example, 16,651 "fatwas" were issued in Urdu in August 2015 and 7,765 were issued in English. Some crossover between languages occurs in the categories and subcategories. The site was designed so that the same categories are found in both the Urdu and English sections of the site. Subjects such as Islamic beliefs, deviant sects, prayer, marriage, and dream interpretation received substantially more opinions in Urdu than in English.

One key question that is addressed within this website is on the conflict between Deobandis and Barelwis, which reflects differences in leadership, interpretation, and opinion that have led to accusations of unbelief and blasphemy on both "sides." The Barelwis were also founded in India, established on the writings of Mawlana Ahmad Reza Khan Barelwi (1856–1921), a "reformer" who sought to remove so-called innovation from Islam—and made good use of printing Urdu texts in order to promote his understanding, which held a strong Sufi orientation.[103] His pronouncements on "deviant" practices have extended to reactions to events in India and elsewhere.

In response to questions emailed to the website, scholars discuss topical themes and present opinions and expertise. Elsewhere, the site reflects on the legitimacy of "sects," including Salafis, and comments on their leaders and media figures. Within the answers, references to other online materials reinforce perspectives. This is an online space where relatively mundane issues are also addressed, such as the analysis of dreams as potential portents of wealth or marriage. The site focuses in microdetail on numerous religious practices associated with ritual, purity, and practice, including advice on food and drink, such as the consumption of squirrel (not permitted), seafood (varied responses according to different schools of thought), and intoxicating drinks and substances (forbidden), and food production issues.[104]

The site emphasizes that all elements of life require explanation, interpretation, and opinion. While the site is based in India, the historical migration of people from the subcontinent means there is substantial demand for

Command and Control in Muslim Digital Worlds

opinions elsewhere. In the UK, it has recently been estimated that 44 percent of UK mosques were linked to Deobandi perspectives.[105] Deobandis are represented by diverse UK organizations and platforms, not necessarily all in line with one another. Some Deobandi-associated elements internationally have had links with the Taliban and al-Qaeda, although this has categorically not been endorsed by other Deobandi groups.

Such diversity is reflected as much online as it is within mosques. The Darul Ulooms are extensively networked: the Haq Islam website hub presents articles and lectures and links to key Deobandi organizations worldwide.[106] In terms of internet representation, within the UK context key figures are utilizing social media. An example is Gujarat-born Sheikh Riyadh ul-Haq, a head imam at Birmingham Central Mosque who was trained at a Darul Uloom seminary in Bury, who has become influential via YouTube and podcasts of recorded lectures.[107]

Decision-making can become more localized, as shown by Mufti Muhammed ibn Adam al-Kawthari, a UK-born scholar trained in Bury, whose opinions are featured on DarulIftaa.com. In addition to providing traditional religious messages and interpretations, this website addresses contemporary concerns such as cosmetic surgery, voting in elections, the use of radio and other media, responses to terrorism, the appropriateness of wearing football shirts with beer logos, and the permissibility of playing musical instruments. A number of questions focus on local concerns. Mufti Muhammed ibn Adam answers questions individually in a detailed fashion. The searchable database is divided into primary categories.[108]

Deobandi thought is communicated via numerous media channels and websites to followers in global and local contexts. This is not the full picture, given the emphasis on dissemination within mosques, printed materials, other media outlets (such as television and radio), and word-of-mouth. India enjoys a high level of digital access, but significant sectors are underrepresented online, including followers of the Darul Ifta Deoband. The web content represents a platform on which the scholarly perspectives are disseminated, in line with improvements in digital literacy and access.

Sistani.org

Sistani.org is based on the authority of Ayatullah al Uzama As-Sayyed Ali al-Husayni al-Sistani, a prominent Iraqi Shi'a cleric. Al-Sistani's followers have been proactive online for many years, developing a database of questions and answers, legal texts, ritual information, and books in Arabic, Azerbaijani,

English, Farsi, French, Turkish, and Urdu. The ritual information is presented thematically, while the Q&A section covers a multitude of themes, including living as a Muslim in a minority context. The website reflects al-Sistani's outlook and the body of knowledge informing Shi'a development, including material on shrines and key figures.[109] There is comparable content across languages, including the central component, where responses are provided to user questions.

In English, Al-Sistani.org's database contains responses to over 770 questions, searchable by topic and in web format; in Arabic, many fatwas were assembled into a PDF/zip file format. Differences might imply different access and user patterns between audiences. Responses can be basic in nature, compared with IslamQA or OnIslam.net. Topics reflect contemporary concerns, such as technology, as well as ritualistic practices and issues. Answers echoing al-Sistani's own approach to Shi'ism include thoughts on who is qualified to provide advice and opinions ("Following a Mujtahid") and how to act according to a Shi'ite approach to taqlid: "Taqlid in religious laws means acting according to the verdict of a Mujtahid. It is necessary for the Mujtahid who is followed, to be male, Shi'ah Ithna Ash'ari, adult, sane, of legitimate birth, living and just ('Adil)."[110]

This opinion represents a specific perspective of Ithna 'Ashari Shi'ism ("Twelver" Shi'ism), not necessarily one that would be embraced by other branches and certainly not one that would be shared with all Sunni Muslims. Particularly significant in the context of Iraq is the discussion about purity, including approaches toward non-Muslims: "The Kitab (that is, the Jews, the Christians and the Zoroastrians) are ritually pure (tahir) as long as you do not know that they have become ritually impure (najis) by coming into contact with an impure object. You can follow this ruling when dealing with them."[111] It is significant that the Zoroastrians are included in this equation, given their presence in (and historical links to) Iraq and Iran.

In addition to Question and Answers, a searchable listing of books provides detailed advice on aspects of Shi'a practice and focuses on ritual purity, leadership, religious practices, transactions, and family law. Each book provides extensive detail, with precedent, and requires more complex reading than do the simple, more accessible question-and-answer options on the site.

Within a listing of institutes are links to thirty-four different affiliated organizations and institutions endorsed by al-Sistani. These also host content relating to his thoughts and interpretations. The Imam Ali Foundation–London networks followers together, with Arabic, Farsi, French, Urdu, Spanish, and

Command and Control in Muslim Digital Worlds

English content.[112] There is an option to "Ask a Question" but no specific searchable database. A list of several pages of questions and answers looks at issues associated with living in Western contexts. Themes include the "purity" of proximity to non-Muslims, finding halal food, burial in non-Muslim cemeteries, finance, locating a job that supports prayer, shopping in supermarkets, consumption of alcohol-free beer, insurance, cheating in exams, and the technicalities of living appropriately within Western contexts.

Al-Sistani's worldview is shared and circulated across different markets, including through the Aalulbayt Global Information Center based in Qom. Founded in 1998, the center has a specific remit to promote Shi'ism under al-Sistani's guidance, with content in twenty-seven languages.[113] The production of fatwas is central, together with information on Islamic sciences and gateways to other sites. The core site is text-based and has not evolved into a social media hub. The English-language site focuses on article distribution, an ethos reflected in other languages presented via the portal. While al-Sistani is represented on Twitter and his official Arabic page has over 20,000 followers, no tweets are available.[114] A Facebook page has a wider reach, with more than 37,000 "likes."[115] The websites are information-rich but dated in terms of social media and the requirements of Web 2.0. Their design has not moved on substantially, compared with other sites; their primary focus is on content rather than on interfacing.

Astan Quds Razavi

Astan Quds Razavi is a key Iranian charitable foundation, with considerable financial and religious influence, based around the Imam Reza Shrine in Mashhad City. Imam Ali ibn Musa al-Reza was the eighth Shi'a imam and is viewed as a martyr by his followers. His shrine attracts millions of visitors every year, making it a distinct focal point for this particular branch of Shi'ism.

The Astan Quds Razavi website acts as a hub for numerous educational, charitable, and business activities. It offers the opportunity for a person to have a pilgrimage undertaken "vicariously" on his or her behalf through the completion of an email form. All aspects of the shrine can be visited virtually through 360-degree images. Live broadcasts from the shrine are facilitated through an app. The invocation of specific prayers relating to the shrine can be selected via the main page, which also has an extensive online library.

The multilingual website acts as a significant focal point for Astan Quds Razavi's regional and international activities.[116] It is important in the way

Home page of the Iranian charitable foundation
Astan Quds Razavi, http://aqr.ir.

it can mobilize substantial resources to communicate to its audiences, and it has integrated multimedia into many of its activities to provide Iranian and other site visitors with a perspective relating specifically to the role of the foundation in Iranian religious life. This role extends into political and economic zones, given its strong relationship with the Iranian government, and it can also be a focal point for detractors. Its conservative outlook was in contention with that of President Hassan Rouhani, with the foundation's leader, Ebrahim Raisi, seen as a possible successor to Rouhani.[117] The 2017 election saw Rouhani as a victor, but Raisi and his supporters continued to reinforce his status, and the vision of the foundation, through Astan Quds Razavi's online activities.

eShaykh.com

Followers of Mawlana Shaykh Nazim Adil Al-Haqqani and the Naqshbandi-Haqqani Sufi Order established eShaykh as part of their extensive international internet presence.[118] Although Al-Haqqani was based in Northern Cyprus, the hub website SufiLive is hosted in the United States, and its primary religious opinions outlet is eShaykh.

Home page of eShaykh.com, http://eshaykh.com.

An emphasis on Islamic mysticism is reflected in the types of questions and responses available with a searchable database. One key area, outside basic religious enquiry and practice, is a focus on dream interpretation (also seen on the unrelated Darul Ifta pages). Nearly 5,000 questions have been delivered on this subject area alone. Questions are anonymous; answers are concise and reference specific Islamic concepts and sources. Some dreams relate specifically to religious experiences, with the presence of the sheikh within them (seen in a very positive light).[119] Dreams provide advice concerning relationships, ritual, and religious obligations. Symbolism is attached to these dreams in different forms. Some general questions elsewhere on the site, in relation to beliefs and practices in particular, also link into the interpretation of dreams.

Technology forms a subtext to a number of issues that are discussed within the pages of eShaykh. A question about computer gaming addiction as a distraction from worshipping elicited the response, "Instead of losing yourself in cyberspace lose yourself in Allah's Grace."[120] Practical matters are also addressed, such as whether it is appropriate to use a website in order to find a marriage partner (generally approved, within certain religious provisos).[121] Concerns regarding lost love have been sent to scholars for attention, the advice being that prayer provides an appropriate solution.[122]

eShaykh.com goes into substantial detail on many aspects of religious practices, especially the requirements of this Naqshbandi-Haqqani branch of Sufism. Among the thousands of opinions and responses, advice is given on how to approach allegiance to the Sufi order, including the benefits in terms of religious practice and understanding, with a focus on this particular order. Divine intercession is also available online, through submitting a prayer request via an online form (this requires logging in to the site).

The website demonstrates how significant the internet can be in the formulation and development of individual beliefs. It assumes a technologically literate approach to religious authority, as part of a wider internet hub associated with this Sufi order, and takes advantage of many aspects of networking, with a resonance in concepts associated with Sufism in general. The hub links into multimedia elements, including the opportunity for online initiation, a media library, and the 24/7 SufiLiveTV with regularly updated film clips of Sufi activity from across the world. A significant performative element is incorporated, with the filming of ritual singing and music.[123] The focus on the order's spiritual leader Shaykh Hisham Kabbani's sermons and pronouncements is reinforced by Twitter, with short statements on authoritative issues. As with many other aspects of the order, it is possible to donate via credit and debit cards, as well as bank forms, via the website. Consequently, in addition to being a hub for spiritual and religious matters, eShaykh.com is a financial hub. This is reflected elsewhere in the order's social media activities.

CONCLUSION

The above survey of question-and-answer-related sites is a snapshot of opinions generated online and of the methods in which information is dispensed. Numerous other examples exist online, offering different perspectives on Islam and operating in diverse cultural, religious, and geographic information marketplaces. From the globally oriented organizations working through multiple networks of authority to the locally oriented concerns within microcommunities, the extent to which advice delivered online is followed is open to question. People may visit a site for different reasons, and there is no feedback as to whether an opinion was observed and acted upon. The sites offer an indication of long-standing religious concerns and issues, as well as contemporary ones requiring an authoritative opinion. In some cases, they present a challenge to traditional frameworks of religious authority, although many of these frameworks are themselves represented online.

Information drawn from online sources is used in conjunction with more traditional channels of authority, from print, other media, mosques, and face-to-face contact. The dynamics of decision-making have shifted in line with the options available to the digitally literate and digitally connected Muslim, who might go online to seek advice in the same way he or she might shop around for a product or look up symptoms online prior to going to a doctor. The results may be spiritual and life changing for some and might simply satisfy the curiosity of others. Because of some of the personal issues frequently expressed, anonymity is often paramount on such sites; they have therefore built up confidence among their audiences for discretion. Within a competitive information marketplace, the investment of time and energy into such question-and-answer websites indicates intensified recognition from religious authorities that a strong digital presence is necessary.

As levels of connectivity increase and the digital divide diminishes, integration of social media into daily discussions on issues of religious authority increases in significance. The ways in which information is promulgated, with many channels promoting concepts of interpretation through phones, tablets, and computers that are always on, suggest that for some consumers of religious information, there are new and evolving patterns of processing Islamic data. The convenience of consumption via digital media may overwhelm the integrity of the content; if the medium does, pace McLuhan, overcome the message, then this may mean that the value of significant, developed theories and opinions from nondigitally literate authorities is lost. These may be destined to emerge in a more rarefied, considered, edited, and traditional format (such as the printed page or a spoken sermon). Over time, the impact of such material may be more substantial than that of a tweet, but it may not reach the same number of readers. The *type* of audience is clearly significant here, rather than the *numbers* reflected in web statistics, followers, and reposts. This again raises questions associated with Habermas, in terms of whether critical perspectives are eroded through manipulation of opinion in these public spheres. It would be problematic to quantify any impact here. Content providers are keen to apply technology to promote specific religious and societal goals through such Q&A sites. These are open to contestation and challenge, in jostling virtual spheres influenced by the power of religious language, imagery, and personality. These factors combine with the ways that different media forms create participatory and interactive elements, *if* they are utilized and designed in such a way to reach a critical mass audience.

Habermas may not have anticipated the *number* of public spheres that might emerge to challenge conventional power and authority and that they would constantly stream (in some cases) with content. Constantly changing content can lead to user concerns about keeping up-to-date with developments and balancing intake of information with demands from other sectors of digital media. The sense of obligation, in order to remain in touch with religious centers online, will vary from individual to individual. The demands on authority centers to produce streaming content and balance digital requirements with traditional perspectives on decision-making and control may be dependent on levels of digital literacy within organizations and platforms. The idea that imams, muftis, and scholars are inputting data themselves used to be unrealistic, in the early days of the internet; now, there is a sense of awareness of the medium and participation in the process of data distribution and content creation from religious actors and individuals.

Smartphone Jihad

Hashtags in Conflict Zones

DEFINING JIHAD

Jihad is a dominant theme in conversations about Islam and the internet. This is particularly true when ascertaining its online manifestations and the pronouncements of prominent activists, ideologues, and organizations. From a contemporary "Western" historical and social perspective, it is the lesser jihad that has made the greatest impact and received the most attention, academically, politically, and socially, in terms of online activities associated with Islam.[1] This may be disproportionate attention compared with the numerous other concerns associated with cyber-Islamic environments that are also significant and influential.

The concept of jihad, erroneously or not, has been a significant element in many Western perceptions of Islam. Its use is synonymous with ultraviolent terrorism and anti-Western political movements seeking a return to Islamic roots. It is also used as a convenient orientalist, reductive label often applied by secular, non-Muslim, and even Muslim societies to explain movements that may or may not have "Islamic" religious motivations behind them.

Jihad is an incendiary term, often applied without consideration of its nuanced meanings, which are worth considering briefly here. The word is the abstract noun of the Arabic verb *jahada* ("exerted"). It is commonly translated (and has transitioned into the English language) as "holy war," a military action sanctioned (purportedly or otherwise) in the name of God, and it is the *lesser jihad*. The *greater jihad* could be explained as a spiritual and religious striving on a path toward God or in the name of God. Understandings of jihad can have both exoteric and esoteric emphases and can be examined on the term's external aspects alone and also on its deeper, exegetical meanings. The greater jihad, when seen as a striving for an inner perfection, is an essential component of Islam. Definitions of greater jihad in Islam may suggest the power of an individual to have an overall effect on the whole society.

The actions and conduct of the Prophet Muhammad offer a source by which the importance of jihad in Islam can be ascertained, with examples drawn from his own experiences being a template for approaches to jihad. The concept of jihad can be as much (or more) about approaches to prayer and spirituality as about the necessary justification for war. In Sunni Islam (where there can be different concepts of religious leadership), the question arises of who has the capacity to judge the instigation (or not) of lesser jihad. Whether this lies in the hands of a caliph, an 'alim (religious scholar), or some other form of ideologue is an open question—especially given the ways in which jihad is articulated online.[2]

In Shi'ism, the roles of Ali ibn Abi Talib and the descendants of the Prophet can be significant in defining approaches to the ideals of jihad, for example through the martyrdom of his grandson Husayn ibn Ali in Karbala. Shi'ism reflects different interpretative approaches toward religious authority, which are frequently articulated online. Historically, in Shi'ism, an imam's sanction was required to justify a jihad, the imam being a descendant of the ahl al-bayt (literally, "people of the Prophet's house," essentially his family). A Shi'a Muslim might have to give allegiance to an imam when undertaking a jihad—an allegiance known as walaya.

Divergence can appear between different Muslim perspectives on jihad, and not just between Sunni and Shi'a but within Sunni and Shi'a factions. The term jihadist has also emerged to promote the militaristic definition of jihad and has to an extent become interchangeable (for some) with Islamist, with attendant negative implications. It has become particularly synonymous with online activism promoting specific militaristically oriented interpretations of Islam. Other terminologies are also applied, associated in particular with permutations of "Salafi" concepts, which themselves can be diffuse.[3]

MOTIVATING JIHAD

The motivation of so-called jihad activity, especially within minority contexts, is related to a multitude of influences and factors that go beyond specifically "Islamic" factors and toward social, economic, cultural, and political elements that have led to disaffection: "The root causes of terrorism and violent radicalism are extremely complex, multifaceted, and often intertwined. They resist simplification and easy categorization."[4] Factors leading individuals to join jihad activity may include perceived empathy with an external cause, especially if it is linked to "Western" foreign policy in a Muslim context, together with disaffection and identity crises.[5] Radicalization itself is subject to a multiplicity of definitions and constructs.[6]

Psychological factors can also play an important part within this process, including ideas associated with group identity formation, which have shifted with the emergence of the internet. Small groups of homogeneous cells can include family members and friends, who may be influenced by internet content, and can be decentralized and semiautonomous.[7] Recent survey research also suggests that issues associated with mental health, depression, and psychiatric illness can influence the radicalization processes.[8] Economic deprivation is not necessarily a factor within the profiles of radicalized individuals.[9]

Clearly, different factors prompt individuals to join jihad activity, albeit with some common themes. Recruiters play up disaffection in their rhetoric, couched within a framework of religious or pseudo-religious terminology, while utilizing trigger themes and emotive language in order to engender levels of affiliation, participation, and support. The BBC, reporting on the activity of a young extremist, commented: "Young people, inevitably curious and not hearing the answers they wanted at home, were looking for solutions. Some became obsessed with the hyper-violence that the IS social media machine began pumping out to the Internet."[10]

Internet-driven elements can contribute to the recruitment paradigm in the ways in which they fuel rebellion and provide a means through which anger and resentment can be expressed. Oliver Roy describes how "they choose to Islamise their own radicalization but none of them was a Salafi or a Muslim fundamentalist before going into terrorism."[11] Jihad has, according to this analysis, become a driver for radicalization rather than its cause. Internet-driven media are able to influence this process, especially given the saturated state of social media as part of popular culture in general and given the forms of jihad discourse in particular. The design of jihad-related content has made a specific effort to tap into these trends and societal concerns.

EVOLVING E-JIHAD

The integration of social media and the internet into jihad campaigning became a key driver within strategic planning and propagation toward diverse audiences. From the images generated by Chechen forces in the 1990s to Osama bin Laden videos, jihad newscasts, and the application of streaming social media during campaigns, expectations of audiences and participants have focused on the utilization of internet-driven media across a variety of conflict zones and contexts.[12] I have previously referred to the electronic jihad ("e-jihad") as a digital sword striking a variety of targets. There is conceptual and methodological continuity between formative iterations of online jihad and more recent social media–driven forms, even if the causes and audiences may differ.

E-jihad content is designed for consumption beyond the boundaries of disparate followers, journalists, media analysts, and security personnel. Rhetorical statements, "justifications" of actions, and video actuality are significant features of it. Capturing content has become embedded in on-the-ground jihad activity, as have the extensively choreographed publicity films. They integrate specific formulations of global and local religious symbolism and utilize religious language drawn from the Qur'an and other sources. As publicity drivers, the use of such materials has been a central element of campaigning.

Alongside these aspects, the internet has been applied for logistical purposes through the production of online magazines promoting jihad and educating readers as to its technical methodologies and practicalities. Such use has become a key element for recruitment, funding, and participation opportunities. Leaders, participants, strategists, and technical operators have in many cases a firm grasp of the potentiality of media use. They encourage good internet practice in terms of improvements in technical production, editing, utilization of multiple distribution channels, and integration of media forms. These improvements emulate practices from creative communities elsewhere and reflect the emergence of a generation of digitally literate participants well versed in the use of information technologies. In a further echo of Marshall McLuhan, the power of messages in this sphere is driven by the medium, although the amount and type of content can be overwhelming to observe.

An ability to work within the frameworks of technology can be as important as familiarity with religious sources. Indeed, the former may be more prominent than the latter in some jihad-oriented contexts, where views of ideologues are repurposed and recycled for the purposes of e-jihad. In some cases, e-jihad has included an aptitude for technological disruption and an ability to evade censorship and control.

Within the infrastructures of diverse campaigns and organizations, technical personnel have increasingly formed part of the hierarchy, integrated rather than a bolted-on element or afterthought to campaigns. From the production of posters and statements by 9/11 participants to the real-time tweets from the Somali al-Qaeda affiliate al-Shabaab during the 2013 Nairobi shopping mall siege and the streaming actuality of "Islamic State" (IS), a complex and intense variety of statements and content has emerged.

The application of social media has had an impact on a number of different zones of conflict: within Nigeria, for example, the emergence of the Nigerian pro-al-Qaeda group Boko Haram saw the use of social media to highlight its campaigning and military activities, including bombings, kidnappings, and other attacks. Boko Haram's social media use, influenced by the online and offline strategies and approaches of IS, surpassed local expectations. Boko Haram pledged allegiance to IS in 2015 and began sharing supportive data.[13]

State security organizations recognized that social media was an effective jihadi recruitment channel in a number of contexts.[14] In the UK, a parliamentary committee saw social media as the most prominent factor in recruitment.[15] In Germany, the impact of online recruitment has been highlighted, including specific psychological approaches and profiling of target audiences, showing German jihadis in action.[16]

Jihad approaches have been shaped and articulated in part through online activities, produced in line with technical innovations and widening access to technologies across a multiplicity of spheres and zones. Online definitions of jihad—including the perspectives in Chechnya, particularly in the late 1990s through early 2000s, where the use of video recordings promoting jihad-oriented activity was in part pioneered—are diffuse and not necessarily in line with one another. Islamic organizations in Lebanon and Palestine have also drawn on internet technologies to promote diverse causes and agendas.

Greatest attention has been paid to al-Qaeda, whose ideologues and affiliates—particularly post-9/11—disseminate interpretations of jihad across multiple media platforms to nuanced audiences. The impact of these has been increased exposure in world media, an immediacy of statements being broadcast, and the integration of online production into all aspects of campaigning (from conceptualization to aftermath). Results have been increased funding, widening recruitment, an interlinking of diverse campaigns and agendas, and a promotion of the concept of globalization in relation to jihad.

Social media, in particular, has become increasingly integrated into jihad campaigns. Many online articulations of jihad have a short life online and disappear from the web. My intention here is to provide a way of navigating through online discourse, particularly that focused on Western audiences. One emphasis is the application of online media by al-Qaeda and its affiliates;

the developments by so-called Islamic State/ISIS/ISIL/Daesh will be discussed in the next chapter.

The Taliban's emergence in late-1990s Afghanistan projected anti-Western, antitechnological interpretations of Islam. However, supporters of the Taliban were utilizing the internet. Despite proclamations against technology, online materials have provided a conduit of propagation, recruits, and finances.[17] Use of social media in a variety of languages and formats predated that of al-Shabaab and ISIS by several years.[18] Very basic pro-Taliban sites emerged in the 1990s, soliciting finance and even providing bank account numbers and addresses. Nowadays, more sophisticated channels are utilized in a strategic and considered manner in a way that—perhaps ironically for observers—has demonstrated a way forward for the application of social media in jihadi contexts. Given limited internet infrastructure in Afghanistan, distribution patterns have incorporated offline models, where files are copied for distribution or played to audiences in zones lacking internet access.[19]

Taliban leaders have used electronic media to facilitate interviews and to broadcast opinions without revealing their location.[20] Taliban outlets have produced online magazines that show activities on different fronts, drawing on embedded reporters. The *Voice of Shariah* and the *Voice of Jihad* include online question-and-answer services.[21] The sites are multilingual, with materials in local languages such as Dari and Pashto as well as in Arabic, Urdu, English, and Persian. Particularly significant are the "official" Emerah.net and Shahamat.info channels, which emerged from their origins in 1990s sites such as Taliban Online.[22] By 2015, Taliban supporters were posting content onto the encrypted Telegram channel, for example through its Alemarah-English-Online account. An Android Alemarah app was also introduced in 2016, while WhatsApp was being used to solicit donations through the traditional *hawala* (informal transfer transaction) payment system (having previously used PayPal).[23]

There is always the possibility of events being set up for the cameras online (as in other media forms), especially for the ironically titled photographic magazine *In Fight*.[24] One magazine sought to proclaim a "caliphate" stretching from Afghanistan to Spain.[25] The magazines are couched in religious messages and languages and specific Taliban-centric definitions of jihad, although magazines themselves have been in part superseded by social media channels.[26] Reliance on the online magazine format is based on access opportunities, restricted literacy, and the digital divide. Whereas some urban settings in Afghanistan have reasonable internet connectivity, outside of urban centers such content would have to be distributed via memory sticks or offline channels (such as Bluetooth circulation via mobile phone).

There remains an audience locally and internationally for the Taliban's internet content, although a primary focus in Afghanistan is on rudimentary mobile radio broadcasts.[27] Along with more traditional propagation routes, the use of Twitter and Facebook has been endorsed by Taliban supporters, with feeds in English, Pashto, and other languages. On occasion, these have been shut down but reemerged.[28] Twitter disputes have also flared up between U.S. agencies and Taliban supporters.[29]

The Taliban and its affiliates have developed a nuanced media strategy, integrating and embedding media into their campaigning and providing regularly updated content in a variety of formats. Emphasis on encryption and secure messaging for logistics and fund-raising processes has grown.[30] There is continuity from offline, more traditional methods of distribution to the use of online and social media, aimed as much at international audiences as at locals. Increases in access and digital literacy and cheaper technology have all been relevant factors in promoting the Taliban's worldview. There is now an approach that draws on social media apps and content in multiple languages for nuanced local and global audiences.

E-JIHAD SOMALIA

Prior to the emergence of IS, some of the most successful jihad applications of social media as a recruitment, fund-raising, and publicity tool were associated with al-Shabaab, an al-Qaeda affiliate in Somalia.[31] Al-Shabaab was also reaching out to diaspora communities for support in what had become a long-term civil war.[32] Al-Shabaab drew on concepts developed by al-Qaeda and had members who had in some cases participated in al-Qaeda activities in other zones. Al-Shabaab sought to impose its interpretations of Islamic law in Somalia, which led to its controlling of territories in the region. The internet was applied to bring al-Shabaab into the bigger al-Qaeda network through official statements and greetings of affiliation. Ayman al-Zawahiri welcomed the group in 2012.[33] One reporter noted that there was a difference between al-Qaeda and al-Shabaab and that this was represented online, in terms of emphasis on domestic agendas,[34] and also shown in the output of @HSMPress on Twitter, a handle derived from Harakat al-Shabaab al-Mujahideen (Movement of Mujahideen Youth).[35]

Al-Shabaab's use of smartphones was out of line with its approaches toward technology in general. In Somalia, there was a reaction to al-Shabaab banning mobile phone use in 2013 in the territories the organization controlled on the basis that phones had potential use for spying activities.[36] Yet technology became an integral part of al-Shabaab activities at every level, including recruitment and propagation of a religious justification for its undertakings.[37] This systems change was also represented in the communications shift, with the use of mobile technology to present streaming updates of al-Shabaab actions—notoriously during the 2013 attack on a Nairobi shopping mall, which was effectively "live tweeted" in real time and included graphic updates and religious justifications for what became a siege that left many shoppers dead.

Al-Shabaab had firmly integrated social media into its strategy for statements and updates, and this became particularly focused during the phases of the Westgate mall siege in Nairobi. Posts appeared in nuanced and relatively sophisticated English, which could counter assumptions about e-jihad. "What is striking about their tweets is their native and even high-brow use of the English-language," noted Rebecca Chao. "Words and phrases like 'minuscule in nature' and 'sangfroid' do not seem to belong to the language of violent jihadists."[38]

The organization was associated with the "white widow" Samantha Lewthwaite, British convert wife of 2005 London bomber Jermaine Lindsay, who absconded to Kenya and developed web content supportive of concepts of jihad. Lewthwaite created the blog *Fears and Tears: The Confessions of a Female Muhajid*. She was implicated in al-Shabaab activities, including at one time being cited as the alleged ringleader of (and participant in) the Westgate mall siege. This was emphasized in a tweet from al-Shabaab (which may go counter to earlier analyses of sophisticated language): "@HSM-PRESSOFFICE2: Sherafiyah lewthwaite aka Samantha is a very vrave [sic] lady," it read; "were [sic] happier to have her in our ranks #westgate #AlShabaab COWARDS!"[39] Attempts have been made to close down al-Shabaab Twitter accounts, but they often reemerge with other identities, a process likened to the "Whac-a-Mole" game.[40]

Al-Shabaab benefited from advice derived from other e-jihad zones.[41] Such information ranged from generic information (not necessarily from jihadi sources) to elements of the Dark Web where passwords were required to access complex encrypted technical information. The Dark Web was a natural zone for the acquisition of a range of logistical information relevant for those participating in militaristic jihad. Googling "jihad" would reveal substantial data, in particular for recruits from nonmilitaristic backgrounds seeking a form of participation that did not require formal membership or allegiances. The dynamics of such activities led to internet-specific forms of recruitment.

Events in Somalia saw the emergence of specific internet "personalities," including American jihadi Omar Hammami (Abu Mansoor Al-Amriki). He produced a number of hip-hop tracks, derided on some channels, aimed toward urban Muslim youth who did not necessarily appreciate his musicality or application of hip-hop. Hammami used Twitter to update his situation when he was under siege—physically and digitally—by his opponents.[42] Having been renounced on al-Shabaab's official Twitter account, @HSMPress, Hammami sought to resolve the conflict with the assistance of scholars through an online video.[43] He had an FBI reward on his head, but it was because of religious and political differences with al-Shabaab leader Ahmed Godane that Hammani paid the ultimate price for factional fighting in al-Shabaab, although his hip-hop attempts live on in cyberspace.[44]

Attempts by social media companies to close down the accounts of al-Shabaab platforms have been sporadic and generally unsuccessful. Media activists have easily established new accounts, even if they have a relatively short shelf life, and transferred their followers across. Hashtags assist across diverse Twitter accounts, supporters receive and repost information, and media from embedded sources are quickly circulated across social media networks. Social media is a natural place for not only supporters but also observers and opponents to acquire data. Social media has drawn attention to an underrepresented jihad conflict zone.

E-JIHAD AL-QAEDA

Participation in jihad on all sides could be motivated by internet content, and information about logistical issues was frequently posted online in social media and other forums. Social media updates and sharing indicated the locations of fighters as they progressed through their training and mobilization, although whether their field commanders appreciated such updating might be open to question.

The use of social media by al-Qaeda raised alarm bells for some online observers, although really it represented a logical progression from the use of other media.[45] Various Facebook pages purported to present Osama bin Laden's Facebook page, suggesting a status as "Prince of Mujahideen" and location as "mountains of the world."[46] In truth, these could have been produced by any number of official or unofficial supporters or even generated as "honeypot" pages to glean information on visitors. The extent to which bin Laden ever used Facebook himself is open to question.

A U.S. Department of Homeland Security report identified the nuanced ways in which al-Qaeda sought to disseminate its message, going beyond the "converted" to reach other audiences, including through Facebook posts: "Given that in terror networks social bonds tend to be more significant than external factors like shared hatred or ideology, social networking interfaces whose purpose is to virtually connect people based on such common social bonds clearly lend themselves to extremist use and recruitment efforts."[47]

The report picked up on the ways in which anonymity and internet security advice were presented through al-Qaeda channels. There were concerns regarding how a government could deal with jihadi online activities and yet *not* suppress free speech.[48]

Within al-Qaeda sectors, there were suggestions that migrations to diverse social media were influencing the traditional online forums and chat rooms, which had previously been hives of activity. More secure, user-friendly, and immediate forms of communication precipitated this decline and led to a diversification of media strategies, including nuanced products for specific audiences.[49] Some within al-Qaeda thought that the quality of the organization's content and its technical delivery had to be improved.[50]

Even dress codes were adjusted to suit specific online audiences. A German-language video in 2009 from al-Qaeda featured former Bonn resident Bekkay Harrach wearing a Western business suit as he addressed his audience with jihad rhetoric.[51] In 2010, Harrach was killed leading a mission on Bagram Air Base in Afghanistan.[52] The impact of a German-language video showing a person in Western dress may have been designed for publicity value as much as for recruitment objectives. It certainly highlighted Harrach's profile and helped publicize al-Qaeda objectives in Afghanistan. Harrach had featured in other videos, although this was the first time he was in a suit, which made an impact on viewers: "What we have here is the most explicit trans-epistemological appeal to Western Muslims from a Western-rooted al-Qaida individual dressed like a Western circus ringmaster (I don't think that's the image they were shooting for). . . . It is their attempt to look, smell, sound and talk like youth in the West albeit they exist on a fundamentally different epistemological plane. He is al-Qaida's epistemological ambassador."[53]

This development became familiar in other jihad-oriented contexts, with a use of colloquial language and the presentation of specific cultural signals and values that sought to attune presenters to specific audiences. In many ways, this marked a generational shift: increasingly digitally literate proponents of jihad were more autonomous than their predecessors in terms of being self-radicalized and trained through online sources.[54] The notion of "lone wolf" operatives, inspired by online content, was initially met with derision by some observers. However, there was evidence that it may have played a role in some prominent jihad-oriented cases, such as the 2013 attack on the Boston Marathon by the Tsarnaev brothers.

The integration of the internet into operations supporting al-Qaeda strategic aims was highlighted in Stockholm in 2010 when the bomb attack by Taimour Abdulwahab al-Abdaly immediately featured on the Shumukh internet forum and al-Hanin website, and a Facebook page was established celebrating al-Abdaly's "martyrdom."[55] It was claimed that al-Abdaly, a naturalized Swede born in Iraq and with a UK education, was supportive of the Islamic State of Iraq, a pro-al-Qaeda organization.[56] Statements were sent to news agencies in Swedish and Arabic, complete with audio files, "justifying" the attack. The Facebook page remained online for several days after the bombing, showing his activities on a dating site, his likes of the Islamic caliphate and Apple iPad, and posts of radical sermons.[57]

In March 2012, Muhammad Merah recorded an attack he undertook in the name of al-Qaeda in France on soldiers and a Jewish school. Merah posted the video on a memory stick to Al Jazeera, which refused to broadcast it. He was killed after a gun battle in Toulouse, but there were fears that the footage would appear online.[58] Merah was commemorated in an online montage, which borrowed from an archive of montages, featuring jihad-oriented *nasheed* recitations alongside images of bin Laden and Ayman al-Zawahiri.[59] A similar film was uploaded in 2009 after Nidal Malik Hasan attacked the Fort Hood army base in Texas. The commemoration of "martyrs" and "heroes" online has a long-standing history from other jihad campaigns, predating (and unlinked to) the emergence of al-Qaeda, such as the galleries of Hamas and Hezbollah "martyrs" emerging on the web in the late 1990s.[60]

The integration of media and campaigning reflects an enduring pattern, utilized on numerous jihadi fronts. In Russia, video was posted by a member of an Ingushetian front of the North Caucasus movement, showing its leader, Said Buryatsky, giving a "farewell sermon"; he was implicated as organizer of a bombing on the Nevsky Express in 2009. This was part of a long-term jihadist campaign linked to the North Caucasus, which had made extensive use of online media.[61] Similar approaches to operations were utilized by IS, prior to suicide missions in Iraq and Syria; an attack on tourists in Sousse, Tunisia, in June 2015 by a supposed "lone wolf" operative later saw an audio statement "justifying" his actions being placed online.

Significant social media use started to play out in a number of campaigns and contexts.[62] The levels of information presented on sites ranged from short statements to more substantial tomes. Attempts were made to provide "corrective" histories of al-Qaeda activities, to counteract negative perceptions and propaganda, and to justify specific ideological approaches (often critical of other jihad interpretations).[63] Through online works, authors such as Abu Yahya al-Libi from al-Qaeda Central—who published a detailed e-book on jihad via the Al-Fajr Media Centre—became jihad "personalities."[64] However, establishing the identities of some online activists could be problematic, as the field was open to fabrication (to varying degrees). One anti-American jihad warrior "fighting" in Iraq turned out to be posting from a public library in Blackburn, Lancashire.[65] The identity issue is an internet-wide phenomenon but holds specific implications in the zones associated with e-jihad.

The flexibility of languages used for statements is demonstrated in other contexts: in Gaza, a pro-al-Qaeda group issued threats in Hebrew.[66] Many statements from al-Qaeda platforms were quickly translated and placed online in a coordinated approach by supporters in diverse locations; this was relevant in particular in Western contexts, where statements would be taken and placed online in a variety of languages by entities such as the Global Islamic Media Front (GIMF), an online advocate of al-Qaeda. GIMF members became subject to prosecutions in Germany and elsewhere.[67] Nuanced videos and other content for specific markets became a feature of al-Qaeda-related media as an extension of the networks derived from the core principles of al-Qaeda. This content might include drawing on a key message, such as an archived speech by bin Laden, and interspersing it with locally derived images and media.[68] Presenting information online could be interpreted in some contexts as a show of strength, especially in campaigns where governments struggled against al-Qaeda and its affiliates.[69] Platforms such as al-Qaeda in the Arabian Peninsula (AQAP) advertised for recruits, including suicide bombers, via web forums and social media.[70] In 2013, al-Qaeda in the Islamic Maghreb (AQIM) was among the numerous al-Qaeda channels consistently using Twitter and other forms of social media to promote its interpretation of jihad.[71]

Al-Qaeda affiliate Lashkar-e-Taiba in Pakistan drew on similar media approaches using video materials to highlight activities, including execution videos. Following the Mumbai attacks in 2008, which led to website closure, the organization resumed its online activities in 2012.[72] It was suggested that the use of private networks and Voice over Internet Protocol by Lashkar-e-Taiba meant that security platforms could not effectively monitor its activities, even when its leaders were in state prisons using smuggled devices to coordinate network activities.[73]

Mobile communications became essential elements for al-Qaeda and its affiliates, and encoding of internet activities associated with al-Qaeda naturally became more sophisticated.[74] Digital methods were detailed in part in online magazines such as *Inspire*, which described encryption keys and other relevant tools. The Global Islamic Media Front Technical Centre also developed encryption tools.[75] User guides were circulated via jihadi magazines, which became influential beyond the supporters of al-Qaeda.[76] Distribution methods for specialist online jihad magazines varied, from traditional file distribution sites to distribution on generic sites such as Internet Archive. Video sharing sites such as Dailymotion, Vimeo, and YouTube became important locations for jihadi video content.

The language in which jihadi messages were articulated became significant. Whether this was through street language and colloquialisms or religious rhetoric, many sites and sources of jihadi knowledge invested thought and resources into this aspect of their development. The placing of Qur'an quotes within these materials was critical, not just in magazines and social media.[77] Gaming could also be an entry point to jihad, including some free-to-play games that were relatively crude but presented specific "Islamic" messages. For example, participation in jihad in Mali was encouraged by the online game Muslim Mali, focused on attacking French fighter jets.[78]

Amid this media diversity, the killing of Osama bin Laden in Abbottabad, Pakistan, in 2011 led to some reflection on the ways in which he and al-Qaeda had utilized social media and the internet over the years in order to facilitate the fulfillment of their objectives. The actual operation in Abbottabad was also the subject of attention on Twitter—inadvertently at first—when a neighbor reported on what he described as military activities taking place above the city, complaining about helicopter noise.[79]

It is significant that bin Laden's voice continued to emerge online following his death in a message praising the so-called Arab Spring.[80] Subsequent anniversaries of 9/11 were marked by videos featuring bin Laden. The emotional response to bin Laden's demise from his supporters was also articulated in detail online, suggesting that his jihadi message would continue in diverse global contexts.[81] Bin Laden was subsequently eulogized in Ayman al-Zawahiri's "Days with the Imam" online series.[82]

Technological devices retrieved from bin Laden's house included evidence of bin Laden rehearsing delivery of his online messages.[83] It was technology that facilitated bin Laden's capture, through the use of social networking software determining his relationships with individuals and networks.[84] There was substantial discussion regarding how bin Laden's hard drives would be analyzed.[85] Its data yield was subsequently released (at least in part) online by authorities.[86] Pornography was among the publicized discoveries on the hard drive, but a number of other materials were not fully in the public domain.[87] His bookshelf included thirty software guides, including for the Dreamweaver web coding package, Adobe Photoshop, and McAfee Virus Scan.[88] Other works included numerous U.S. government publications, such as the "9/11 Report" and a report into the use of the internet for violent extremism.[89]

E-JIHAD: OTHER CONFLICT ZONES

Prior to a discussion on IS, it is useful to survey the application of the internet within other conflict zones associated with jihad, not all affiliated with al-Qaeda, and to determine how these applications have informed e-jihad developments.

E-Jihad Palestine

Hamas has had a long-standing and developed approach to the ways in which the internet could be utilized to promote its concept of jihad. It could distribute its approach regarding religious concepts and values to regional and global audiences, especially in the Gaza Strip and Palestine. In the 1990s, Hamas was using discussion lists and early internet sites to provide listings of operations, details of "martyrdom operations," and logistical information. Within contemporary contexts, the application of social media has been particularly significant. Despite requests from the Israeli state in 2011 requesting Hamas's removal from Facebook, it utilized social media in order to promote its perspective.[90] In 2014, it introduced #AskHamas on Twitter as an invitation to ask questions. However, the campaign was unsuccessful in that it was "trolled" by sarcastic questions (although it did go viral).[91] Hamas developed material for diverse audiences online, including children, through the website Al-Fateh.[92]

Other Palestinian platforms have been proactive, with varying degrees of religious content in their output. Some of this has been innovative in scope. The release in 2010 of animation by the Ezzeddine al-Qassam Brigade titled "The Sentiment in the Zionist Society Regarding Schalit" was based around the intended fate of then-kidnapped soldier Gilad Schalit. The animation, showing Schalit's father walking through empty streets, was part of a campaign of psychological warfare that indicated what would happen if the brigade's demands were not met.[93]

Social media became a significant element in the campaigning on all sides, with Israel Defense Forces banned from taking mobile phones into Gaza for fear of the leak of strategic or other data.[94] Attacks could be in the form of hacking as much as physical attacks, although sometimes (as with attacks in the analog world) these could be misplaced too. Pro-Palestinian hackers issued a retraction when they hacked the website of the newspaper *Haaretz* in 2012, stating that they did not know it was a "good newspaper."[95] This did not prevent hacking elsewhere, although this was not necessarily synonymous with specific religious hacktivism. In 2012, the Anonymous collective hacked Israeli governmental websites protesting attacks on Gaza.[96]

Israeli security agencies have also used the internet as an information-gathering tool.[97] Representatives from Israel and Palestine have used social media to attack each other, but there have also been initiatives aimed at more constructive dialogue.[98] In sustained Israeli attacks on Gaza in 2014, people in Gaza tweeted in real time, showing the impact of bombing on civilians. This became a primary source for broadcasters, who did not have reporters embedded on-site.[99]

E-Jihad Pakistan

Support for jihad-oriented activities could manifest themselves in different ways. When Pakistani neuroscientist and al-Qaeda supporter Aafia Siddiqui was sentenced to prison for eighty-six years in 2010 for attacking U.S. interrogators following her abduction, her fate became a major cause on social media. Protesters included Pakistani politicians and human rights groups.[100] Al-Qaeda sought her release on a hostage swap—and also named a battle after her (as filmed for release online).[101]

Elements of Pakistan cyberspace mobilized in diverse factions following the assassination of Punjab governor Salmaan Taseer in 2011. A group emerged on Facebook, in the immediate aftermath of his shooting, praising his assassin, Mumtaz Hussain Qadri. An intriguing profile of Qadri's supporters emerged, suggesting professional qualifications and an appreciation of popular Western culture and sport. The Kala Kawa blog suggested that many supporters of Qadri were middle-class professionals.[102] The idea that digitally literate, educated individuals were proactive in their support of jihad online may run counter to some stereotypes about jihad activities. In contrast, a prominent voice against jihad from Pakistan was Shaikh Muhammad Tahir-ul-Qadri of Minhaj ul-Qur'an, who received death threats following the publication of a fatwa against terrorism, which featured on his organization Minhaj al-Qur'an's website.[103]

The Tehreek-e-Taliban Pakistan's (TTP) emergence in Swat Valley, Pakistan (affiliated with the Taliban in Afghanistan), came to international attention when video allegedly of a local woman being flogged appeared on YouTube. This had apparently been filmed surreptitiously and led to accusations that it was fabricated or based on another event. Whatever its provenance, the video galvanized public opinion in Pakistan, especially among the Pakistan Taliban's opponents.[104]

The TTP also used social media to broadcast film of the 2012 jailbreak from Bannu Central Jail, where more than four hundred prisoners were able to escape; this showed grateful prisoners being released and getting onto coaches, together with statements from leaders.[105] The freeing of prisoners was a significant element of Taliban activities, and the formation of the Ansar al-Aseer unit to fulfill this objective was announced online.[106] In 2014, a photo of the TTP unit responsible for a school massacre in Peshawar appeared on its social media. Further, in 2016, responsibility for a major attack on Bacha Khan University in Khyber Pakhtunkhwa province was claimed online, although this was contested by another party in a reflection of TTP's fractured leadership.[107]

E-Jihad Mali

The expansion of al-Qaeda activities in Mali, specifically attacks and a period of occupation of regions including the ancient city of Timbuktu, had a subtext in which the internet became a key element for dissemination of propaganda for local and international audiences. For those who found themselves ruled by al-Qaeda, the internet was a tool with which to discuss the occupation and share images of punishments under #Mali.[108] A period when internet services went down in Timbuktu caused protests on all sides, with jihad groups harassing the service provider.[109]

The internet became the place to review ongoing campaigns and issues. In Timbuktu, concerns regarding the destruction of shrines and mausoleums led to an online debate as to whether this was an "Islamically correct" strategy. Some felt that it ran counter to Mali's cultural and religious heritage, especially its long tradition of Sufism. Others believed that this was an action that was in line with Islamic law, where worship at tombs may be seen as innovative and un-Islamic.[110] Images of Mali's cultural heritage being destroyed were distributed online, potentially influencing subsequent Western policies concerning intervention.

Muslim Minority Contexts

Social media became an integrated element of online jihadi activities in numerous contexts where Muslims were in the minority. This reflected earlier patterns where support manifested itself online and was part of a package of recruitment, logistics, propaganda, and religious justification for campaigns. Jihad activists in minority settings could link themselves with wider international networks.

An example of this was the integration of the internet into "operations" during an attack in London in May 2013. Two converts murdered British army soldier Lee Rigby on the streets of Woolwich using a machete; one attacker (with blood-covered hands) then made jihad-oriented statements to spectators, who filmed his statements on mobile phones. These were quickly circulated through conventional and social media and screenshots to become the focus of subsequent newspaper coverage.[111] It was clear that the attack had been planned with the aim of demonstrating a model of lone wolf attack and the integration of real-time actuality into campaigns via social media.

In a further case, a jihad cell in Britain sought to launch a sustained attack on British soil, which was thwarted; participants had been influenced by lectures and other materials that had been downloaded and copied.[112] The internet had become a channel for self-radicalization and dissemination of an interpretation of jihad, which went beyond the control and confines of more traditional routes of Islamic knowledge, such as mosques and imams.[113] As a natural location for the acquisition of information for digitally literate individuals, the internet had become integral to sustaining concepts of jihad.

This was despite the fact that numerous international prosecutions related either to the possession of or to the development of online jihad materials. The high-profile case of Babar Ahmad focused on allegations of him developing web content supportive of the Taliban in the 1990s. Much of the content was produced in a pre-9/11 period, where there was less attention to the manifestations of jihad appearing online. It was easy to determine the site's location, given it provided bank details and a postal box address, indicative of a more "innocent age" online. Ahmad spent several years on remand in UK prisons, was finally extradited to the United States in 2013, and was prosecuted and jailed in 2014.[114] Ahmad was released in 2015, after a sustained online campaign of support for his release.

The UK Terrorism Act 2000, Section 58, made it a criminal offense to copy, download, or possess materials that might incite acts of terrorism.[115] Such might include content of a religious nature. In the UK, simple possession of material supportive of al-Qaeda could lead to imprisonment. There were discussions on the feasibility of prosecution of owners of online propaganda materials. In 2008, British police held a student for several days on a charge of downloading an al-Qaeda manual, which he was using for his postgraduate research; after a court case, in 2011 the police paid damages to the student.[116] In 2011, Mohammed Gul was convicted for activities on an internet forum and for posting jihad-oriented videos onto YouTube in 2008.[117] Also in 2011, five men had been accused of planning a bombing campaign in London, in which possession of the *Inspire* magazine (discussed below) and related tracts were pivotal elements in the evidence of the case.[118] In 2012, a woman was jailed for a year for possessing al-Qaeda materials on her cell phone.[119] In Yorkshire, a Muslim couple were convicted in 2012 of an anti-Jewish bomb-making plot, influenced by viewing online materials.[120]

In France, President Nicolas Sarkozy in 2012 sought to crack down on online postings relating to jihad.[121] In Belgium, eight people were convicted of sending people to jihad training camps in Waziristan. The leader, Malika El Aroud (originally from Morocco), utilized the internet in order to facilitate this activity and went against the stereotype of "internet jihadists" by being in her fifties and female. She received an eight-year sentence.[122] The real impact of online content manifested itself in extreme fashion in prosecutions in Germany, when a Kosovar Albanian sentenced for killing two American military personnel at Frankfurt Airport testified that online materials had radicalized him.[123] A number of posters of Islamic content were also prosecuted and imprisoned in Germany.[124] In Canada, an activist received a life sentence for online activities.[125]

In the United States, prominent among several prosecutions was the case of Tarek Mehanna, who received a seventeen-year sentence in 2012 for writing materials for a jihad webpage.[126] According to prosecutors, this was after he had traveled to Yemen seeking a training camp; having failed to do this, he returned to the United States and offered himself as an online representative of al-Qaeda. The Mehanna case raised specific issues in the United States associated with translation, the production of online content, and possessing and distributing printed materials under the concept of the freedom of speech.[127]

The transition from reader of jihad content online to participant could also lead to prosecution. The Colleen LaRose case in the United States, which received much publicity, saw a housewife become an alleged terrorist via net consumption. Using her alias, Jihad Jane, she sought to involve herself in a campaign: "She said her blond hair and blue eyes were assets that would allow her to 'blend in with many people.'"[128]

There were risks for online actors and armchair jihadis who chose to go into the field, away from their laptops and online discourse; a number were killed.[129] These and numerous other cases indicated at some level the impact that online content could have on "real world" events—and that the production and distribution of e-jihad materials did not diminish despite the risks for those posting content. However, since these cases, technological interfaces with greater encryption—such as Telegram and WhatsApp—became preferred tools for the anonymous posting of e-jihad content by a variety of jihadi groups.[130]

EVALUATING E-JIHAD

Numerous cases in which internet materials have been deemed as radicalization tools have led to their viewers/owners and instigators being prosecuted. Determining the levels of influence in some cases have proven problematic, including for academic researchers.[131] The types of data available are granulated for different audiences and levels of knowledge, including primers on jihad concepts and theoretical ideas as well as more detailed and academic sources.[132] The nature of this information flow crosses formats and interfaces, with a particular focus on social media outlets. Online, pro-jihad content outweighs that seeking to counter jihad arguments.[133]

There may be a generational gap, in terms of those analyzing the data and those producing content, where expectations may be different.[134] The data flow also has had an impact on perceived levels of religiosity and understanding about jihad, with suggestions that exposure to multiple contexts of jihad activities via the internet will lead to an increase in fervor.[135] Those who are most web-literate in utilizing social networking for disseminating Islamic content are best able to present their worldviews. An absence of "moderate" information about Islam is perceived as being problematic, with the information marketplace dominated by other interpretations provided by web-literate organizations and individuals.[136] Concerns about this have been articulated in a variety of languages and contexts,[137] and such dialogues have been the subject of concern for agencies, communities, organizations, and individuals in Western and other contexts.[138] Observation of these channels have been analyzed by a variety of governmental and other agencies and institutions.[139] Beyond social media channels and websites, agencies have sought to infiltrate alternative spaces to evaluate jihad chatter, such as the World of Warcraft and Second Life virtual worlds.[140]

There has been evidence that aspects of online jihad influenced or radicalized people who were not Muslims, such as the Norwegian far-right terrorist Anders Breivik, responsible for killing seventy-seven people in Oslo on the island of Utøya on July 22, 2011: "Insisting that 'universal human rights' gave him the mandate to carry out his acts, he described himself as a 'militant nationalist' and, using the pronoun 'we' to suggest he was part of a larger group, added: 'We have drawn from al-Qaeda and militant Islamists.'"[141]

The evolution of e-jihad has gone beyond its foundations on email listings and chat rooms and continues to develop in line with technological innovations, software shifts, and differing forms of internet consumption. While it is not the only factor in relation to radicalization, e-jihad has played a significant role and has a specific relationship to the emergence of wider access to digital materials in diverse markets. It is specifically integrated into discourse, at a core level, within all aspects of campaigns—from logistics and finance to radicalization, delivery of an objective, and its subsequent publicity.

A critical element has been the production of online magazines produced for different audiences and on specific topics. These included a first-aid manual for jihadists, which sought to project an Islamic approach to generic medical content.[142] Women's magazines, such as *al-Shamika* (The majestic woman), presented fashion advice alongside militaristic content.[143] AQAP's Al-Malahem Media arm produced the *Expectations Full* jihad manual online in English; specialist magazines such as *Al-Qaeda Airlines* focused on issues such as the manufacture of chloroform.[144] However, more traditional forms of magazine distribution were also utilized, especially in areas with low internet connectivity—such as in Pakistan, where its *Hiteen* magazine was distributed by post.[145] Online magazines were a core element of numerous campaigns, at every level, as will be seen in the next section.

Inspire was a reference point for online jihad activities, radicalization, and re-lated campaigns, in particular in English-language contexts. Its primary driver in its formative phase was Anwar al-Awlaki, a key ideologue and recruiter for AQAP. Born in New Mexico of Yemeni heritage, he and his followers built a significant online jihadi profile while he was in self-imposed exile in Yemen. The impact of his English-language online sermons and other digital output made him a target for assassination by American forces.[146] He acted as a channel for making al-Qaeda ideology more accessible for English-language speakers through translating and distributing the work of other key al-Qaeda figures, including Yusuf al-Ayiri.[147]

Al-Awlaki's own output was redistributed widely on jihadi forums, relat-ing to different global campaigns, and he was a central figure within the publi-cation *Inspire*. This magazine was developed by Samir ibn Zafar Khan, a U.S. citizen born in Saudi Arabia and resident of North Carolina who relocated to Yemen. Khan's online output via English-language blogs and video posts supporting al-Qaeda and jihad captured substantial media attention in the United States and elsewhere, prior to his reemergence with *Inspire* magazine.

Inspire sought to present a user-friendly format, using colloquial lan-guage designed to appeal to a youthful readership. Posters, graphics, and pho-tographs gave a contemporary edge. Distribution patterns on jihadi forums and blogs in easily downloadable formats—as well as through channels such as Kindle and YouTube—allowed for rapid and discrete circulation. It was suggested that early editions were hosted on American servers.[148]

Inspire was first published online in summer 2010; it featured articles such as "Make a Bomb in the Kitchen of Your Mom," "What to Expect in Jihad," and "Sending and Receiving Encrypted Messages" and interviews with prominent jihadis.[149] By issue number 5, *Inspire* was offering quick reac-tions to events in Palestine, Egypt, and Libya and gave a summary of critical comments and reviews of previous issues from analysts and experts. Readers were invited to submit questions by email to the magazine; the intention was to put these to Anwar al-Awlaki for use in a video interview. Although al-Awlaki did not manage, organize, or produce all the content (that being the editorial responsibility of Samir Khan), *Inspire* was a high-profile addition to al-Awlaki's media output and influence. Even after he was killed (along with Khan) in a U.S. drone military strike in Yemen on 30 September 2011, al-Awlaki's output continued to have a presence online. It was noted that although it received sustained coverage in Western media, al-Awlaki's demise was less significant in Arabic-language contexts.[150]

The *Inspire* title, in new editorial hands, continued to have a substantial circulation of new issues. These were often cited in prosecutions of jihadis, the possession of the magazines implicating their owners, who may have downloaded and distributed the content to store offline. Al-Awlaki's work was also found in conventional media outlets, at least for a while, with a report in 2012 claiming its availability on Amazon (it remained available in 2014).[151] Distribution problems led to *Inspire* issue 11 being released via Twitter, which stopped it from being removed altogether from online forums.[152]

Samir Khan's own work was significant for English-speaking audiences in terms of the ways in which he had drawn upon various forms of social media and the internet in order to promote a version of jihad, on occasion in an innovative fashion as a content creator and networker.[153] Khan was not the first person to take the route from the United States to facilitating al-Qaeda websites abroad: Moeed Abdul Salam, a naturalized American citizen, was killed in Pakistan in 2012 but had established himself as a key individual in al-Qaeda's online activities.[154]

There were claims that the audience for *Inspire* included inmates at Guantanamo,[155] and al-Awlaki was also cited as influential in the UK: Stephen Timms, a member of Parliament, was stabbed in his east London constituency office in 2010. The perpetrator, Roshonara Choudhry, was an English-language university student who had downloaded and listened to a complete series of al-Awlaki's lectures.[156] Attempts at removing these materials from YouTube in the UK were unsuccessful, in that they were quickly replaced. In 2013, a plot to use a remote-controlled toy car (containing explosives) to attack an army center in Luton, UK, was also linked directly to the magazine.[157]

Al-Awlaki's influence was felt elsewhere too, such as in the attempted bombing in Times Square, New York.[158] Al-Awlaki additionally expressed pride in training Umar Farouk Abdulmutallab, the failed "underwear bomber" who sought to down a flight from Amsterdam to Detroit in 2009.[159] A video emerged on al-Malahem Media in 2015 of al-Awlaki talking to Abdulmutallab.[160] U.S. Army Medical Corps psychiatrist Nidal Hasan, who killed thirteen people at Fort Hood, Texas, was himself apparently influenced by al-Awlaki's online content.[161] *Inspire* magazine was further implicated in relation to the 2013 Boston Marathon bombings, as the Tsarnaev brothers used advice from the magazine to construct their devices.[162] Al-Awlaki was also a model for other online ideologues of jihad in the English language, including Adam Gadahn, who encouraged Muslims in Western contexts to make attacks; Gadahn's death was described by J. M. Berger as the end of "Al-Qaeda's American Dream."[163]

The twelfth issue of *Inspire*, released in 2014, included a question-and-answer session with al-Awlaki, based on questions sent to him as part of a special feature prior to his death. It posthumously featured an article authored by Samir Khan. The magazine continued the format of earlier issues, artistically and in terms of content. It provided further logistical advice, such as in an article on manufacturing car bombs inside America, and additional details on suggested targets across Western contexts. The 2015 Paris attacks on *Charlie Hebdo* offices by al-Qaeda supporters were linked to *Inspire*, which had encouraged attacks on the satirical magazine and named cartoonist Stéphane Charbonnier ("Charb")—among others—as a principal target. An article discussing the strategic organization of the attacks later featured in a September 2015 issue of *Inspire* is likely to have influenced the November 2015 attacks in Paris by IS affiliates.

The release of the sixteenth issue in 2016 marked the "lone wolf" Bastille Day truck attack in Nice, which killed eighty-six people.[164] It suggested strategies for "lone Mujahid" attacks in the United States, drawing on photos of attacks in New Jersey, Manhattan, and Minnesota. "The Rulings of Lone Jihad" featured the opinions of Sheikh Hammed al-Tameemi, a U.S.-born associate of al-Awlaki, imprisoned for life in 2005 for organizing jihad camps. *Inspire* also described the making of a pressure bomb and gave a retrospective account of 9/11. In an article on American Muslims, it looked back at its coverage of African American issues and focused on antiglobalization concerns.

A contestation of online jihad space meant that, to an extent, *Inspire*'s impact was challenged by the emergence of new channels for the articulation of definitions of jihad, including IS. This is covered in the next chapter.

CONCLUSION

The greatest influence in terms of methodologies associated with social media and jihad has been on IS, although it does not take all elements of the approach to jihad from al-Qaeda and has in some cases opposed its affiliates in Syria and Iraq. In many ways, online pronouncements by al-Qaeda and its networks were subsumed by the global interest in IS. IS shifted boundaries in terms of the ways in which social media and the internet were applied and integrated into campaigning, and while these were not the only factors associated with its impact, they were certainly relevant and significant developments. In some cases, these factors may in the long term make al-Qaeda and its affiliates more competitive on the internet and proactive in the ways in which they apply different media forms in order to fulfill their numerous objectives. Al-Qaeda and its followers benefited from the relative lack of focus their activities had since the emergence of IS. As a central brand for e-jihad, they continue to be proactive in many ways online and in numerous conflict zones.

#ChapterSix

E-Jihad and Gen-ISIS

DEFINING THE CYBER CALIPHATE

Perceptions of twenty-first-century Islam have been indelibly colored by the emergence of the "Islamic State" and especially its utilization of social media. The Islamic State was also known as ISIS (the Islamic State of Iraq and Al-Sham) and ISIL (the Islamic State of Iraq and the Levant) and by its Arabic acronym Daesh (al-Dawlah al-Islamiya fi-Iraq wa'l Sham, or the Islamic State in Iraq and al-Sham/Syria). The acronym had negative connotations for IS, with the lexical association of "one who creates disunity."[1]

It is not intended here to chart every proclamation or electronic missive by IS or every action within its campaigns. Rather, it is to determine how the internet influenced elements of its actions and strategy, especially during its formative phase, and its representation of Islam and use of religious rhetoric.

The group proclaimed a "caliphate" in parts of Syria and Iraq that it had conquered in 2013–14 under Abu Bakr al-Baghdadi's leadership. The caliphate concept holds a resonance that goes back to the formative phase of the emergence of Islam, related to an ideal of leadership within the nascent Muslim community of the seventh century CE. The Arabic word *khalifa* means "successor" and is synonymous with issues of leadership of the Muslim community following the death of the Prophet Muhammad in 632 CE. The term later became linked with the Ottoman caliphate, which lasted from 1517 to 1924, and also had an association with other rulers and dynasties in diverse contexts.[2]

The adoption by al-Baghdadi of the "caliph" mantle was simultaneously provocative and strategic, attracting publicity and generating discussion about the notions of religious authority and accountability. It was not a proclamation received with unanimous support from other Muslim sectors, being condemned outright by Yusuf al-Qaradawi and other influential religious leaders in 2014, including through online channels.[3] Al-Baghdadi's proclamation led to ideological conflict between supporters of al-Qaeda and IS for superiority, some of which inevitably played out online.[4]

Every sequence of IS activities, from fighting on front lines to its leaders' proclamations, has been accompanied by social media output. This has led to terms such as "hashtag warriors" being applied to IS, which in itself may have added to a cachet of "jihadi chic" that presents IS in a favorable light to supporters and potential recruits. Internet coverage has included the conquests of strategic cities such as Mosul, the positive reactions of (some) inhabitants, and the subsequent "benefits" for supportive elements of the population.[5] The extent to which such scenes have been stage-managed and insightfully edited is open to discussion. Some images have been disseminated not just by supporters but taken as actuality by media elements unable or unwilling to report from such locations.

IS has demonstrated an understanding of the nuanced requirements of different audiences for internet materials, as well as (in some cases) technical proficiency, ranging from photographs of cats posed next to weapons (under hashtags relating to cats and jihad) to detailed logistical reports of IS activities. Quotations from the Qur'an and other Islamic sources have been slickly integrated into video montages and soundtracks. An IS annual report projected the financial and logistical details of a multimillion dollar enterprise, albeit one centered on an interpretation of jihad.[6] Videos and other content encompass media production values adopted from other broadcasters, such as a news broadcast using the style of familiar radio stations.[7] Nuanced propaganda reaches several markets, including sign language content.[8]

Significant personalities have articulated views about approaches to jihad via the internet, such as Jihadi John, associated with the filmed executions of various hostages. He was one of four British fighters, the other three also acquiring Beatles nicknames in grim recognition of their origins. Masked and brandishing a knife, he was recorded making statements regarding IS activities prior to beheading hostages. Each execution was carefully staged, with the victim dressed in an orange jumpsuit synonymous with prisoners in Guantanamo Bay. Prior to being killed, victims were required to address the camera and make a statement. Such "theater," filmed in high definition and rapidly circulated to supporters via social media and in edited form by world media, gave IS substantial publicity.

Threats were made to future individual hostages in the clips, which in some cases were enacted in later videos. Clips showing mass executions of soldiers and other victims were filmed with careful consideration of lighting, audio, and media factors—as well as shock value. Victims were often

Twitter page of Islamic State of Cat, http://twitter.com/ISILCats.

paraded in front of cameras. The brutality of IS was demonstrated when bodies were cast into a ravine, gathering sustained coverage in the media not just because of the group's murderous campaign but because of Islamic principles associated with respect for the dead and appropriate burial.[9] The footage was combined, in many cases, with religious justification for such activities and a soundtrack of Qur'anic recitation and *nasheeds*—chants based on Islamic verses usually performed without instrumentation or with simple percussion.

In 2015, al-Baghdadi asked video producers to tone down violent content for the sake of Muslim audiences; this edict requested that full executions not be shown. In addition to such content considerations, the "evolution" of jihad media and attendant improvements in technical quality were linked to factors such as the impact of cinema and gaming media on presentation, promotion, and production factors.

Jihadi John's anonymity did not last, and he was later identified as Mohammed Emwazi, born in Kuwait and educated from a primary level in London. Emwazi was a computing science student at the University of Westminster prior to being radicalized. After the execution activities, he maintained a low profile until being killed in a targeted drone attack in Syria in November 2015. With his British accent and awareness of the shock value of the images he generated (especially online), Emwazi presented his interpretation of jihad in a cinematic and staged way. Guaranteed to go viral and difficult to censor, his recorded activities were taken and utilized by traditional media outlets as well as jihad-oriented sites. This developed awareness of the power of social media, influenced by Emwazi's own computing skills, set a bloody benchmark for others to follow.

Other individuals also became personalities and generated a following or interest online. Georgian jihadist Omar al-Shishani, a veteran of the conflict in Chechnya, made headlines because of his distinctive red beard. He generated substantial media coverage after Mosul's capture, being filmed inspecting American Humvees captured from Iraqi forces.[10] The charismatic senior IS military commander was killed in 2016. Islam Yaken, a previously cosmopolitan Egyptian recruited into IS, was photographed on a horse and flourishing a curved sword and acquired a social media following prior to his death in 2014.[11] Other media figures became fatalities; British jihadis featured prominently in IS videos were also killed.[12] Despite this grim trend, or perhaps because of the desire for martyrdom, there was no shortage of individuals willing to go in front of the cameras or appear on social media. In these images, the inadvertent disclosure of location by IS combatants through the use of social media held negative implications, with one careless tweeter providing sufficient data for a subsequent air strike on his "hidden" base.[13]

IS "DIGITAL NATIVES"

High levels of technological literacy were embedded into IS, demonstrating its awareness of the implications for propaganda, recruitment, finance, and logistical support. Common tools for production and editing of media materials were drawn upon. Many IS participants were clearly "digital natives," for whom such social media expression was a natural extension of daily digital lives. Consequently, what was perceived as sustained levels of technical adeptness was simply the result of a generation encultured in mobile data systems.[14] In some cases, their technical knowledge probably superseded their knowledge of Islam.

Technically high-quality content produced on mobile phones was supplemented by professionally edited and produced materials from dedicated media units—often presented by the Al-Hayat Media Group. As with other e-jihad expressions, such outputs were quickly distributed via social media and dedicated web channels to be circulated by world media (albeit on occasion in a censored format). The immediacy of the IS digital message frequently led to countermessages and responses generated by opponents and observers, adding to the conversation about the "caliphate." Hacking was applied as part of the intelligence-gathering process, particularly in Iraq.[15] Given the levels of technological awareness among different factions, this should not be surprising. Online rivalry and conflict between IS factions were reflected at ground level. IS continued to expand its activities and make strategic gains in 2014 in Syria and Iraq, although debates on its legitimacy dominated online media. Recognition of the internet's significance as a driver for jihadi activity was coupled with the realization that its impact was hard to control.[16]

Muslim parents in some contexts found it difficult to stop their children from being influenced by the jihad-oriented messages viewed online. In one of the numerous cases that emerged, social media was seen as influential in the recruitment of two teenage girls from Austria.[17] The girls were apparently later regretful of their action but were unable to escape their weddings to IS activists. One girl was subsequently killed in a bombing raid. This case led to substantial Austrian media attention, including a Facebook interview with a jihadi.[18] An imam from Austria, Mamdouh El Attar, responded, "Those who have gone to Syria and Iraq didn't attend religious classes or prayers. They are easily manipulated because they have no idea what Islam really is."[19] This was not the only high-prominence case of "jihadi-brides" influenced by internet recruitment patterns. In Colorado in 2014, Twitter was deemed a motivating factor in influencing teenage girls seeking to travel to Iraq, one with a "SlavesOfAllah" Twitter handle.[20] Encouraged by idealistic depictions of IS, three London girls were recruited via social media, traveling to Syria via Turkey.[21] Research identified how potential IS female recruits in the West were plied with gifts to encourage them.[22] A "manifesto" was published online for women, focusing on marriage and motherhood as a defining goal.[23]

Nasheeds were a critical element in this romanticized fusion of religious values with emotive images and sounds. The use of the human voice in this way is seen as acceptable, even if some interpreters discourage music.[24] *Nasheeds* have been featured in al-Qaeda and other videos but have taken on a greater emphasis within IS jihad soundtracks. A prominent example is in the 2014 video *Flames of War*. IS activities are graphically demonstrated in this one-hour montage of military victories, executions, and religious justification for actions. The high-definition cinematic production takes e-jihad to a dramatic new level.[25]

The production values continued, with consideration of filming location, lighting, and choreography. In 2015, video of a mass murder of prisoners in Palmyra took advantage of its staging in an ancient amphitheatre.[26] A video of captured Jordanian pilot Moaz Kasasbeh presented him walking past IS fighters and the ruins of air bombing before being immolated in a cage. The IS publicity drive gained momentum when the sequence was shown on Western media, including uncut on Fox News.[27] The Kasasbeh film played on big screens in IS zones, each high-definition moment emphasizing the violence to encourage further recruits and support. A preemptive "public relations" online campaign sought to counter criticism of the murder. Further online controversy was generated when some clerics denounced the murder.[28] Imams in IS territory who condemned the murder were themselves executed.[29]

IS devised new ways of execution, in part to attract new views and develop viral potential. Drowning people in cages, filming an occupied car being bombed, and showing executions with bomb-necklaces all became part of the macabre online repertoire. The videos not only generated further publicity but also were a warning to opponents. Children were shown executing prisoners. While not every video could be classified as a high-end production, in general they provided a sense of organization and authority comparable with broadcasters' output. Strata of production levels were featured online, ranging from phone video providing a ground floor/grassroots perspective ("Anyone can do this . . .") to HD productions. These played to the expectations of diverse audiences, from broadcasters (regional and international) to general and casual viewers. The raw quality suggested that technical expectations of different audiences can vary: some films became big productions, with documentation and HD footage, in line with the capacity for internet streaming and file-sharing possibilities. In these zones of streaming jihad, the immediacy of content meant that technical perfection was not always a requirement. Videos were produced in line with data usage factors and improvement in mobile phones across international markets.

Activities by supporters outside of IS geographical boundaries were also promoted online. Social media was central in synchronous attacks in Tunisia, Kuwait, and France. Seifeddine Rezgui was the perpetrator of the Sousse beach massacre in Tunisia, killing thirty-eight holidaymakers in 2015. Rezgui made a filmed statement with a Kalashnikov rifle backdrop. The actuality of the attack was also featured online from other sources.[30] On the same day, a French IS supporter who severed his former manager's head posted a selfie of the aftermath.[31] IS then released an audio message, accompanied by Qur'anic recitation, from the perpetrator of the bombing of a Kuwaiti Shi'a mosque.[32] A separate attack that killed a priest in a church in Saint-Étienne-du-Rouvray, France, was attributed to pair of IS supporters who had met online, one of whom actively promoted jihad via Facebook.[33]

Video clips were used to mourn the passing in battle of fighters. A young boy described as the "Cub of Baghdad" was featured on YouTube.[34] Social media recorded numerous "martyrdom operations," including Abu Yusuf al-Britani, the nom de guerre of the "UK's youngest ever suicide bomber."[35] Distribution of such clips led to international prosecutions.[36] In the UK, a woman proactive online on behalf of ISIS was jailed for three and a half years, having posted over 45,000 supportive messages and images.[37] In India, former Google software engineer Munawad Salman was arrested for supporting IS through alleged redistribution and creation of Twitter content.[38] Despite numerous prosecutions, supporters on social media have continued to pump the IS media synthesis of *nasheed*, ideology, and actuality.

DIGITAL JIHADI LIFESTYLES

The "positive" elements of life under IS has been featured in social media in order to encourage recruits. Londoner Abu Rumaysah al-Britani's *A Brief Guide to the Islamic State 2015* features photos of familiar food brands and discussion of lifestyle elements such as cappuccino availability.[39] One critical element of the recruitment process has been the development of one-to-one relationships between potential recruits and IS via social media. Tones of romance and relationship building are developed (along religious lines), especially among vulnerable individuals.[40] "Normal" images promoting IS life, such as babies sleeping next to weapons alongside the ubiquitous jihadi cats, have fueled some Western media perceptions of IS.[41] These images contrast with the increasingly extreme and violent cinematic-style images of execution videos.

The proliferation of pro-IS social media accounts means that information circulates rapidly and is difficult or impossible to control or censor. One investigation suggested that 60,000 pro-IS Twitter accounts had been established between May and September 2014, although exactly how proactive those accounts were was difficult to verify.[42] They did not always work in conjunction with one another. The execution of Steven Sotloff in September 2014 caught some in IS unawares when the video apparently "leaked" online.[43]

Attempts at censorship and content control in specific conflict zones or their vicinity have been generally unsuccessful. They simply draw participants and supporters into the Dark Web or closed sections of the internet. Technologically literate IS supporters are adept at finding ways around authorities' censorship tools, which are often out of synch with their opponents' online proficiency.[44] IS has provided supporters with technical advice via online help desks to prevent them from being spied on.[45] Specific IS training has sought to develop secure internet use.[46]

Facebook restrictions, together with a suggestion that the platform's ethos was "un-Islamic," led to the announcement in 2015 of the short-lived Kelafabook, which drew on a generic software platform.[47] That same year an online IS television channel was also promised,[48] and IS supporters developed apps to disseminate strategic information and encourage recruitment.[49] This global media strategy developed news apps such as "The Dawn of Glad Tidings" and online guidance on traveling to the Islamic State.[50] Multilingual IS jihad content circulated through thousands of IS-affiliated Twitter feeds. The IS cyberstrategy was refined and—according to experts—could not be underestimated.[51] Technological innovations were being applied at all levels, including the use of encrypted funding tools such as Bitcoin to support IS.[52] Secret film emerged of a "grooming headquarters" generating communications between IS and potential recruits.[53] IS had concerns that intelligence and infiltration could occur through uncensored internet systems, leading to the closure of phone and net facilities in some locations.[54] This general fear across IS and other jihad-oriented platforms resulted in efforts to cloak some online activities.[55]

The application of specific hashtags have denoted IS campaigns and brought together conversation strings. The #CalamityWillBefallUS campaign sought to project the damage that would be caused to the United States if it was to engage directly against IS.[56] It promoted ideas of how future conquests would change the Middle East map.[57] The concept of Twitter as a tool for publicizing jihad was celebrated by IS activists, who praised God rather than the site's founders.[58] Despite being keen users of Twitter, IS threatened to kill Twitter employees when attempts were made to block content.[59]

WhatsApp, Telegram, Ask.fm, Snapchat, Instagram, and Kik are alternative online social media tools utilized to publicize and recruit IS agendas in public zones as well as to personally connect, one to one, with individuals. They offer varied levels of encryption and security, with Telegram becoming prominent for media distribution, a pattern also reflected in al-Qaeda online content propagation. They are additionally significant in terms of logistics, with invitation-only areas for tactical discussions and virtual meetings.[60] Concerns have surfaced in IS that this is leading supporters into a more insular online environment.[61] Activists can be reached by Skype for one-to-one video conversations. IS policies on IT use have evolved. Rather than individuals posting in an uncoordinated fashion, there is a developing awareness of the need for integrated social media approaches for activism, campaigns, and filming content. In comparison with other platforms, IS net literacy and use has had a sustained regional and global impact on recruitment, radicalization, funding, adherence, and profile-raising. Its supporters have utilized gaming imagery and popular culture as a means of promoting the IS message, such as the echoes of Call of Duty within an IS online poster.[62] IS has developed as a distinct brand, strategically oriented, with its specific application of religious language and symbolism maintained by a dedicated group of staff working 24/7 on aspects ranging from personal communication to individuals to preparing material for global audiences.

COUNTERING E-JIHAD ONLINE

Governments, religious organizations, and other platforms have developed online strategies to counter IS. Sermons have been delivered against perceived IS propaganda.[63] Religious organizations encourage internet training for imams, developing awareness and counterstrategies against technologically literate and mobile opposition.[64] Efforts have been made by activists with varying degrees of success to hack and counter IS activities online, including the use of "honey traps" and identity theft.[65] One activist sought to trick IS and its opponents in an online battle in 2015.[66] Hacktivist network Anonymous launched a cyberwar against IS via its GhostSec branch in the same year.[67] A result was the release of a listing of IS Twitter accounts.[68] Other unidentified hacktivist groups further announced their intention to disrupt IS in 2016—although it was difficult to ascertain the full impact of these activities.[69] Governmental agencies have drawn on hacker expertise covertly and in public spheres.[70]

Some governments have sought to filter online activities through regulation and introduction of software, although such monitoring has drawn accusations of challenging freedom of speech through a Big Brother governmental mentality.[71] Human intervention has been a more effective mechanism to prevent online recruitment, with religious authorities and individuals seeking to identify vulnerable individuals and counter IS messages.[72]

Pressure has been placed on service providers to shut down expressions of e-jihad on social media. In 2016, Twitter suspended almost a quarter of a million accounts linked to the Islamic State.[73] The U.S. government sought in the same year to disrupt online recruitment through search engines, using specific targeted advertising that linked to anti-radicalization videos. This strategy included identification of 1,700 "radicalizing" keywords, which led searchers to anti-IS content.[74]

Through the use of social media, independent individuals have generated a counternarrative to IS. For instance, "Average Mohamed" is an animated cartoon with content focusing against ISIS. Produced by Somali American gas station manager Mohamed Ahmed, it has achieved a sustained online and media profile. Average Mohamed is also credited with engaging Facebook users on issues associated with gender and identity/identities, for example through the video "Be Like Aisha."[75] Government agencies have become involved, with the Iranian government launching its own cartoon campaign online against IS in 2015.[76] The Open Your Eyes video series shows young UK Muslims presenting advice to peer groups to dissuade radicalization and commenting on film clips, suggesting that IS does not represent "mainstream" Islam. The website includes the voices of IS victims in Arabic. Viewers are encouraged to send in their own videos for use in neighborhoods and schools. The videos highlight the impact on families of radicalization and provide religious justification for abstaining from militaristic jihad.[77] Counternarratives have also emerged from broadcast channels. The Middle East Broadcasting Center aired the satirical *Selfie* show online, with an ironic take on ISIS and radicalization in the context of Saudi Arabia.[78] Even from within Syria, YouTube was being applied to satirize the conflict in 2015, with a nine-year-old being the focus of "Umm Abduh."[79]

Governments have also become involved in social media activities. The Jordanian government's Jordan Knights app facilitated reporting of suspicious activities in 2015.[80] A hashtag campaign and YouTube video in 2014 demonstrated that IS did not speak for all Muslims.[81] British Muslims introduced *Haqiqah* magazine to address the IS narrative.[82] Saudi Grand Mufti Sheikh Abdul Aziz Al Sheikh encouraged internet use to combat IS and other jihad platforms.[83] In Malaysia, an online *pondok* or religious school was established to counter IS messages, which some traditional authorities had been "extremely reluctant" to challenge.[84]

Despite these initiatives, IS could still counteract technological and other barriers to the presentation of its message. The role of technology companies in this is open to scrutiny, raising the question of the extent to which major players should become involved in the censoring and shutting down of jihad-oriented materials and whether they have an obligation to do this. The employment by Google of an Arabic speaker in 2015 to counter jihadi messages was very small in scale, considering the breadth of the issues and content.[85] The European Union developed an Internet Referral Unit, via Europol, to remove jihad-oriented material from the internet.[86] Some governments have used the jihad issue to silence critics or the platforms they used, such as the Russian blacklisting of the Wayback Machine because its archive included an IS video.[87] In doing this, the Russian government also effectively censored a channel of online opposition to its own activities.

INTEGRATED E-JIHAD

On 13 November 2015, IS activities entered another sphere when IS fighters (with European Union citizenship) attacked several targets in Paris, killing 130 people and injuring many more. This came a few weeks after IS affiliates bombed a Russian airliner, heading from Egypt to Russia, killing 224 passengers and crew. These events led to escalations in militaristic activities against IS in Iraq and Syria as well as to targeting of its supporters elsewhere. Significantly, mission statements allegedly from IS appeared online—in Arabic, English, and French—"justifying" the attacks.[88]

Much of what played out in the massacre at the Bataclan theater, Stade de France, and cafés in the 10th and 11th arrondissements in Paris quickly surfaced on social and internet media, generated by eyewitnesses as well as by conventional media and used by jihad-oriented sites. The IS online English-language magazine *Dabiq* marked the Paris attacks with photographs and an editorial, promoted on Twitter and on file-sharing sites. On social media, hashtags commemorating the victims jostled online with IS statements linking these attacks with French (and other) attacks in Syria and Iraq. The real fight on the ground was mirrored digitally online.

Some of the technical IS input may have come from fighters with western European origins, especially those who had skillfully picked up on the relevance of social media in pro-jihad campaigns in Europe. Trial evidence suggested in 2014–15 that Sharia4Belgium sent people to fight for IS; the group's leader, Fouad Belkacem, received a twelve-year sentence.[89] Belkacem had previously met with Anjem Choudary and Omar Bakri Muhammad, prominent UK-based leaders of jihad-oriented groups al-Muhajiroun and Sharia4UK in the 1990s and early 2000s.[90] These figures were pioneering users of internet media to promote their interpretation of jihad.[91] Belkacem used social media to recruit people; forty-three supporters were tried in Antwerp, some in absentia, either dead or in Syria (or elsewhere).

In May 2017, a single suicide bomber killed twenty-two people and injured many more leaving an Ariana Grande music concert at Manchester Arena. The British-born perpetrator, Salman Abedi, was apparently radicalized through viewing internet material, including YouTube videos.[92] The following month, an attack at London Bridge and the adjacent Borough Market by three attackers left at least eight people dead; the attackers used a vehicle and knives on their victims before being shot dead by police. It was subsequently alleged that at least one of the attackers, Khurram Butt, had been radicalized through viewing the "hate videos" of American preacher Ahmad Musa Jibril.[93] Another of the attackers, Moroccan Italian Youssef Zaghba, was described as having IS videos on his phone and of showing them to his mother—who tried to dissuade his allegiance.[94]

In August 2017, attacks in Catalonia were attributed to IS, including the use of a van to kill 13 pedestrians and injure more than 100 in Las Ramblas, Barcelona; this attack drew on a modus operandi promoted by IS via social media in previous months. IS supporters quickly voiced their support of the attacks via social media.[95] Warning signs of potential radicalization had already appeared on social media but had not been picked up by authorities or service providers.[96] While not the only factor contributing to radicalization, online materials are significant in inspiring some people to participate in activities. For some digitally literate individuals, this is a natural zone to develop allegiances and be further motivated to participate in (a definition of) jihad.

Following an IS-related attack on the Jewish Museum in Brussels, which killed four people in May 2014, Belgian IS supporters were implicated in the 2015 Paris attacks (among others), including "ringleader" Abdelhamid Abaaoud. In February 2015, Abaaoud featured in an issue of the

Dabiq cover, issue 10, July 2015.

English-language *Dabiq* magazine under the nom de guerre "Abu Umar al-Baljiki," in which he described evading police capture. Abaaoud was photographed alongside "Abuz-Zubayr" and "Abu Khalid," fellow compatriots killed in a joint Belgium-France operation. A photo of Abaaoud from *Dabiq* featured in global media coverage of the Paris attacks, showing him holding a Qur'an and an IS flag next to a military vehicle. Shortly after the Paris attacks, *Dabiq* released a photo of the bomb that had allegedly downed the Russian airplane.

Table of contents from *Rumiyah*, issue 7.

IS had also promoted the utilization of trucks and other vehicles as weapons in the *Rumiyah* (Rome) online magazine, launched in September 2016 and superseding the *Dabiq* title, perhaps in recognition that the anticipated IS battle in the town of Dabiq was less likely given sustained IS territorial losses in the region. By June 2017, this had run to nine issues, with the familiar format of its predecessor. The first issue included screenshots from ten IS videos, along with lengthy treatises on jihad, the role of women in warfare, and hajj etiquette. An article explaining that "the kafir's blood is halal for you" set the tone for other editions of *Rumiyah*. Issue 8 contained an infographic highlighting the March 2017 attack on Westminster Bridge and how it was carried out by one person with a knife and a car. It also provided statistical representation of fatalities in its Iraq operations. The lengthy ninth issue outlined the use of trucks as weapons, with an infographic explaining acquisition and ideal targets; it provided a synopsis of how to gain hostages in the article "Just Terror Tactics," explaining how to lure and execute targets even without conventional weapons. Throughout the series, *Rumiyah* railed against the "scholars" who opposed its views, drawing on religious language and imagery in an attempt to justify its perspective.[97]

E-Jihad and Gen-ISIS

IS started sending out real-time actuality of its operations. An attack in June 2017 in Tehran on the Iranian parliament and the shrine of Ayatollah Khomeini included a short film clip distributed by the IS Amaq agency showing assailants shouting in Arabic within the parliament building and the body of a victim. This trend set a precedent, likely to be continued in future operations.[98]

The integration of social media with IS activities, whether in Europe or the Middle East, suggests a formulated approach that is significant for the group's cause. As IS faces pressure from sustained attacks in various locations, there remains a strategy of high-level social media activity as a publicity and promotional tool.

CONCLUSION: PROCESSING E-JIHAD

The entire output relating to IS represents a case study in itself of how an organization oriented around a specific religious worldview has integrated different levels of social media and online content to mobilize, recruit, finance, publicize, and justify its activities to diverse audiences in Muslim and other contexts. It demonstrates a nuanced approach to online media. Precedents from Muslim and other contexts have been utilized. IS ensured its activities were recorded and effectively distributed online during its formative phase. It showed awareness that specific content would draw other media attention. By presenting content of a high technical quality, edited with subtitles and religious soundtracks, IS was a ready-to-transmit movement with internet technology at its core, alongside its specific (but not universal) interpretations of jihad and Islam.

IS online strategists knew that specific audiences, especially within younger demographics, would respond with enthusiasm to specific forms of presentation of religiously couched information. These were often compacted messages, precise and with a veneer of religious authority, not necessarily backed up with footnotes or appropriate source attribution. Audiences themselves can be technologically sophisticated consumers. Their attention span has been attuned to specific forms of knowledge dissemination, including graphic images and ideas about religious identity and affiliation outside of the mainstream. Perhaps this audience is, in some cases, seeking answers to their concerns, and searching top-level content on the internet often offers ready-to-fit solutions. As with other online products, the internet provided IS recruitment and affiliation opportunities by drawing readers further down the chain of knowledge and information.

By 2017, counteroffensives against IS in Iraq and Syria had led to a loss of territory, control, and influence in the region. This did not necessarily indicate the demise of IS but a shift, in which the online element may become more vital in terms of logistics, recruitment, and publicity. A prepackaged operational template has been made available for download via online magazines and social media, with evidence of it being utilized by self-radicalized affiliates and operatives. The IS brand has shifted to other locations, such as Afghanistan and sub-Saharan Africa, led by members who were dispersed from Syria and Iraq. The emergence of radicalized returnees in Muslim-minority contexts has also been flagged as a risk, especially given that their connectivity could be maintained online.

Without social media, it would have been more problematic for IS to achieve its objectives (which were still fluid), although no doubt alternative routes for recruitment and finance could have been facilitated. Indeed, in relation to IS, the internet was not the only channel through which people were attracted to its cause. However, the use of Twitter, Telegram, Facebook, Instagram, Snapchat, WhatsApp, and other smartphone channels have no doubt been effective, especially in well-publicized cases of recruitment and as a way of promoting the "benefits" of the "Islamic State" to others.

Some of this content was from individuals, but there was also a coordinated approach through central media groups using generic technology. These motifs were familiar through other forms of online e-jihad and reinforced specific jihad identities of the content creators: the application of religious language, quotations from sources, graphic images of the "victims" of their enemies, presentation of a sense of religious authority (through reference to "scholars"), and utilization of specific logos, images, and color schemes.

The symbiosis of software and hardware providers with jihad content providers continues. Some of the most enthusiastic early adopters of social media present themselves on the jihad battlefield, and the recognition of the implications for tools such as Telegram, Snapchat, WhatsApp, and Instagram as means of circumnavigating forms of censorship has been a significant development. There has also been a sense of the need to develop specific IS platforms in the areas of social media and encryption; the popularity of generic tools supersedes any options. They provide a window for IS e-jihad into world media and public opinion, which has presented difficulties for authorities to counter. Muslim religious authorities have been challenged, especially if they lack refined awareness of the implications of this digital jihad revolution/evolution. This familiar pattern played out with the online activities of other (not necessarily directly related) jihad-oriented platforms in the past, such as al-Qaeda and Hamas.

E-jihad required a countermessage from religious authorities, scholars, and Muslims from within communities speaking the same language as the erstwhile audiences for IS. In order that such a countermessage could be effectively delivered, there was a need for an extension of digital literacy. It would not necessarily stem recruitment or the impact of ingenious IS social media output but would provide a sense of competition. As IS territory shifted in 2017, potentially away from Iraq and Syria, the globalization of the brand shifted its emphasis and support further into dark areas of cyberspace. There was an indication that a contestation for online credit for operational activities between al-Qaeda and IS affiliates was also developing.[99]

Online discourse and a variety of apps and packages have shaped the formulation and presentation of key IS concepts, highlighting Marshall McLuhan's concept in which the media shapes the message. The extent to which one might apply Jürgen Habermas's concept of the "public sphere" in relation to IS is problematic, given the different notion of the state (or "caliphate"), its violent agenda, a lack of democracy, and the lack of equality within dialogues. Its adherents might be private individuals, but their public sphere can function only in safe territories where IS held military dominance. It also operates on one level as a "virtual state" whose adherents identify with propaganda and authority models, which are projected through choreographed displays in a way to demonstrate domination of ideals as a form of stage-managed imagery. In an echo of Roland Barthes's concepts surrounding the structuring of signs and images, these ideals are articulated in language and symbols that IS adherents identify rightly or wrongly as representing core Islamic values and association with specific ideologues. This projection is contested by other authorities and IS opponents, who may also use the public sphere to present their own conceptual framework. Rather than a single sphere, there are multiple spheres, which represent parallel if not complementary forms of electronic *ummah* (the ideal of the Muslim community, dating back to the Prophet Muhammad and articulated in the Qur'an).

This presentation of electronic jihad is simply the latest chapter in an evolving media form, where cyber-Islamic environments shift and diversify in response to world events and technological innovations, including improvements in digital access. It is natural that these media forms are integrated into activities; what should not be surprising is that IS has paid so much close attention to digital media. While internet engagement was not the only element, it offered a route to facilitate IS's activities. As a CIE zone, it was one that could be maintained and developed in different ways by IS, its peers, and its successors—despite attempts made at censorship, countermessage, and closure.

#Conclusion

Hashtag Islam

A transformation is clearly taking place within the Muslim contexts in which internet access is available.[1] Electronic media are having a significant effect on approaches toward religious authority, interpretation, control, power, and the dissemination of specific political and religious understandings. This effect can appear in different ways, and clearly, it is difficult to analyze every form of influence, especially given that some of these influences may be subtle or revealed only with the benefit of long-term hindsight. Nevertheless, since the emergence of the World Wide Web, there has been a progression in the ways in which Muslims have articulated religious knowledge and values through cyber-Islamic environments.

These CIEs create new ways for the communication of Islam that go beyond dominant and long-standing tropes. They maintain a continuity of values and principles associated with spectrums of the Islamic understandings going back to the foundations of the divine revelation, presented to the Prophet Muhammad and contained within the Qur'an. Traditional understandings of the ways in which Islam and Muslims operate and communicate (both from insider and outsider perspectives) have been challenged in profound and revolutionary ways through the emergence of the World Wide Web in general and in particular through widening access, increased digital literacy, and enhanced social networking through a variety of media tools.

Even a decade ago, it would have been difficult to have anticipated the way in which, for example, jihad-oriented platforms have embedded social media within their activities at every stage while adopting new apps and software to develop their digital boot-print. This has included the introduction of help desks to service users' technical questions and requirements.[2] The use of secure and encrypted generic tools, such as Telegram, have countered the efforts of authorities to censor and limit the digital output of the "Islamic State." Technological application and innovation has resulted in a cat-and-mouse sequence of actions and responses in cyberspace at a frenetic speed that would not have been anticipated during the early days of the internet. Marshall McLuhan's global village is now a megalopolis, with hidden channels and alternate universes enmeshed between and within elements of the internet. This is reflected in particular in CIEs, digitally reflecting the notion of a multitude of parallel *ummahs*.

There is also the related consciousness of image associated with these platforms, which can mirror design considerations that locate their aesthetic within gaming. The relationship between images derived in part from Call of Duty and other games and the presentation of images of militaristic jihad present a synthesis that could resonate within a younger game-playing demographic (although it is appreciated that it is not *just* teenagers who play on gaming platforms). The extent to which this synthesis might affect issues of recruitment and logistical support is open to analysis. A blurring between the violence presented within some games and the potential "real world" participation in a battle or other forms of conflict opens up substantial issues in which a negotiation between the cinematic aesthetic and its impact on susceptible individuals could be explored. Of course, this conversation relating to the impact of diverse forms of media on consumers is a long-standing one. The impact of gaming media provides the latest iteration of a debate about media influence, but it could be suggestive of some form of transformation in our understanding of the psychology and dynamics of immersion in electronic media and their real-world impact.[3] Consideration can be given here to Jean Baudrillard's hyperreality concept and the construction of zones where boundaries between reality and representation are blurred—if not breached.

Religious authority's articulation via social media reflects a further change, especially in terms of impact on traditional networks, when new and innovative approaches toward religious messages are constantly being presented. Take, for example, the way in which the phone app Snapchat was applied in 2016 as a way to answer religious questions in an extremely condensed video format (of about eight seconds in length); the American imam Suhaib Webb was delivering "snapwas," recorded in a variety of contexts in a streetwise and informal manner.[4]

Elsewhere, the stereotypical images of religious authorities and scholars were undergoing something of a digital transformation, when imams in Iran were represented on Instagram interacting with the public in nonreligious contexts. Whether people were bricklaying, feeding ostriches, playing basketball, or taking selfies, the use of this particular form of social media was offering a challenge to the stereotypical models often associated with religious authorities.[5] That is not to say that these examples are necessarily typical. It does suggest that internet media offer potential for a greater insight of, and access toward, religious figures. The construction of meaning, as conveyed within this social media landscape, requires an understanding of the codes and symbols of religion and their specific interpretations as articulated by Roland Barthes.

The images of religious authorities and figures have themselves, in some cases, undergone a shift: certain authorities have acquired near celebrity status through social media, beyond the traditional reverence for religious figures. The promotion of individuals who are media savvy and perform well through a variety of media forms (if not necessarily the most religiously knowledgeable or qualified) has amplified the way in which the confines of more traditional and controlled media forms have been transcended. Individuals and organizations, from minority and majority contexts, have developed personalities through the application of the World Wide Web in general and social media in particular; this phenomenon has been observed in the evolution of different forms of religious authority and knowledge. That digitally literate individuals and organizations present their scholars and authorities in an accessible and immediate format is significant.

Opportunities for marginalized interpretations and voices have also become available to varying degrees, depending on context. This is not to present an idealistic picture, as clearly censorship, as well as technical issues and traditional cultural barriers, can impede the opportunities for individuals to express their views online. Religious leadership through the use of hashtags in order to generate conversations and strings of tweeted opinions has in some contexts reframed approaches to authority; the nuances of religious opinion have burst into cyberspace. For example, the multiple identities associated with so-called Salafi Islam transcend political restraints and censorship in local and global contexts in order to initiate conversations (not necessarily complementary or agreeing with each other) in which there is a presentation of forms of religious authority online. Where this occurs in the various online channels associated with definitions of Salafi Islam, opportunities are presented for the delivery of information that had been limited or nonexistent prior to the emergence of the World Wide Web.

In these contexts, the models have changed, paralleling the dramatic shifts within the real-world analog contexts on the ground. It is important to stress that the internet reflects activities and even initiates developments in analog contexts but is not the full picture in relation to religious or political developments. It would be simplistic to say that the internet was the only cause, but there are areas in which it forms a digital pulse for developments in terms of immediacy, mass distribution, evading censorship, and opening up channels of knowledge to broad audiences. In some ways, it also offers opportunities for an evaluation of diverse Muslim perspectives between and within the so-called Muslim world(s), as well as for outsiders, in terms of the levels of access to updated news, information, and actuality that go beyond previously traditional channels.

The expectations from followers of specific shades of belief within the Islamic spectrum that they should be able to connect to religious authority and opinion via digital interfaces means that even platforms that were previously reluctant to go online have taken on—if not embraced—the utilization of social media as a cost-efficient and effective tool to disseminate particular worldviews. Within this environment, the challenges to the existing frameworks also include forms of opposition presented through social media and in some cases through direct cyberattack. The contestation for audiences and authority plays out not only in the streets, public spaces, institutions, and mosques but also in cyberspace. Those players who are digitally effective and possess the resources have demonstrated that influence can be generated in ways that can challenge the status quo. Former hierarchies have adjusted to this technological evolution, while attempts by others to censor and control have not always met with success. For example, according to some critics, substantial investments in Iranian censorship of the World Wide Web did not necessarily present the anticipated results, especially given the high levels of technical aptitude many users and content generators were able to apply to evade control.[6]

The impact on perceptions of Islam and Muslims within a twenty-first-century context is significant, as is the underpinning role that information technology can have on developing a holistic understanding of contemporary Islamic issues. The impact relates to perceptions at the level of media, where one can observe an increasing reference to internet content in journalistic and other analyses. Its influence is also significant in relation to academic perceptions, in contemporary analyses of Muslim expression within a range of applications and contexts. There is considerable scope for expanding the ways in which the impact of the internet can be approached, for example within legalistic contexts as having an influence on religious authority and personal decision-making. Notions of debate within Muslim public spheres and the dynamics of opinion—as outlined by Jürgen Habermas—may have a resonance within contemporary online CIE discourse. Ideas surrounding potential manipulation are also prevalent. Whether these debates are "democratic" is open to question. Marshall McLuhan asked whether the medium overcomes the message, a notion that could be applied to CIEs. The medium is to an extent shaping discourse in CIEs and influencing its presentation, format, and distribution—but is not necessarily *overcoming* the message. The source code of Islam is retained at the core, in a multiplicity of formats and encoding (technical and religious). Users may be loyal to specific digital tools and apps, which inform their understanding.

A tendency toward compartmentalizing internet themes, rather than seeing them as an integrated element within a contemporary discourse about Islam and Muslims, has occurred at personal, institutional and international levels. This would suggest that in some areas of discourse, there is a need for a maturity of academic approach in relation to how (if at all) the internet can play a role as a catalyst for influence and change. By contrast, in other areas, there has been an integration of internet issues within wider analyses of contemporary Islam and Muslim societies. This growing acceptance of the importance of the field is important in developing a sense of engagement with the complexities of a digital discourse that can be difficult to capture or at times ephemeral in nature.

There is, however, a role for considering the bytes of influence and knowledge transmission that might fall under the radar when looking at the texts, tweets, Facebook posts, Instagram exchanges, and even the visits to Ask the Imam question-and-answer sites. A multiplicity of information pulses and exchanges, taking place every second, including dialogues about Islam and Muslim issues, with opportunities (for some) to engage on specific religious issues that were unavailable to previous generations. This raises specific concerns, in terms of the levels of control within Muslim societies of these different influences, some of which can be deemed by certain authorities (and wider society) as negative in nature. Examples of such negativity could range from feminist religious activism to jihad-oriented recruitment, a spectrum that is difficult to judge in broad generalizations, especially from external perspectives. The issues of censorship and filtering content mean that a range of other materials can be blocked, under the suggestion that they are concerned with preventing terrorism, ignoring the fact that they can also inhibit other elements associated with freedom of speech.

Within all of this discourse and consideration, within an academic context one might raise concerns that the ephemeral nature of internet content means that substantial materials are lost from view for future academics and historians. Capturing and managing terabytes of information necessary to complete a picture of the development of CIEs is beyond the scope of a single scholar but could be an activity that some form of open-source collaboration could facilitate, in which the capture of materials for scrutiny (and posterity) might contribute to a fuller understanding of the real impact of the internet on Islam. Such an activity would require great hindsight, engendered over a decade or two.

Given that some have suggested that the World Wide Web has had as big an impact on societies as a whole as the introduction of the printing press and that the emergence of concerns about Islam and Muslims has also become a dominant theme within academic and other contexts, a fusion of these elements and a more granulated understanding would surely be a relevant ambition for future scholarship. This would require a reframing of the models associated with the study of Islam in order that specialists of religion, language, and culture could focus on internet materials as part of their studies and research. This reframing is as relevant within minority contexts, where Muslims are part of a small but growing population, as within majority contexts, where more conventional studies of Islam occur.

The internet cannot be reduced to specific nation-state frameworks, and neither can its study in relation to Islam and Muslims. The internet is a globalizing phenomenon, where influences are drawn from dispersed and at times obscure sources in conjunction with more traditional authoritative materials, and it is relevant for academics to try to ascertain the way in which CIEs are shaping discourse about and understanding of the interpretation of Islam for Muslims and others. This exchange of bytes of knowledge can be an intra-Muslim concern, not necessarily one that is seen as an activity for mutual benefit, where material derived from the internet can be used by religious and political opponents as part of a form of "flaming," which can spill over into other forms of abuse and violence.

Despite the impact of digital innovations in communications, traditional forms of communication maintain a significant role, and one cannot talk about forms of networking being exclusively digital. A synthesis of different forms still continues to play a role in communications, even though online media have become dominant in particular for generations of digital natives.

This book is indicative of the different forms that communication can take, having been written not only with traditional tools (including a fountain pen) but also in a variety of contexts—on iPads, mobile phones, laptops, and desk-bound machines. Speech recognition software, as well as handwriting, has formed a significant tool within the development of this book. When I started working on the issue of Islam and the internet, back in the 1990s, the assumption was that internet access could be facilitated only through a desk-bound machine and that it would come (very erratically) down a phone line. This in itself was a considerable advance for people working from home, given that previously it was usually possible to access the internet only through institutional interfaces (certainly in the 1980s).

One must consider what possible leaps there might be in the future for information technology and how further technological leaps are going to affect ideas about Islamic religious expression. Will there be future transformative shifts associated with technology? For many perspectives and orientations associated with Islam, the internet in different forms is extremely important. In the future, whether that access is going to be facilitated more through wearable devices, constant streaming, or even implants is a subject for conjecture (and even science fiction).

One projected future that could be more realistic would be to see a greater proportion of the Muslim world(s) having access to and developing digital literacy, which in itself will influence ideas about the momentum of religious knowledge and influence. Depending on the types of systems installed, digital literacy might also facilitate forms of control and monitoring, given some of the more dystopian ideas about how information technology will manifest itself in the future. The sense of religious obligation and the need to observe pronouncements from specific sources and networks may become an extension of individual digital identity. There could be further shifts when concepts associated with identity transcend physical/national boundaries and frameworks and become even more manifest within virtual contexts. While the influence of virtual worlds such as Second Life may be negligible, enhanced virtual realities in the future with embedded religious content could change the dynamics of networking and religious identity, including within notions of the performance of ritual and interaction with religious authorities. Interfaces for question-and-answer sessions may not just be made up of textual sources and responses but could increasingly incorporate avatars operating within realistic virtual contexts.

Mobilization of militaristic jihad may also develop a more immersive edge, with the experiential element of an individual being embedded within a specific battle zone or conflict becoming more and more feasible. The sustained cinematic productions developed by IS have already provided an indicator of technological awareness, in which the value to the protagonists of investment of time and resources to develop the films and put them in place online has provided rewards in terms of the ways in which these media products have extended the organization's profile and impact beyond its geographical borders. While some campaigns and activities have been filmed using smartphones or HD cameras, there is potential for jihad to be presented through streaming immersive actuality, seen through the perspective of combatants (using action cameras in real time).

The processes of interaction between leaders and followers have been enhanced through technology, with campaigns being conducted thousands of miles away from the heartlands of IS. In 2016, the attacks in the Brussels airport, following the Paris attacks in 2015, demonstrated a linkage in relation to the ways in which social media feeds associated with IS quickly took responsibility for the actions, and supportive comments emerged through a myriad of networks, not just in western Europe but within global contexts. Similarly, it was not a surprise when, following an "operation," a Taliban-affiliated platform was quick to present images of a suicide bomber who had attacked a target in Lahore, killing more than seventy people.[7]

It is natural for media to seek out these images and present them online and increasingly for researchers and others to look to the internet for statements "justifying" such activities. Even those platforms previously adverse to use of information technology have used modern tools to facilitate access to such information: the Taliban announced the development of a smartphone app, featured on the Google Play store in April 2016, with which supporters could network and locate information.[8] This is in marked contrast to some of its previous approaches toward the internet and forms part of its multilanguage hub website.

Whatever the positive and negative implications of such online activities, clearly the issue of any sense of controlling internet output is limited at best. For academics and observers, this can mean some form of information overload, as one struggles to collect, interpret, and absorb the implications of daily—and even minute-by-minute—updates. As I write, on my desk there are several devices streaming different forms of social media and updates, which I continue to collect (and share) as I write this chapter. Part of the analytical process includes the sharing of information and reposting of relevant sources, given that one is dependent in part methodologically on the findings of a multiplicity of sources and feeds.

The role of academics as gatekeepers for information is particularly pertinent when exploring online religious discourse, especially when one deals with students and others who are seeking to interpret this information in a coherent and organized fashion. Unlike other disciplines, which may have more fixed data sets and sources of information, when looking at CIEs the river of data is constant and fluid, with occasional floods. Given my location in the heart of Wales, this may be an appropriate analogy. The flood reaches me, despite the notion of distance from some core Muslim activities.[9]

One is able to observe and record the conversations in a multiplicity of contexts and at times contribute to these dialogues, wherever one is located.

This sense of engagement and of Islam being always "on" continues to be a significant issue. Technological advances mean that we have more devices that are internet-enabled, which can provide (if desirable) continual updates of news, tweets, updates, and information. One significant question is how one becomes functional given this data overload, especially within religious circles, when one risks a bombardment of authorities, advice, commands, and suggestions of control. It is tempting to respond to this data overload by retreating to more traditional print sources or other forms of information, especially given that knowledge distributed on the internet always has issues of authenticity as a principal concern. Different interfaces also provide reading experiences and knowledge acquisition, which can be diffuse and different in nature: there is a distinct difference between reading a printed source and looking at its online equivalent. The ways in which printed texts are mediated and absorbed are different from digital encounters. One experience may be more intense and absorbing, while another may be more peripheral and fleeting, especially if that encounter is through a portable digital device accessed in a public space.

Islam has always been mediated via a variety of channels and approaches. The Qur'an is recited, read, listened to, written about, and reflected on within diverse contexts and methods by a variety of advocates; it can be memorized by heart, presented in a sermon, or drawn upon for prayer, ritual, and legal interpretive processes. Its mediation might be as part of a mystical or esoteric ritualistic encounter. The nature of its interpretation varies according to culture, school, history, language, and political influence. Translation and interpretation have a role to play in ways in which the divine is mediated. All of these factors now have a digital edge and interface while retaining the core revelation and consistency of text.

This model of consistency in relation to core content is durable enough to survive and thrive, even if the frameworks in which it is presented shift in line with technological development and specific ideological and religious influences. The multiplicity of interfaces and devices through which there is potential for this information to be distributed is dependent on human interfaces, from content originators and platform developers to the volition of the individual consumer to locate, read, and absorb the specific message in the way desired by its creator (or Creator).

In an increasingly complex digital souk of ideas, it is only through creativity and innovation that some messages will ever be heard, while others require the momentum of support (and perhaps a popular hashtag) in order to reach audience momentum. The marketing of religious knowledge and ideas goes beyond the strength of its content, with reliance on algorithms and digital dynamics in order that it can reach a target audience. It is this relationship between religion, technology, and innovation that will be a critical element within the future study of contemporary Islam and Muslim societies, in majority and minority contexts. Within shifting CIEs, the application of diverse forms of information technology surrounding hashtag Islam will increasingly influence command and control within Muslim digital—and actual—worlds.

#Notes

INTRODUCTION

1. Huawei Global Connectivity Index, " 'Digital Divide Is Now a Digital Chasm': Inequality Widens in Technology, Reports Huawei Global Connectivity Index 2017," Huawei, 17 April 2017, http://www.huawei.com/en/news/2017/4/Huawei-Global -Connectivity-Index2017.

CHAPTER 1

1. BBC News, "Migrant Crisis: 'We Would Be Lost without Google Maps,' " YouTube, 9 September 2015, https://youtu.be/Zcr-GWv3Qbs; Andrew Byrne and Erika Solomon, "Refugees Seek Help from Social Media," *Financial Times*, 11 September 2015, http://www.ft.com.

2. John Dewey and F. W. Garforth, *John Dewey: Selected Educational Writings* (London: Heinemann, 1966).

3. Marshall McLuhan and Quentin Fiore, *War and Peace in the Global Village* (1968; London: Simon and Schuster, 1989).

4. Marshall McLuhan and Bruce R. Powers, *The Global Village: Transformations in World Life and Media in the 21st Century* (New York: Oxford University Press, 1989).

5. Jean Baudrillard, *Simulations* (New York: Semiotext(e), 1983).

6. Christopher Helland, "Religion Online/Online Religion and Virtual Communitas," in *Religion on the Internet: Research Prospects and Promises*, ed. Jeffrey K. Hadden and Douglas E. Cowan (New York: Elsevier Science, 2000), 205–24. Also see Douglas E. Cowan and Lorne L. Dawson, eds., *Religion Online: Finding Faith on the Internet* (New York: Routledge, 2004).

7. Michel Foucault and Alan Sheridan, *Discipline and Punish: The Birth of the Prison* (London: Allen Lane, 1977).

8. Roland Barthes and Annette Lavers, *Mythologies* (London: Cape, 1972).

9. Jürgen Habermas, *The Structural Transformation of the Public Sphere: An Inquiry into a Category of Bourgeois Society* (Cambridge, Mass.: MIT Press, 1989). Also see Nicholas Garnham, *Emancipation, the Media, and Modernity: Arguments about the Media and Social Theory* (2000; Oxford: Oxford University Press, Oxford Scholarship Online, 2011).

10. James Bohman and William Rehg, "Jürgen Habermas," in *The Stanford Encyclopedia of Philosophy* (2014), ed. Edward N. Zalta, http://plato.stanford.edu/ archives/fall2014/entries/habermas/.

11. William Outhwaite, *Habermas: A Critical Introduction* (Cambridge: Polity Press, 2009).

12. John B. Thompson, *Ideology and Modern Culture: Critical Social Theory in the Era of Mass Communication* (Cambridge: Polity, 1990).

13. Kevin Williams, *Understanding Media Theory* (London: Arnold, 2003).

14. Anthony Giddens and Simon Griffiths, eds., *Sociology*, 5th ed. (Cambridge: Polity, 2006), 118.

15. Anthony Giddens, *Modernity and Self-Identity* (Cambridge: Polity, 1991), 53.

16. Giddens, 244.

17. David Buckingham, ed., *Youth, Identity, and Digital Media*, John D. and Catherine T. MacArthur Foundation Series on Digital Media and Learning (Cambridge: MIT Press, 2008).

18. Giddens, *Modernity and Self-Identity*, 5. Also see Giddens and Griffiths, *Sociology*, 602; and Kehbuma Langmia, Tia C. M. Tyree, Pamela O'Brien, and Ingrid Sturgis, eds., *Social Media: Pedagogy and Practice* (New York: University Press of America, 2013), 65.

19. Howard Rheingold, *The Virtual Community: Homesteading on the Electronic Frontier* (Reading, Mass.: Addison-Wesley, 1993).

20. Gary R. Bunt, *Virtually Islamic: Computer-Mediated Communication and Cyber Islamic Environments* (Cardiff: University of Wales Press, 2000).

21. Manuel Castells, *The Rise of the Network Society*, 2nd ed. (Oxford: Blackwell, 2000).

22. Manuel Castells, *The Internet Galaxy: Reflections on Internet, Business, and Society* (2001; Oxford: Oxford University Press, Oxford Scholarship Online, 2011), 117.

23. Castells, *Internet Galaxy*.

24. Stewart M. Hoover and Lynn Schofield Clark, eds., *Practicing Religion in the Age of the Media: Explorations in Media, Religion, and Culture* (New York: Columbia University Press, 2002); Stewart M. Hoover, *Religion in the Media Age* (London: Routledge, 2006); Stewart M. Hoover, *Mass Media Religion: The Social Sources of the Electronic Church* (London: Sage, 1988); Stewart M. Hoover, *Religion in the News: Faith and Journalism in American Public Discourse* (London: Sage, 1998); Stewart M. Hoover and Knut Lundby, *Rethinking Media, Religion, and Culture* (London: Sage, 1997).

25. Jeffrey K. Hadden and Douglas E. Cowan, eds., *Religion on the Internet: Research Prospects and Promises* (New York: Elsevier Science, 2000).

26. Douglas E. Cowan and Lorne L. Dawson, eds., *Religion Online: Finding Faith on the Internet* (New York: Routledge, 2004); Morten T. Højsgaard and Margit Warburg, eds., *Religion and Cyberspace* (London: Routledge, 2005); Göran Larsson, ed., *Religious Communities on the Internet* (Stockholm: Swedish Science Press, 2006).

27. Bruce B. Lawrence, *The Complete Idiot's Guide to Online Religion* (Indianapolis: Alpha Books, 1999); Gary R. Bunt, *The Good Web Guide to World Religions* (London: Good Web Guide, 2001).

28. Gwilym Beckerlegge, *From Sacred Text to Internet* (Burlington, Vt.: Ashgate, 2001).

29. Brenda E. Brasher, *Give Me That Online Religion* (San Francisco: Jossey-Bass, 2001).

30. *Online: Heidelberg Journal of Religions on the Internet*, Institute for Religious Studies, 2005, http://journals.ub.uni-heidelberg/index.php/religions/.

31. Christopher Helland, "Virtual Tibet: Maintaining Identity through Internet Networks," in *The Pixel in the Lotus: Buddhism, the Internet, and Digital Media*, ed.

Gregory Grieve (New York: Routledge, 2014), 213–41; Douglas E. Cowan, *Cyberhenge: Modern Pagans on the Internet* (New York: Routledge, 2005); Heidi Campbell, *When Religion Meets New Media* (New York: Routledge, 2010); Heidi Campbell, *Exploring Religious Community Online: We are One in the Network* (New York: Peter Lang, 2005).

32. Bunt, *Virtually Islamic*; Bunt, *Islam in the Digital Age: E-jihad, Online Fatwas and Cyber Islamic Environments* (London: Pluto Press, 2003); Bunt, *iMuslims: Rewiring the House of Islam* (Chapel Hill: University of North Carolina Press, 2009); Bunt, "From Mosque to YouTube: Cyber Islamic Networks in the UK," in *Postcolonial Media Cultures*, ed. Ros Brunt and Rinella Cere (London: Palgrave Macmillan, 2011), 68–81; Bunt, "Mediterranean Islamic Expression and Web 2.0," in *Arab Society in Revolt: The West's Mediterranean Challenge*, ed. Olivier Roy and Cesare Melini (New York: Brookings Institution Press, 2012), 76–95; Bunt, "#Islam, Social Networking and the Cloud," in *Islam in the Modern World*, ed. Jeffrey T. Kenney and Ebrahim Moosa (New York: Routledge, 2014), 177–208; Bunt, "Studying Muslims and Cyberspace," in *Studying Islam in Practice*, ed. Gabriele Marranci (New York: Routledge, 2014), 190–203; Bunt, "Islamic Spirituality and the Internet," in *Wiley-Blackwell Companion to Islamic Spirituality*, ed. Bruce B. Lawrence and Vincent Cornell (New York: Wiley-Blackwell, 2018; Bunt, "Decoding the Hajj in Cyberspace," in *The Hajj: Pilgrimage in Islam*, ed. Eric Tagliacozzo and Shawkat M. Toorawa (Cambridge: Cambridge University Press, 2015), 231–49.

33. miriam cooke and Bruce B. Lawrence, eds., *Muslim Networks from Hajj to Hip Hop* (Chapel Hill: University of North Carolina Press, 2005); Bruce B. Lawrence, "Allah On-Line: The Practice of Global Islam in the Information Age," in *Practicing Religion in the Age of the Media: Explorations in Media, Religion, and Culture*, ed. Stewart M. Hoover and Lynn Schofield Clark (New York: Columbia University Press, 2002; Bruce B. Lawrence, *Who Is Allah?* (Chapel Hill: University of North Carolina Press, 2015).

34. Dale F. Eickelman and Jon W. Anderson, eds., *New Media in the Muslim World* (Bloomington: Indiana University Press, 2003); Dale F. Eickelman and James Piscatori, *Muslim Politics* (Princeton: Princeton University Press, 1996); Noha Mellor and Khalil Rinnawi, eds., *Political Islam and Global Media: The Boundaries of Religious Identity* (London: Routledge, 2016).

35. Jon B. Alterman, *New Media, New Politics? From Satellite Television to the Internet in the Arab World* (Washington, D.C.: Washington Institute for Near East Policy, 1998); Noha Mellor and Khalil Rinnawi, eds., *Political Islam and Global Media: The Boundaries of Religious Identity* (London: Routledge, 2016).

36. In particular, see Albrecht Hofheinz, "The Internet in the Arab World: Playground for Political Liberalisation," *Internationale Politik und Gesellschaft / International Politics and Society* 3 (2005): 78–96, http://fesportal.fes.de/pls/portal30/docs/FOLDER/IPG/IPG3_2005/07HOFHEINZ.PDF; Deborah L. Wheeler, *Digital Resistance in the Middle East: New Media Activism in Everyday Life* (Edinburgh: Edinburgh University Press, 2017); and Wheeler, *The Internet in the Middle East: Global Expectations and Local Imaginations in Kuwait* (New York: State University of New York Press, 2005).

37. Roxanne D. Marcotte, "The New Virtual Frontiers: Religion and Spirituality in Cyberspace," *Australian Religion Studies Review* 23, no. 3 (2010): 247–54, http://www.equinoxjournals.com/ARSR/article/view/10060/pdf; El-Sayed El-Aswad, *Muslim Worldviews and Everyday Lives* (Lanham, Md.: AltaMira Press, 2012); Sariya Cheruvallil

Contractor, "'Online Sufism'—Young British Muslims, Their Virtual 'Selves' and Virtual Reality," in *Sufism in Britain*, ed. Ron Geaves and Theodore Gabriel (London: Bloomsbury Academic, 2013), 161–76; Thomas Hoffmann and Göran Larsson, eds., *Muslims and the New Information and Communication Technologies: Notes from an Emerging and Infinite Field* (Amsterdam: Springer, 2013); Smeeta Mishraab and Gaby Semaan, "Islam in Cyberspace: South Asian Muslims in America Log In," *Journal of Broadcasting and Electronic Media* 54, no. 1 (2010): 87–101.

38. Christopher M. Schroeder, *Startup Rising: The Entrepreneurial Revolution Remaking the Middle East* (New York: Palgrave Macmillan, 2013).

39. Vit Šisler, "Video Games, Video Clips, and Islam: New Media and the Communication of Values," Digital Islam, 9 November 2009, http://www.digitalislam.eu/article.do?articleId=2550; Glen Dalakian II, "Arab Heroes Can Now Battle on the iPhone in Falafel Games' New Mobile MMO Knights of Glory," Wamda, 16 May 2013, http://www.wamda.com/2013/05/falafel-games-launches-mobile-mmo-knights-of-glory.

40. Heather Marie Akou, "Interpreting Islam through the Internet: Making Sense of Hijab," *Contemporary Islam* 4, no. 3 (2010): 331–46.

41. Dorthe Høvids Possing, "A Politics of Place: How Young Muslims Frame Global and Local Events in Online Communication," Center for Global Studies, George Mason University, Global Migration and Transnational Politics Series Working Paper no. 11, 2010, http://cgs.gmu.edu/publications/gmtpwp/gmtp_wp_11.pdf.

42. Anna Piela, *Muslim Women Online: Faith and Identity in Virtual Space* (New York: Routledge, 2012); Piela, "Piety as a Concept Underpinning Muslim Women's Online Discussions of Marriage and Professional Career," *Contemporary Islam* 5, no. 3 (2011): 249–65; Eva F. Nisa, "The Internet Subculture of Indonesian Face-Veiled Women," *International Journal of Cultural Studies* 16, no. 3 (2013): 241–55, http://ics.sagepub.com/content/16/3/241.short.

43. Vahideh Golzard and Cristina Miguel, "Negotiating Intimacy through Social Media: Challenges and Opportunities for Muslim Women in Iran," *Middle East Journal of Culture and Communication* 9 (2016): 216–33; Chiara Bernardi, "Saudi Bloggers, Women's Issues and NGOs," *Arab Media and Society*, 2010, http://www.arabmediasociety.com/?article=757.

44. Andrea L. Stanton, "Islamic Emoticons: Pious Sociability and Community Building in Online Muslim Communities," in *Internet and Emotions*, ed. Tova Benski and Eran Fisher (London: Routledge, 2013), 80–98.

45. Rita Wan-Chik, Paul Clough, and Mark Sanderson, "Investigating Religious Information Searching through Analysis of a Search Engine Log," *Journal of the American Society for Information Science and Technology* 64, no. 12 (2013): 2492–506.

46. Marie Gillespie, John Herbert David Eric, and Anita Greenhill, *Social Media and Religious Change* (Berlin: De Gruyter, 2013).

47. Evgeny Morozov, *The Net Delusion: How Not to Liberate the World* (London: Allen Lane, 2011).

48. *CyberOrient: Online Journal of the Virtual Middle East*, http://www.cyberorient.net; *Arab Media and Society*, http://www.arabmediasociety.org; Andrew Helms, "Politics of Information: The Internet and Islamist Politics in Jordan, Morocco and

Egypt," *Journal of Middle East Media* 5 (Fall 2009), http://jmem.gsu.edu/2014/09/29/volume-5-issue-1/.

49. Wissam S. Yafi, *Inevitable Democracy in the Arab World* (New York: Palgrave Macmillan, 2012).

50. Philip N. Howard, *The Digital Origins of Dictatorship and Democracy: Information Technology and Political Islam* (Oxford: Oxford University Press, 2010); David Faris, *Dissent and Revolution in a Digital Age: Social Media, Blogging and Activism in Egypt* (London: I. B. Tauris, 2012).

51. Sean Aday, Henry Farrell, Marc Lynch, John Sides, and Deen Freelon, "Blogs and Bullets II: New Media and Conflict after the Arab Spring," United States Institute of Peace, 2012, http://www.usip.org/publications/blogs-and-bullets-ii-new-media-and-conflict-after-the-arab-spring; Sahar Khamis, Paul B. Gold, and Katherine Vaughn, "Beyond Egypt's 'Facebook Revolution' and Syria's 'YouTube Uprising': Comparing Political Contexts, Actors and Communication Strategies," *Arab Media and Society* (2012). http://www.arabmediasociety.com/articles/downloads/20120407120519_Khamis_Gold_Vaughn.pdf ; Bunt, "Mediterranean Islamic Expression and Web 2.0," 76–95; Laila Shereen Sakr, "A Digital Humanities Approach: Text, the Internet, and the Egyptian Uprising," *Middle East Critique* 22, no. 3 (2013): 247–63, http://www.tandfonline.com/doi/abs/10.1080/19436149.2013.822241.

52. Bruce Etling, John Kelly, Rob Faris, and John Palfrey, 2009. " Mapping the Arabic Blogosphere: Politics, Culture and Dissent," Berkman Klein Center for Internet and Society at Harvard University, 16 June 2009, http://cyber.law.harvard.edu/publications/2009/Mapping_the_Arabic_Blogosphere.

53. Racha Mourtada, Fadi Salem, and Sarah Alshaer, *Citizen Engagement and Public Services in the Arab World: The Potential of Social Media* (Dubai: Mohammed Bin Rashid School of Government 2014).

54. Sumayyah Amar, "Pornography, Internet Freedom and Shariah," FMT News, 6 December 2013, http://www.freemalaysiatoday.com/category/opinion/2013/12/06/pornography-internet-freedom-and-shariah/.

55. Liz Halloran, "King Hearings to Revisit 'Radical Muslim' Question," NPR, 10 March 2011, http://www.npr.org/2011/03/10/134374186/king-hearings-revisit-radical-muslim-question.

56. Glenn Greenwald, "The Sham 'Terrorism Expert' Industry," *Salon*, 15 August 2012, http://www.salon.com/2012/08/15/the_sham_terrorism_expert_industry/.

57. Philip Seib and Dana M. Janbek, *Global Terrorism and New Media: The Post–Al Qaeda Generation* (New York: Routledge, 2010); Aaron Y. Zelin, Jihadology, http://jihadology.net; Christopher Anzalone (@Ibn Siqilli), Twitter, http://twitter.com/ibnsiqilli.

58. James A. Danowski, "Counterterrorism Mining for Individuals Semantically-Similar to Watchlist Members," *Counterterrorism and Open Source Intelligence, Lecture Notes in Social Network* (2001), 223–47, https://link.springer.com/chapter/10.1007/978-3-7091-0388-3_12.

59. Hassan Hassan and Michael Weiss, *Isis: Inside the Army of Terror* (London: Regan Arts, 2015); Abdel Bari Atwan, *Islamic State: the Digital Caliphate* (London: Saqi Books, 2015); Charlie Winter, "Documenting the 'Virtual Caliphate,' " (London: Quilliam Foundation, 2015), http://www/quilliamfoundation.org.

1. Madhavi Bhasin, "Muslims and New Social Media," *Huffington Post*, 11 March 2010, http://www.huffingtonpost.com/madhavi-bhasin/muslims-and-new-social-me_b_ 493748.html.

2. "Facebook Frenzy Beats Out Newspapers in ME," *Arab News*, 1 June 2010, http:// arabnews.com/world/article60057.ece [link deleted].

3. "Residents in Saudi Arabia Spend Almost a Quarter of Their Day on Social Media," YouGov, 4 July 2016, http://research.mena.yougov.com/en/news/2016/07/04/ saudi-residents-spend-quarter-day-social-media/.

4. Everette E. Dennis, Justin D. Martin, and Robb Wood, "Media Use in the Middle East," Northwestern University in Qatar, 15 August 2015, http://www.mideastmedia .org/2015/.

5. Stephanie Baker, "The Arab World's Silicon Valley: Jordan Emerges as an Internet Hub," *Bloomberg Markets/Washington Post*, 17 October 2012, https://www .washingtonpost.com/.

6. Hind Mustafa, "Google: Arabic Content Ranks Eighth on the Internet," Al Arabiya News, 1 December 2013, http://english.alarabiya.net/en/media/digital/2013/12/ 01/Google-Arabic-content-ranks-eighth-on-the-internet.html.

7. "ICANN Bringing the Languages of the World to the Global Internet, Fast Track Process for Internationalized Domain Names Launches Nov 16," ICANN, 30 October 2009, http://www.icann.org/en/announcements/announcement-30oct09-en.htm.

8. Hannan Taha, "Qatar Receives Approval for Arabic Internet Domains," GlobalArabNetwork.com, 30 March 2010, http://www.english.globalarabnetwork. com/201003305332/Technology/qatar-receives-approval-for-arabic-Internet-domains. html; "'Historic' Day as First Non-Latin Web Addresses Go Live," BBC News, 6 May 2010, http://news.bbc.co.uk/1/hi/technology/10100108.stm.

9. Dana Khraiche, "Arabic Fastest Growing Language on Twitter: Study," *Daily Star*, 24 November 2011, http://www.dailystar.com.lb/Article.aspx?id=155083; Mohamed Marwen Meddah, "Arabic Language Domains and Internet Growth in the Arab World," StartUpArabia, 6 August 2009, http://www.startuparabia.com/2009/08/arabic -language-domains-Internet-growth-in-the-arab-world/.

10. Renad Ghanem, "'Arabizi Is Destroying the Arabic Language,'" *Arab News*, 19 April 2011, http://www.arabnews.com/node/374897.

11. "Twitter Enables Right to Left Writing," ArabCrunch.com, 13 August 2011, http:// arabcrunch.com/2011/08/twitter-enables-right-to-left-writing.html.

12. Gaith Saqer, "Translation War Intensifies: Microsoft Launched Translator Widget in 32 Languages Including Arabic and Chinese," ArabCrunch.com, 25 March 2010, http:// arabcrunch.com [link deleted].

13. Gaith Saqer, "Google to Push for a Larger Expansion in the Arab Region," ArabCrunch.com, 8 March 2010, http://arabcrunch.com [link deleted].

14. Farid Hossain, "Internet Rolls into Bangladesh Villages on a Bike," Associated Press/*San Diego Tribune*, 31 October 2012, http://www.sandiegouniontribune.com/sdut -Internet-rolls-into-bangladesh-villages-on-a-bike-20120ct31-story.html.

15. "Samsung to Bring 'Solar' Laptop in Bangladesh: Official," bdnews24.com, 9 January 2012, http://bdnews24.com/bangladesh/2012/01/09/samsung-to-bring-solar-laptop-in-bangladesh-official.

16. International Telecommunications Union, "ICT Facts & Figures," May 2015, https://www.itu.int/en/ITU-D/Statistics/Documents/facts/ICTFactsFigures2015.pdf.

17. International Telecommunications Union, "ICT Facts & Figures."

18. "Egypt Blogger Wins Euro-Mid Online Media Prize," Al Arabiya News, 16 October 2010, http://www.alarabiya.net/articles/2010/10/16/122476.html; Dalia Ziada, "A Space for Unveiling the Minds of Young Muslim Women," *Dalia Ziada: World from the Perspective of an Egyptian Human Rights Activist* (blog), 8 November 2009, http://daliaziada.blogspot.com/2009/11/space-for-unveiling-minds-of-young.html.

19. "Headscarf Emoji Proposed by 15-Year-Old Saudi Girl," BBC News, 14 September 2016, http://www.bbc.co.uk/news/world-middle-east-37358719; "Meet the New Arab Emojis Perking Up Dubai's WhatsApp Chats," BBC News, 28 February 2017, http://www.bbc.co.uk/news/world-middle-east-39079974; Halla Walla, http://hallawalla.com/.

20. Sheikh Ahmed Chienda, Programs Officer of the Islamic Information Bureau (IIB), cited in "Malawi Muslim Leaders Fight Pornography," OnIslam.net, 13 November 2013, http://www.onislam.net [link deleted].

21. Jonathan Zittrain and John Palfrey, "Internet Filtering: The Politics and Mechanisms of Control," in *Access Denied: The Practice and Policy of Global Internet Filtering*, ed. Ronald Deibert, John Palfrey, Rafal Rohozinski, and Jonathan Zittrain (Cambridge: MIT Press, 2008), 29–56.

22. Julie Ruvolo, "How Much of the Internet Is Actually for Porn (Interview with Ogi Ogas)," *Forbes*, 7 September 2011, https://www.forbes.com/sites/julieruvolo/2011/09/07/how-much-of-the-internet-is-actually-for-porn.

23. Ogi Ogas and Sai Gaddam, *A Billion Wicked Thoughts: What the World's Largest Experiment Reveals about Human Desire* (New York: Dutton, 2011).

24. Zurairi Ar, "Social Media a Threat to Islam, Internet Controls a Must, Muslims Told in Friday Sermon," *Malay Mail Online*, 15 November 2013, http://www.themalaymailonline.com/malaysia/article/social-media-a-threat-to-islam-Internet-controls-a-must-muslims-told-in-fri.

25. AFP, "Saudi Arabia to Halt BlackBerry Services," 6 August 2010, http://www.google.com/hostednews/afp/ [link deleted]; Ben Parr, "UAE to Ban BlackBerry E-mail, Web Browsing and Messaging," Mashable, 1 August 2010, http://mashable.com/2010/08/01/blackberry-banned/.

26. Tech2, "YouTube to Remain Blocked in Pakistan Indefinitely, Says Official," FirstPost.com, 9 February 2015, http://tech.firstpost.com/news-analysis/youtube-to-remain-blocked-in-pakistan-indefinitely-says-official-253728.html.

27. ABC Australia, "Egyptian Jailed over 'Insulting' Facebook Posts," ABC, 23 October 2011, http://www.abc.net.au/news/2011-10-23/egyptian-jailed-over-facebook-posts/3595622.

28. Rebecca Wanjiku, "Online Activists Tap Tools to Escape Censorship," *PC World*, 26 September 2010, http://www.pcworld.com/article/206131/online_activists_tap_tools_to_escape_censorship.html; Gary R. Bunt, "Mediterranean Islamic Expression

and Web 2.0," in *Arab Society in Revolt: The West's Mediterranean Challenge*, ed. Olivier Roy and Cesare Melini (New York: Brookings Institution Press, 2012), 76–95.

29. Golnaz Esfandiari, "Trial of Iran's 'Blogfather' Begins, 20 Months after His Arrest," *Persian Letters* (blog), 24 June 2010, http://www.rferl.org/content/Trial_Of _Irans_Blogfather_Begins_20_Months_After_Arrest/2080946.html; Robert Mackey, "Trial of Iran's 'Blogfather' Begins in Tehran," *The Lede* (blog), *New York Times*, 24 June 2010, http://thelede.blogs.nytimes.com/2010/06/24/trial-of-irans-blogfather-begins-in -tehran/; Free Hoder, http://freehoder.wordpress.com/.

30. "Netizen Report: Are Blogger Assassinations Becoming Routine in Bangladesh?," *Slate*, 14 May 2015, http://www.slate.com/blogs/future_tense/2015/05/14/netizen _report_are_blogger_assassinations_becoming_routine_in_bangladesh.html.

31. Daniel Moritz-Rabson, "Pakistani Social Media Icon's Brother Arrested in Her Death," *PBS NewsHour*, 16 July 2016, http://www.pbs.org/newshour/rundown/ pakistani-social-media-icon-strangled-suspected-honor-killing/; "Qandeel Baloch Stirs Storm with Selfies," *The News*, 21 June 2016, https://www.thenews.com.pk/latest/ 129556-Qandeel-Baloch-stirs-storm-with-selfies.

32. "Sheikh Khaled Denies Monitoring Twitter Users," *AlWatanDaily*, 9 May 2011 [link deleted].

33. "Darwin Censored by the Turkish Government's Porn Filter," *Telegraph*, 12 December 2011, http://blogs.telegraph.co.uk/news/tomchiversscience/100123035/ darwin-censored-by-the-turkish-governments-porn-filter/.

34. "Turkey Goes into Battle with Google," BBC News, 2 July 2010, http://www.bbc .co.uk/news/10480877.

35. Andrew Griffin, "WhatsApp, Facebook, YouTube, Twitter and More Down in Turkey in Apparent Internet Ban," *Independent*, 4 November 2016, http://www .independent.co.uk/life-style/gadgets-and-tech/news/whatsapp-facebook-youtube -twitter-down-turkey-Internet-outage-problems-a7396856.html.

36. Helmi Noman, "In the Name of God: Faith-Based Internet Censorship in Majority Muslim Countries," OpenNet Initiative, 1 August 2011, http://opennet.net/ sites/opennet.net/files/ONI_NameofGod_1_08_2011.pdf.

37. Matthew Green, "Afghanistan to Launch Internet Crackdown," *Financial Times*, 28 April 2010, http://www.ft.com/.

38. Luke Allnutt, "How Western Companies Help Middle Eastern Governments Censor the Web," Radio Free Europe/Radio Liberty, 29 March 2011, http://www.rferl .org/content/how_western_companies_help_middle_eastern_governments_censor _the_web/3540582.html; Helmi Noman and Jillian C. York, "West Censoring East: The Use of Western Technologies by Middle East Censors, 2010–2011," OpenNet Initiative, March 2011, http://opennet.net/west-censoring-east-the-use-western -technologies-middle-east-censors-2010–2011.

39. "Protecting Arabs Online," *Digital Frontiers* (blog), Voice of America, 9 April 2011, http://blogs.voanews.com/digital-frontiers/2011/04/09/protecting-arabs-online/.

40. "Anonymity Online," TorProject.org, 7 February 2017, https://www.torproject.org/.

41. Azam Ahmed, "YouTube Ban, Spurred by Anti-Islamic Video, Is Met with Shrugs," *New York Times*, 5 December 2012, http://www.nytimes.com/2012/12/06/world/asia/ youtube-ban-is-shrugged-off-in-afghanistan.html.

42. Huma Imtiaz, "Hate on the Internet," Dawn.com, 8 October 2010, https://www
.dawn.com/news/958080.

43. "Editorial, Internet Censorship," Dawn.com, 25 May 2010, http://www.dawn
.com; "1,200 URLs Remain Blocked Even after YouTube Ban Lifted," *Daily Times*, 28 May
2010, http://www.dailytimes.com.pk.

44. Amber Rahim Shamsi, "Pakistan Unplugged," Dawn blog, 28 May 2010, https://
www.dawn.com/news/813271.

45. Associated Press, "Pakistan Censors Twitter over Muhammad Images," CBC
News, 21 May 2012, http://www.cbc.ca/news/technology/story/2012/05/21/twitter
-pakistan-blocked-facebook-images-muhammad.html; Jon Russell, "Pakistan Turns to
Interpol after Twitter Declines to Help Manage 'Anti-Islamic Material,'" The Next Web, 21
May 2012, http://thenextweb.com/twitter/2012/05/21/pakistan-turns-to
-interpol-after-twitter-declines-to-help-manage-anti-islamic-material/; Doug Bernard,
"Why Did Pakistan Shut Off Twitter?," The Cutting Edge, 24 May 2012, http://www
.thecuttingedgenews.com/index.php?article=73734&pageid=28&pagename=Sci-Tech.

46. Mahesh Sharma, "Pakistani Activists Smell a Mole in Government's Proposed
YouTube Filtering Plan," TechCrunch.com, 16 September 2013, http://techcrunch
.com/2013/09/16/pakistani-activists-smell-a-mole-in-governments-proposed-youtube
-filtering-plan/.

47. "Mufti Aijaz Arshad Qasmi v. Facebook and Ors (Order Dated December 20,
2011)," Centre for Internet and Society, 20 December 2011, https://cis-india.org/
internet-governance/resources/order-2011-12-20-mufti-aijaz-arshad-qasmi-v
-facebook-and-ors.

48. AFP, "Google to Block Jordan Links to Anti-Islam Film," Ahram Online, 23
September 2012, http://english.ahram.org.eg/NewsContent/2/8/53576/World/Region/
Google-to-block-Jordan-links-to-antiIslam-film.aspx.

49. A. N. M. Nurul Haque, "Facebook Furore," *Daily Star* (Bangladesh), 8 June 2010,
http://www.thedailystar.net/newDesign/news-details.php?nid=141804.

50. Victor Ulasi, "Update: Nigerian Religious Court Bans the Use of Facebook and
Twitter," World News Vine, 30 March 2010, http://worldnewsvine.com [link deleted].

51. Yvonne Lim, "Face It, You Can Be Virtually Spooked via Facebook," *Star Online*,
14 November 2011, http://www.thestar.com.my/news/nation/2011/11/14/face-it-you
-can-be-virtually-spooked-via-facebook/.

52. Dubai School of Government, *Arab Social Media Report 2014* (2014), http://
www.arabsocialmediareport.com.

53. Simon Kemp, "Special Reports: Digital in 2016," We Are Social, 27 January 2016,
http://www.wearesocial.com/special-reports/digital-in-2016.

54. "Riyadh the Most Active Twitter City in the Middle East," Al Arabiya News, 2
August 2012, http://english.alarabiya.net/articles/2012/08/02/230037.html; "Twitter
Reaches Half a Billion Accounts, More Than 140 Millions in the U.S," Semiocast, 31 July
2012, http://semiocast.com/en/publications/2012_07_30_Twitter_reaches_half_a
_billion_accounts_140m_in_the_US.

55. Matt Smith, "Young Saudis Getting Creative on YouTube," Reuters, 18 November
2013, http://www.reuters.com/article/2013/11/18/us-saudi-youtube
-idUSBRE9AH0GY20131118.

56. "HRH Prince Alwaleed Bin Talal Bin Abdulaziz Alsaud Reports 4.9 Percent Passive Stake in Twitter," Reuters, 6 February 2017, http://www.reuters.com/article/idUSFWN1FR0U1.

57. Al Jazeera English, "Top Saudi Cleric Says Twitter Is for Clowns," Al Jazeera, 24 March 2013, http://www.aljazeera.com/news/middleeast/2013/03/20133246150585567.html.

58. Barbara Slavin, "Saudi Arabia Faces New Challenge from Its Restive Youth," Al-Monitor, 7 January 2013, http://www.al-monitor.com/pulse/originals/2013/01/saudi-arabia.html.

59. Ben Hubbard, "Young Saudis, Bound by Conservative Strictures, Find Freedom on Their Phones," *New York Times*, 23 May 2015, http://www.nytimes.com/2015/05/23/world/middleeast/saudi-arabia-youths-cellphone-apps-freedom.html.

60. Press Trust of India, "On Facebook, Young Muslims Turn Away from Islam," NDTV, 7 September 2010, http://www.ndtv.com/article/world/on-facebook-young-muslims-turn-away-from-islam-49951

61. Kim-Mai Cutler, "Men Outnumber Women among Facebook Users in Muslim Majority Countries," InsideFacebook.com, 13 October 2010, http://www.insidefacebook.com/2010/10/13/men-outnumber-women-among-facebook-users-in-muslim-majority-countries/.

62. Chuck Holmes, "Change Comes to Saudi Arabia, in Slow Motion," NPR, 21 May 2012, http://www.scpr.org/news/2012/05/21/32507/change-comes-to-saudi-arabia-in-slow-motion/.

63. Rima al-Mukhtar, "Women Bloggers Express Themselves on Web," *Arab News*, 8 June 2010, http://www.arabnews.com/node/347118.

64. Ahmed Al-Omran, "Twitter Is Big in Saudi. The Professor Detention Debate Shows Why," Mideastposts.com, 7 December 2010, http://mideastposts.com/2010/12/07/law-professor-detained-over-saudi-succession-article/.

65. Index on Censorship, "Saudi Arabia: New Regulation Censors Internet Content," Index: The Voice of Free Expression, 12 January 2011, http://www.indexoncensorship.org/2011/01/saudi-arabia-new-regulation-censors-Internet-content/.

66. "Saudi Arabia: Forced into Extinction," *Economist*, 21 January 2013, http://www.economist.com/blogs/pomegranate/2013/01/saudi-arabia.

67. Sarah Elzeini, "Social Media's Fruitful Exchange with Gulf Women," Your Middle East, 9 February 2015, http://www.yourmiddleeast.com/culture/social-medias-fruitful-exchange-with-gulf-women_29777.

68. Sheera Frenkel, "Saudi Women Ready to Take to the Streets," BuzzFeed News, 23 September 2013, http://www.buzzfeed.com/sheerafrenkel/saudi-women-ready-to-take-to-the-streets; Alaa Wardi, "No Woman, No Drive," Facebook, 26 October 2013, https://youtu.be/aZMbTFNp4wI.

69. Rachel Hosie, "Meet the Saudi Arabian Woman Fighting for Women's Right to Drive," *Independent*, 12 June 2017, http://www.independent.co.uk/life-style/saudi-arabia-women-drive-right-fight-manal-al-sharif-a7785326.html.

70. Sarah E. Needleman, "Saudi Girls Finally Get to Drive, but Only in a Videogame," *Wall Street Journal*, 22 May 2015, http://www.wsj.com/articles/saudi-girls-finally-get-to-drive-but-only-in-a-videogame-1432248063.

71. Ahmad Al-Shagra, "Facebook Is Not Where You Want to Hide," The Next Web, 15 November 2010, http://thenextweb.com/me/2010/11/15/facebook-is-not-where-you-want-to-hide/AP/Technet; Abdullah Al-Shihri, "Saudi Arabia Blocks Facebook over Moral Concerns," Technet, 15 November 2010, http://technetyes.blogspot.co.uk/2010/11/saudi-arabia-blocks-facebook-over-moral.html.

72. Abeer Allam, "Online Law Curbs Saudi Freedom of Expression," *Financial Times*, 6 April 2011, http://www.ft.com.

73. "Saudi Arabia: New Terrorism Regulations Assault Rights," Human Rights Watch, 20 March 2014, https://www.hrw.org/news/2014/03/20/saudi-arabia-new-terrorism-regulations-assault-rights.

74. Ahmed Al Omran, "Saudi Gov Releases New Law for Online Media," Saudi Jeans, 12 January 2011, http://saudijeans.org/2011/01/01/saudi-gov-law-online-media/.

75. Ian Black, "Saudi Expectations High before Friday's 'Day of Rage' Protests," *Guardian*, 10 March 2011, http://www.guardian.co.uk/world/2011/mar/10/saudi-expectations-high-day-rage; "We Support Saudi 'Day of Rage,'" Facebook, 10 March 2010, http://www.facebook.com/Saudis.Revolution [link deleted].

76. AFP, "Saudi Hamza Kashgari Faces Death Calls after Prophet Tweets," News.com.au, 10 February 2012, http://www.news.com.au/technology/saudi-faces-death-calls-after-prophet-tweets/news-story/3d15ec11536d5b30587e910a40f21cce; "Malaysia Defends Deporting Saudi Journalist for Tweet," BBC News, 13 February 2012, http://www.bbc.co.uk/news/world-asia-17008738.

77. "Saudi Blogger Faces Lashes for 'Insulting Islam,'" *China Daily*, 1 August 2013, http://usa.chinadaily.com.cn/world/2013-08/01/content_16859810.htm.

78. "Saudi Arabia, Free Raif Badawi," Amnesty International, 16 June 2015, https://www.amnesty.org.uk/actions/saudi-arabia-free-raif-badawi-flogged-blogger.

79. Jamillah Knowles, "58 Percent of Iranians Use Facebook Despite Blocks and Censorship, Study Finds," The Next Web, 8 November 2012, http://thenextweb.com/me/2012/11/08/iranian-online-research-panel-releases-its-latest-study-into-attitudes-and-behaviours-online-inside-iran/.

80. Telegram Messenger, https://telegram.org.

81. MohammadReza Azali, "Infographic: Social Media Demographics in Iran," TechRasa, 26 August 2016, http://techrasa.com/2016/08/26/infographic-social-media-iran/. Based on statistics from Iranian Students Polling Agency, 2016, http://ispa.ir/.

82. *Filterwatch*, Episode 8, "Iran's National Internet," Small Media, 23 September 2016, https://smallmedia.org.uk/news/filterwatch-episode-8-irans-national-internet.

83. Matthew Hughes, "Iran's One Step Closer to Launching Its Own Internal Internet," The Next Web, 29 August 2016, http://tnw.to/2bMa5LG.

84. Emaun Kashfipour, "Religious Cyber Activism: Video Calls Iranian Youth to an Internet Battlefield," *Views from the Occident* (blog), 14 October 2010, http://occident.blogspot.com/2010/04/religious-cyber-activism-video-calls.html [link deleted].

85. "Internet Censors Target Ayatollahs, Feminists and Students," Reporters without Borders, 6 October 2010, https://rsf.org/en/news/internet-censors-target-ayatollahs-feminists-and-students.

86. Thomas Erdbrink, "Iran Cyber Police Cite U.S. Threat," *Washington Post*, 29 October 2011, http://www.washingtonpost.com/world/middle_east/iran-cyber-police -cite-us-threat/2011/10/27/gIQA1yruSM_story.html.

87. Jim Finkle, "Conficker Worm Could Be Key to Stuxnet Attack on Iran," Al Arabiya News, 1 December 2011, http://english.alarabiya.net/articles/2011/12/02/ 180395.html.

88. Brid-Aine Parnell, "US Whacks Sanctions on Iranians for Web, TV Censorship," *Register*, 9 November 2012, https://www.theregister.co.uk/2012/11/09/us_sanctions _iran_for_internet_censorship/.

89. AFP, "Iran to Allow Google to Operate if It Respects 'Cultural' Values," *Guardian*, 1 March 2015, http://gu.com/p/468em/stw.

90. Saeed Kamali Dehghan, "Digital Age Poses a New Challenge to Iran's Relentless Book Censors," *Guardian*, 15 May 2015, http://www.theguardian.com/world/2015 /may/15/digital-age-poses-a-new-challenge-to-irans-relentless-book-censors.

91. Zachary Davies Boren, "Iran's Leaders Fight over 'Immoral' Mobile Internet," *IB Times*, 1 September 2014, http://www.ibtimes.co.uk/irans-leaders-fight-over -immoral-mobile-Internet-1463507.

92. "Iran to Launch Its First Ever National Data Network on Sunday: Minister," Islamic Republic News Agency, 27 August 2016, http://www.irna.ir/en/News/ 82205234/.

93. Hamed Jafari, "86 Percent of Iran's Cybercrime Takes Place on Telegram and Instagram," TechRasa, 11 December 2016, http://techrasa.com/2016/12/11/86-irans -cybercrime-takes-place-telegram-instagram/.

94. Waqar Hussain, "Pakistanis Create Rival Muslim Facebook," AFP/ABS-CBN, 28 May 2010, http://news.abs-cbn.com/lifestyle/gadgets-tech/05/28/10/pakistanis-create -rival-muslim-facebook; AFP, "Businessmen Unveil Plans for 'Muslim Facebook,'" Al Arabiya News, 1 December 2011, http://english.alarabiya.net/articles/2011/12/01/180340.html.

95. "'Muslim Face' to Be Launched in Spring," OnIslam.net, 26 January 2015, http:// www.onislam.net/english/news/global/482345-muslim-face-to-be-launched-in-spring .html [link deleted].

96. Muslim Face, http://www.muslimface.com.

97. Ummaland, http://www.ummaland.com; Salamyou, http://turntoislam.com/; Masjidway, http://en.masjidway.com.

98. A. J. Dellinger, "Islamic State Starts Its Own Social Network after Being Banned on Facebook and Twitter," Digital Trends, 18 March 2015, http://www.digitaltrends.com/ web/islamic-state-starts-social-network-after-ban/.

99. Jon Leyne, "Egypt's Muslim Brotherhood Launches 'Islamic Facebook,'" BBC News, 24 August 2010, http://www.bbc.co.uk/news/world-middle-east-11064326.

100. Nancy Messieh, "Naqeshny: A Debating Platform to Help You Make Informed Decisions," The Next Web, 7 May 2012, http://thenextweb.com/me/2012/05/07/ naqeshny-a-debating-platform-to-help-you-make-informed-decisions/.

101. Golaz Esfandiari, "Iranian Social Networking, Hard-Line Style," RFE/RL, 28 July 2010, http://www.rferl.org/content/RFERL_In_The_News_Golnaz_Esfandiari _In_Council_For_Foreign_Relations_Iran_Cyber_War_Social_Networking_Must _Read/2113559.html.

102. Ary Hermawan, "In Culture War, Web 2.0 Offers New Hope for Indonesia," *Jakarta Post*, 25 February 2011, http://www.thejakartapost.com/news/2011/02/25/in-culture-war-web-20-offers-new-hope-indonesia.html.

103. AFP/Dawn, "Welcome to Indonesia—the 'Fesbuk' Country," Dawn, 2 February 2012, https://www.dawn.com/news/692644.

104. Karishma Vaswani, "Indonesia's Love Affair with Social Media," BBC News, 16 February 2012, http://www.bbc.co.uk/news/world-asia-17054056.

105. Kate Lamb, "Welcome to Twitter City: Is There No Limit to Jakarta's Social Media Obsession?," *Guardian*, 21 November 2016, https://www.theguardian.com/cities/2016/nov/21/twitter-city-facebook-jakarta-live-week-social-media-obsession-. Also see Victor Lipman, "The World's Most Active Twitter City? You Won't Guess It," *Forbes*, 30 December 2012, https://www.forbes.com/sites/victorlipman/2012/12/30/the-worlds-most-active-twitter-city-you-wont-guess-it/; and "Geolocation Analysis of Twitter Accounts and Tweets," Semiocast, 2012, http://semiocast.com.

106. Deloitte, *The Digital Islamic Services Landscape: Uncovering the Digital Islamic Services Opportunity for the Middle East and the World* (2012), http://www2.deloitte.com/content/dam/Deloitte/xe/Documents/financial-services/me_Islamic-Digital-Services.pdf.

107. Thamer Al Subaihi, "Islamic Website Aimed at Young Emiratis Would Provide Relationship Guidance," *National*, 3 May 2015, http://www.thenational.ae/uae/islamic-website-aimed-at-young-emiratis-would-provide-relationship-guidance. Also see Al Subaihi, "'Haqqathon' Builds Apps for Islamic Youth," *National*, 28 April 2015, http://www.thenational.ae/uae/heritage/haqqathon-builds-apps-for-islamic-youth.

108. Gary R. Bunt, "Surfing the App Souq: Islamic Applications for Mobile Devices," *CyberOrient: Online Journal of the Virtual Middle East* 4, no. 1 (2010), http://www.cyberorient.net/article.do?articleId=3817; Ahmad Al-Shagra, "5 Apps You Need to Use This Ramadan," The Next Web, 12 August 2010, http://thenextweb.com/me/2010/08/12/5-apps-you-need-to-use-this-ramadan/; Haroon Siddique, "Ramadan Goes Hi-Tech with Phone Apps to Help Muslims Fast and Pray," *Guardian*, 11 August 2010, http://www.guardian.co.uk/world/2010/aug/11/ramadan-apps-iphone-ipad.

109. Qiblafinder, https://qiblafinder.withgoogle.com.

CHAPTER 3

1. Muhammad Ibn Ishaq and Alfred Guillaume, *The Life of Muhammad: A Translation of Ibn Ishaq's Sirat Rasul Allah* (1955; Oxford: Oxford University Press, 1996), 181–87.

2. Ratri Adityarani, "How Mobile Devices Help Indonesians Return to Hometowns for Eid," Tech in Asia, 23 August 2011, http://www.penn-olson.com/2011/08/23/eid-mobile/.

3. Ramin Mostaghim, "Key Cleric Calls for More Prayer, Less Web Surfing," *Los Angeles Times*, 20 September 2011, http://latimesblogs.latimes.com/babylonbeyond/2011/09/iran-cleric-says-more-prayer-less-web-surfing.html, citing Ayatollah Mesbah-Yazdi, a conservative Islamic cleric and chairman of the Imam Khomeini Research and Education Institute in Qom.

4. Mehrdad Balali, "Time to Embrace the Internet, Iran President Says," Reuters, 20 May 2014, http://reut.rs/1nsSGeU.

5. Tariq Ramadan, "Being Muslim in the Age of Globalisation," *Gulf News*, 6 August 2012, http://gulfnews.com/opinions/columnists/being-muslim-in-the-age-of -globalisation-1.1058633.

6. Jonathan Bloom, *Paper before Print: The History and Impact of Paper in the Islamic World* (New Haven: Yale University Press, 2001). For a discussion on translated versions of the Qur'an online, see Bruce B. Lawrence, *The Koran in English* (Princeton: Princeton University Press, 2017).

7. Quran (@quran), Twitter, http://twitter.com/quran; Daily Qur'an (@dailyquran), Twitter, http://twitter.com/dailyquran; "Tweeting the #Quran-#Ramadan [Updated]," Islamicate, 20 July 2009, http://www.islamicate.com/2009/07/tweeting-the-quran ---ramadan.html.

8. "Qur'an for Deaf American Muslims," OnIslam.net, http://www.onislam.net/ english/news/americas/460286-quran-for-deaf-american-muslims.html [link deleted]; muslimdeaf.org, http://muslimdeaf.org; Global Deaf Muslim, http://globaldeafmuslim .org/

9. "Islamic Manuscripts," Cambridge Digital Library, University of Cambridge, http://cudl.lib.cam.ac.uk/collections/islamic; "Technology Reunites One of World's Largest Korans," University of Manchester, 19 January 2011, http://www.manchester .ac.uk/aboutus/news/display/?id=6586; "Online Gallery, Sacred Texts: Islamic," British Library, 8 October 2015, http://www.bl.uk/onlinegallery/sacredtexts/sacredthemesionly .html; "Virtual Manuscript Room: Mingana Collection," University of Birmingham, 8 October 2015, http://vmr.bham.ac.uk/Collections/Mingana/part/Islamic_Arabic/; "Islamic Manuscript Studies," University of Michigan Library, 15 February 2017, http:// guides.lib.umich.edu/islamicmsstudies/onlinecollections; "Islamic Manuscripts Catalogue Online," Fihrist, 17 February 2017, http://www.fihrist.org.uk; Harvard University Islamic Heritage Project, http://ocp.hul.harvard.edu/ihp/.

10. Rym Ghazal, "Fatwa Allows Quran Reading on Smartphones," *National*, 29 March 2012, http://www.thenational.ae/news/uae-news/fatwa-allows-quran-reading -on-smartphones; Authority of Islamic Affairs and Endowments, http://www.awqaf.ae.

11. Guided Ways, http://www.guidedways.com/.

12. Guided Ways, "iPray," Apple.com, 17 February 2017, https://itunes.apple.com/ us/app/ipray-prayer-times-qibla-compass/id288054534?mt=8.

13. "Search: koran," Google Play, 8 October 2015, https://play.google.com/store/ search?q=koran&c=apps&hl=en.

14. iPhoneIslam, http://www.iphoneislam.com/?p=3511.

15. "The Kindle Qur'an," Amazon, http://www.amazon.co.uk/Al-Quran-Definitive -Unabridged-Reproductions-ebook/dp/B004HFS62I; "Al-Nawawi Forty Hadiths and Commentary," Amazon, http://www.amazon.co.uk/; "Qur'an Translations," Internet Sacred Text Archive, http://www.sacred-texts.com/isl/index.htm.

16. Spotify, "Quran," http://spotify.com.

17. IslamAwakened, http://islamawakened.com.

18. Tanzil.net, http://www.tanzil.net.

19. Assabile.com, http://www.assabile.com.

20. Gary R. Bunt, *Virtually Islamic: Computer-Mediated Communication and Cyber Islamic Environments* (Cardiff: University of Wales Press, 2000), 123–30.

21. "Al-Azhar Message on Satellite, Internet," OnIslam.net, 16 December 2011, http://www.onislam.net/english/news/africa/455023-al-azhar-message-on-satellite-Internet.html [link deleted].

22. Rahila Bano, "Is It Safe for Children to Study the Koran Online?," BBC News, 26 June 2013, http://www.bbc.co.uk/news/uk-23060976. Also see Jon Boone, "Concerns over Online Qur'an Teaching as Ex-Pakistan Militants Instruct Pupils," *Guardian*, 17 June 2013, http://www.guardian.co.uk/world/2013/jun/17/online-quran-teaching-pakistan.

23. Tim Craig, "By Way of Computers and Headsets, Islamic Teaching Flows Out of Pakistan," *Washington Post*, 1 February 2016, http://www.washingtonpost.com.

24. "Qur'an-Pooya/Ali Commentary 2:1," Al-Islam, http://quran.al-islam.org.

25. Online Ahlulbayt Quran Center, http://www.shiatutor.com/.

26. LionOfGod, "Shia Qur'an Recitation, Usama al-Karbalai-LIVE in Karbala," YouTube, 2 February 2012, https://youtu.be/VhvfrS385OQ; mp3knuckle, "Karbala Quran Recitation," 6 June 2015, http://www.mp3knuckle.info/file/music/mp3/karbala-quran-recitation.html; Dashtizay, "Recitation at Imam Ali Shrine at Najaf Iraq," Twitter, 2 February 2012, https://twitter.com/dashtizay/ [link deleted].

27. Madhusree Chatterjee, "Religion Goes Digital: Saudi Arabia Connects with Instant Quran," TwoCircles, 5 February 2013, http://twocircles.net/2013feb05/religion_goes_digital_saudi_arabia_connects_instant_quran.html, citing former Jamia Millia Islamia professor and writer Zubair Ahmad Farooqi.

28. Gary R. Bunt, "Decoding the Hajj in Cyberspace," in *The Hajj: Pilgrimage in Islam*, ed. Eric Tagliacozzo and Shawkat M. Toorawa (Cambridge: Cambridge University Press, 2015), 231–49.

29. Syed Faisal Ali, "Technology Revolutionizes Communication in Haj," *Arab News*, 17 November 2010, http://www.arabnews.com/node/360705.

30. Saudi Gazette, "Free Wi-Fi in Saudi Arabia's Makkah Haram Courtyard," Al Arabiya News, 1 July 2015, http://ara.tv/mvta4.

31. Saudi Gazette, "Saudi Arabia May Soon Issue e-Bracelets for All Hajj Pilgrims," Al Arabiya News, 24 May 2016, http://english.alarabiya.net/en/variety/2015/05/24/E-bracelets-on-the-way-for-hajj-pilgrims-.html; Al Jazeera English, "Hajj 2016: Saudi Arabia Introduces Bracelets for Safety," Al Jazeera, 30 June 2016, http://www.aljazeera.com/news/2016/06/saudi-arabia-introduces-bracelets-hajj-safety-160630131905794.html.

32. "AMIR Personal Hajj Assistant for Men," iTunes, 14 September 2017, http://itunes.apple.com/ph/app/amir-personal-hajj-assistant/id473935680?mt=8.

33. Lisa Siregar and Tasa Nugraza Barley, "Indonesian Muslims Surf Internet for a Sacrifice," *Jakarta Globe*, 25 November 2009, http://thejakartaglobe.com/home/indonesian-muslims-surf-Internet-for-a-sacrifice/343764 [link deleted].

34. "Goat with the Arabic Inscription 'Allah' on His Coat Goes on Sale for N32.4m," Information Nigeria, 27 October 2012, http://www.informationng.com/2012/10/photos-goat-with-the-arabic-inscription-allah-on-his-coat-goes-on-sale-for-n32-4m.html.

35. See the discussion on al-Mawashi's app in Kaveh Waddell, "How New Technology Is Changing Eid Celebrations," *Atlantic*, 31 August 2017, https://www.theatlantic.com/international/archive/2017/08/technology-changing-eid/538491/. Also see Al Mawashi

Meat Processing Plant, "Al Mawashi Kuwait," YouTube, 4 May 2016, https://youtu.be/ZMeSoponHQ8; Al Mawashi, "Al Mawashi App, Google Play," Google Play, 5 September 2017, https://play.google.com/store/apps/details?id=com.almawashi&hl=en_GB; Sajila Saseendran, "Dubai Municipality Introduces App to Preorder Sacrificial Animals," *Gulf News*, 9 September 2016, http://gulfnews.com/news/uae/health/dubai-municipality-introduces-app-to-preorder-sacrificial-animals-1.1893988.

36. Kaaba (@HolyKaaba), Twitter, https://twitter.com/HolyKaaba.

37. Sebastian Usher, "Hajj Disaster Fallout Puts Pressure on Saudis," BBC News, 25 September 2015, http://www.bbc.co.uk/news/world-middle-east-34361757.

38. See the collection of photos of Islamic sacred spaces here: "Sacred Spaces: A Photo Essay on Mosques," Salam Stock, 13 June 2012, http://www.salamstock.com/community/sacred-spaces-the-mosque/.

39. Ahmed Al Majaida, "Friday Sermons in English Soon in Mosques," *Khaleej Times*, 25 October 2010, http://khaleejtimes.com/article/20101025/ARTICLE/310259894/1002.

40. Nidhal Guessoum, "How Will Facebook and Twitter Impact Islam?," *Huffington Post*, 29 November 2011, http://www.huffingtonpost.com/nidhal-guessoum/new-media-and-islam_b_1077496.html.

41. "YouTube Starts Live Streaming Prayers from Mecca," ArabCrunch.com, 1 August 2011, http://arabcrunch.com/2011/08/youtube-starts-live-streaming-prayers-from-mecca.html [link deleted].

42. "App Launched for Holy Month," *National*, 24 June 2014, http://www.thenational.ae/uae/technology/app-launched-for-holy-month.

43. "Ramadan," Google, 1 July 2014, https://www.google.com/landing/ramadan/.

44. "Index," Moonsighting.com, 1 July 2014, http://moonsighting.com.

45. Islamic Crescents' Observation Project, http://www.icoproject.org/.

46. "Ramadan Begins Today," *National*, 11 August 2010, http://www.thenational.ae/apps/pbcs.dll/article?AID=/20100811/NATIONAL/708109830/1001/SPORT [link deleted].

47. Shelina Zahra Janmohamed, "Online Is the Place to Be for Ramadan," *National*, 13 July 2013, http://www.thenational.ae/thenationalconversation/comment/online-is-the-place-to-be-for-ramadan#ixzz36EQcB46i.

48. "Dar Al-Arqam—A New Muslim Safe Haven (Part 2)," OnIslam.net, 12 December 2013, http://www.onislam.net/english/reading-islam/living-islam/first-steps/testimony-of-faith/466771-dar-al-arqam-a-new-muslim-safe-haven-part-2.html [link deleted].

49. "Can I Convert in Secret?," OnIslam.net, 1 May 2013, http://www.onislam.net/english/ask-about-islam/new-to-islam/166135-can-i-convert-in-secret.html [link deleted].

50. Mspiration, "Imam Sulaiman Wang and Islam in Hong Kong," MuslimVillage.com, 7 April 2014, http://muslimvillage.com/2013/04/07/38075/imam-sulaiman-wang-and-islam-in-hong-kong/.

51. Rukmini Callimachi, "ISIS and the Lonely Young American," *New York Times*, 27 June 2015, https://www.nytimes.com/2015/06/28/world/americas/isis-online-recruiting-american.html.

52. Anna Piela, "Piety as a Concept Underpinning Muslim Women's Online Discussions of Marriage and Professional Career," *Contemporary Islam* 5, no. 3 (2011): 249–65.

53. "Piety Tops Marriage Criteria among Muslims," Middle East Online, 24 June 2010 http://archive.fo/ZWOcB.

54. SingleMuslim, http://www.singlemuslim.com.

55. HalfOurDeen.com, http://www.halfourdeen.com.

56. Suhaib Webb, "Online Dating: A Muslim Guide on How to Be Safe," Mideast Posts, 22 March 2011, http://mideastposts.com/2011/03/22/online-dating-a -muslim-guide-on-how-to-be-safe/.

57. Ustaz AbdulJaleel Solaudeen, "Courtship in Islam," *Nigerian Tribune*, 1 July 2012, http://tribune.com.ng/index.php/muslim-sermon/43362-courtship-in-islam [link deleted].

58. Nassim Hatam, "Iran: Internet Dating Website Launched by State," BBC News, 28 March 2015, http://www.bbc.co.uk/news/world-middle-east-32833363.

59. Jasper Hamill, "Tinder for Muslims Dating App Asks Singletons to Find Love without Posting a Pic," *Mirror*, 5 March 2015, http://www.mirror.co.uk/news/technology -science/technology/tinder-muslims-targets-religious-singletons-5277497.

60. Muzmatch, https://muzmatch.com/; Natasha Lomas, "YC-Backed Muzmatch Definitely Doesn't Want to Be Tinder for Muslims," TechCrunch.com, 3 August 2017, https://techcrunch.com/2017/08/03/yc-backed-muzmatch-definitely-doesnt -want-to-be-tinder-for-muslims/.

61. Matchbox, http://www.yoursearchendshere.com; Arti Patel, "Canadian Women Create 'Offline Dating' Service for Muslims Looking for Love," *Global News*, 24 July 2017, http://globalnews.ca/news/3608893/muslim-dating-match-making/.

62. Second Wife, https://www.secondwife.com, discussed in Aisha Gul, "Looking for Halal Love? Here Is a Website for People Who Want Second Wives," *Star*, 2 June 2016, https://www.phoneworld.com.pk/looking-for-halal-love-here-is-a-website-for-people -who-want-second-wives/.

63. All India Muslim Personal Law Board member Maulana Asghar Ali Imam Mahdi Salafi, interviewed in "Cleric Calls for Ban on Net Talaq," *Times of India*, 17 March 2011, http://articles.timesofindia.indiatimes.com/2011-03-17/bhubaneswar/29138161_1 _triple-talaq-word-talaq-muslims. Also see "Divorce by Text Message Sparks Legal Battle," *Arab News Blog*, 12 October 2012, http://www.arabnewsblog.net/2012/12/10/ divorce-by-text-message-sparks-legal-battle/; "Talaq Delivered through Skype, WhatsApp, SMS, Email or Phone Valid," Zee News, 7 February 2016, http://zeenews .india.com/news/india/talaq-delivered-through-skype-whatsapp-sms-email-or-phone -valid_1853221.html.

64. Kathryn Westcott, "Can You Get Married Over the Phone?," BBC News, 8 April 2010, http://news.bbc.co.uk/1/hi/world/south_asia/8608878.stm.

65. "'Talaq' Joke during Internet Chat May Cost Uttar Pradesh Youth His Marriage," DNA India, 27 October 2010, http://www.dnaindia.com/india/report-talaq-joke-during -Internet-chat-may-cost-uttar-pradesh-youth-his-marriage-1458648.

66. "Divorce: Chatting Are among of the Contributors?," AllVoices.com, 15 November 2010, http://www.allvoices.com/contributed-news/7344509-divorce -chatting-are-among-of-the-contributors [link deleted].

67. "Wife Involved in Extra Marital Affairs on Internet," OnIslam.net, 11 March 2011, http://www.onislam.net/english/ask-the-scholar/family/marital-relationships/461723 -accept-wifes-apology-from-Internet-relations.html [link deleted].

68. Ingrid Wassmann, "Cyber Infidelity in Egypt's Virtual World," *Arab Media and Society* 10 (30 March 2010), http://www.arabmediasociety.com/?article=738.

69. Imaan, http://www.imaan.org.uk/.

70. "Gay Marriage: Islamic View," OnIslam.net., 19 April 2015, http://www.onislam .net/english/ask-the-scholar/crimes-and-penalties/sexual-perversity/170236-gay-marriage-islamic-view.html [link deleted].

71. Steve Williams, "Saudi Arabia Is Using Social Media to Entrap LGBTs," Care2 .com, 31 July 2014, http://www.care2.com/causes/saudi-arabia-is-using-social-media-to -entrap-lgbts.html.

72. See Anna Piela, *Muslim Women Online: Faith and Identity in Virtual Space* (New York: Routledge, 2012).

73. "Cleric Says Avoid e-Chat, Women's Groups See Red," *Times of India*, 15 December 2013, http://articles.timesofindia.indiatimes.com/2013–12–15/mumbai/ 45215519_1_beauty-parlours-noorjahan-safia-niaz-haseena-khan.

74. Muzammil Siddiqi, "OnIslam, Internet Chats between Males and Females," OnIslam.net, http://www.onislam.net/english/ask-the-scholar/morals-and-manners/ social-manners/relationship-between-sexes/174343-Internet-chats-between-males -and-females.html.

75. "Saudi Sheikh: Women Can Log In Online without 'Guardian,'" Ahram Online, 16 September 2012, http://english.ahram.org.eg/NewsContent/2/8/53070/World/ Region/Saudi-sheikh-Women-can-log-in-online-without-guard.aspx.

76. Ayesha Shahid, "Another Face of Internet Islam," Dawn, 4 April 2012, http:// www.dawn.com/news/707932/another-face-of-Internet-islam-2.

77. Mohammed Jamjoom and Laura Smith-Spark, "Saudi Arabia Women Defy Authorities over Female Driving Ban," CNN, 26 October 2013, http://edition.cnn .com/2013/10/26/world/meast/saudi-arabia-women-drivers/.

78. "Saudi Woman to Members of the Religious Police Who Harass Her for Wearing Nail Polish: This Is None of Your Business, I Am a Free Woman and Will Expose You on Twitter and Facebook," MEMRI TV, 23 May 2012, https://www.memri.org/tv/saudi-woman-members-religious-police-who-harass-her-wearing-nail-polish-none -your-business-i-am.

79. Opheera McDoom, "Sudan Police Arrest Women Protesting at Flogging Video," Reuters, 14 December 2010, http://af.reuters.com/article/topNews/ idAFJOE6BD07U20101214.

80. Amie Ferris-Rotman, "Afghanistan Opens First Women-Only Internet Cafe," Reuters, 8 March 2012, http://www.reuters.com/article/2012/03/08/us-afghanistan -women-Internet-idUSBRE8270X520120308.

81. Rob L. Wagner, "Saudi-Islamic Feminist Movement: A Struggle for Male Allies and the Right Female Voice," Peace and Conflict Monitor, 29 March 2011, www.monitor .upeace.org/innerpg.cfm?id_article=789.

82. Ted Thornhill, "Muslim Cleric Declares Selfies a Sin under Islamic Law," DailyMail.com, 27 January 2015, http://www.dailymail.co.uk/news/article-2928368/

Muslim-cleric-declares-selfies-sin-Islamic-law-criticises-women-particular-shameless
.html.

83. Alan White, "An Indonesian Cleric Said Muslim Women Shouldn't Take Selfies So They Trolled Him Mercilessly," *BuzzFeed News*, 28 January 2015, http://www.buzzfeed .com/alanwhite/an-indonesian-cleric-said-muslim-women-shouldnt-take-selfies.

84. Madeline Grant, "Dar al-Ifta in Egypt Issues Fatwas against 'Selfies' and Online Mixing," MuslimVillage.com, 6 September 2014, http://muslimvillage.com/2014/ 09/06/57553/dar-al-ifta-in-egypt-issues-fatwas-against-selfies/.

85. Gianluca Mezzofiore, "Aliaa Magda Elmahdy, Egypt's Nude Blogger, Hiding in Fear for Her Life," *International Business Times*, 1 December 2011, http://www.ibtimes .co.uk/aliaa-magda-elmahdy-nude-blogger-hiding-fear-259312.

86. Aliaa Elmahdy (@aliaaelmahdy), Twitter, 13 July 2015, https://twitter.com/ aliaaelmahdy.

87. Mona Haydar, "Hijabi (Wrap My Hijab)," YouTube, 27 March 2017, https:// youtu.be/XOX9O_kVPeo; Mona Haydar (ft. Jackie Cruz), "Dog," YouTube, 17 July 2017, https://youtu.be/idMJIEFH_ns. Lyrics for these tracks were available on http://www .monahaydar.com.

88. Deen Squad, "Cover Girl (Rockin' That Hijab)," YouTube, 7 March 2017, https:// youtu.be/ER-Si3ceQFs.

89. Deen Squad, http://deensquad.com; Karter Zaher, "Hijabi Queen (Official Music Video)," YouTube, 20 November 2013, https://youtu.be/uNerdm9Cwr8.

90. Sam Bradpiece, "Hipsters in Hijabs: Inside the Multibillion-Dollar World of Muslim Fashion," *SEA Globe*, 27 December 2016, http://sea-globe.com/islamic-fashion.

91. Elle, "4 Muslim Beauty Influencers on Breaking Stereotypes," YouTube, 19 April 2017, https://youtu.be/dXNjIMz3GUU

92. Dina Tokio, https://www.instagram.com/dinatokio/.

93. Mariam Moufid (@hijabmuslim), http://www.instagram.com/hijabmuslim; Mariam Moufid, https://www.instagram.com/mariammoufid/; Mariam Moufid, http:// nouw.com/mariammoufid. Also see Harmeet Kaur, "Hijabistas: Young Muslim Women Meld Fashion and Faith," CNN, 16 September 2016, http://edition.cnn.com/style/ article/cnnphotos-hijabistas/index.html.

94. Zukreat, https://www.instagram.com/zukreat/; Chinutay, https://www .instagram.com/chinutay/; Chinutay & Co., https://www.chinutayco.com.

95. Stef Van den Branden and Bert Broeckaert, "Living in the Hands of God: English Sunni e-Fatwas on (Non-)Voluntary Euthanasia and Assisted Suicide," *Medicine, Health Care and Philosophy* 14, no. 1 (1 September 2010): 29–41, http://www.springerlink.com/ content/x863106859270230/.

96. "Cell Phones Fatwa Invites India Uproar," OnIslam.net, 1 January 2013, http:// www.onislam.net/english/news/asia-pacific/460694-cell-phones-ban-sparks-india -debates.html [link deleted].

97. David Jones, "Fatwa Issued against 3G Internet Operator in Iran," Al-Monitor, 19 February 2013, http://www.al-monitor.com/pulse/originals/2013/02/iranian-ayatollahs -issue-fatwa-against-3g-company.html.

98. Chris Anderson, "The Long Tail," *Wired*, October 2004 http://www.wired.com/ wired/archive/12.10/tail.html.

99. "Sira," FaithFreedom.org, http://www.faithfreedom.org/Articles/sira/index.htm.

100. Carl W. Ernst, "Ideological and Technological Transformations of Contemporary Sufism," in *Muslim Networks from Hajj to Hip Hop*, ed. miriam cooke and Bruce B. Lawrence (Chapel Hill: University of North Carolina Press, 2005), 191–207.

101. "African Salawat / Rap / Hadrah," SufiLive, 10 May 2008, http://sufilive.com/African-Salawat-Rap-Hadrah-1104.html; Gary R. Bunt, "#Islam, Social Networking and the Cloud," in *Islam in the Modern World*, ed. Jeffrey T. Kenney and Ebrahim Moosa (New York: Routledge, 2014), 177–208.

102. Qadiri Sufi Order, http://www.qadiriyya.com; Ayhan Karaca, "Kermes Zikir 2 HD," YouTube, 5 October 2010, http://youtu.be/ylicZcB6iQI.

103. "Life Story of Sheikh Ahmed Tijani, May ALLAH Be Pleased with Him," Tidjaniya.com, 5 June 2015, http://www.tidjaniya.com/en/ahmed-tijani.php.

104. "Hadra du Vendredi Sidi Abdelmoutaleb Tidjani—*Zaouia Tijaniya Pekine Sénégal*," *wwwtidjaniyacom YouTube Channel*, 13 June 2011, https://youtu.be/ES3ZDDRQnUE.

105. Zaouiya Tidjaniya, Facebook, 6 June 2015, http://www.facebook.com/pages/Zaouiya-Tidjaniya-de-F%C3%A8s/151971234869880.

106. Tivaoune, Facebook, 4 June 2015, http://www.facebook.com/Tivaoune.

107. "Martyrdom of Ali Akbar A.S[.] in Karbala (Documentary)," YouTube, 13 July 2015, https://youtu.be/NBK2JF6fOS4. Also see Alexander Kolbitsch, "The Reciprocal Relationship between the Ritualistic Ta'zie Role-Play and Twelver Shi'ite Collective Identity in Iranian History" (PhD diss., University of Wales Trinity Saint David, Lampeter, 2016).

108. Maaref Foundation, https://www.hilmi.eu/islam/books/maaref-foundation/www.maaref-foundation.com/english/library/index.htm.

109. Hazrat Ali Ibne Abi Talib (A.S.)—The Commander of Faithful, Facebook, 4 June 2015, http://www.facebook.com/pages/Hazrat-Ali-Ibne-Abi-Talib-AS-The-Commander-Of-Faithful/57826295542.

110. Why I Am Not a Shia, Facebook, http://www.facebook.com/pages/Why-I-Am-Not-A-Shia/202674303139867.

111. Ahlulbayt TV, YouTube channel, 11 March 2017, https://www.youtube.com/user/ahlulbaytTV; Ahlulbayt TV, YouTube channel, 11 February 2017, http://ahlulbayt.tv; Ahlulbayt TV, YouTube channel, "General Q&A," 11 March 2017, https://www.youtube.com/channel/UCvbRhYjhlYl2PW7qChc3a4w.

112. Imam Ali Foundation–London, http://www.najaf.org/english/. Al-Sistani is discussed in chapter 4.

113. Specialist Studies Center of al-Imam al-Mahdi [A.S.], http://www.m-mahdi.com.

114. Bunt, *Virtually Islamic*, 51–52; The Sun's House, http://server32.irna.com/occasion/ertehal/index-e.html.

115. Ayatollah Ruhollah Khomeini, Facebook, 22 February 2017, https://www.facebook.com/Grand-Ayatollah-Ruhollah-Khomeini.

116. AFP, "Instagram Reopens Account of Iran Revolutionary Leader," Al Arabiya News, 1 June 2015, http://english.alarabiya.net/en/media/digital/2015/06/01/Instagram-reopens-account-of-Iran-revolutionary-leader.html.

117. Ayatullah Sayyid Ali Khamenei, "Speeches and Quotes," Facebook, http://www
.facebook.com/pages/Ayatullah-Sayyid-Ali-Khamenei-Speeches-and-Quotes/
339249472755055; "Waiting for the Reappearance of Imam Mehdi," Facebook, 4 June
2015, http://www.facebook.com/pages/Waiting-for-the-Reappearance-of-Imam
-Mehdi-as/207949665903363?sk=info.

118. AFP, "Iran Ex-President Sees Facebook as a 'Blessing,' " *Nation*, 1 June
2012, http://www.nation.com.pk/pakistan-news-newspaper-daily-english-online/
entertainment/01-Jun-2012/iran-ex-president-sees-facebook-as-a-blessing.

119. "Press Freedom Violations Recounted in Real Time (from 1st January 2012),"
Reporters without Borders, 20 January 2012, https://rsf.org/en/news/press-freedom
-violations-recounted-real-time-1st-january-2012.

120. Mir Hossein Mousavi, Facebook, 5 June 2015, http://www.facebook.com/
mousavi.

121. Ali Mamouri, "Facebook Use among the Seminary in Qom," Al-Monitor, 3
January 2014, http://www.al-monitor.com/pulse/en/originals/2014/01/qom-seminary
-facebook.html; Islamic Azad University Qom, Facebook, 7 June 2015, http://www
.facebook.com/qomuni

122. Amir Tataloo, "Energy Hasteei," YouTube, 22 May 2017, https://youtu.be/
koN9ARqkuFU; Pure Stream Media, "Hamed Zamani—The Shield," YouTube, 24
September 2016, https://youtu.be/FebvTi2fzcE. See the article by Thomas Erdbrink, "As
'Death to America' Chants Lose Power, Iran Retools Propaganda with Rap Videos," *New
York Times*, 27 August 2017, https://www.nytimes.com/2017/08/26/world/middleeast/
iran-propaganda-persian-gulf.html.

123. Husayni Center, Facebook, 5 June 2015, http://www.facebook.com/husayni.center.

124. Warriors of Imam Mehdi, Facebook, 4 June 2015, http://www.facebook.com/
warriors.of.imam.mehdi.

125. YaShaheed, "Saf matam Karbala 2011 Arbaeen," YouTube, 22 February
2017, http://www.youtube.com/watch?v=s_d-EowxRww. Also see ali119j, "Shaheed
safe matam AZHAR SIAL and FAHEEM SIAL (matmi dasta mazloom-e-karbala)
D.G.Khan," YouTube, 22 February 2017, https://youtu.be/HLseF5gwbbg.

126. Salmanraja110's channel, "28 safar Babul ilm 2011.mp4," YouTube, https://youtu.be/
W7YZLPtZ6wY.

127. "Sina zani Kabul New 2014 HD (Abdullah Ansari Sayed Azim+2)," wn.com, 1
November 2014, https://wn.com/sina_zani_in_afghanistan.

128. Jonah Blank, *Mullahs on the Mainframe: Islam and Modernity among the Daudi
Bohras* (Chicago: University of Chicago Press, 2001).

129. Malumaat, http://www.malumaat.com.

130. Mumineen, http://www.mumineen.org.

131. This differential is discussed in ShiaChat.com, 9 December 2010–, http://www
.shiachat.com/forum/index.php?/topic/234982506-how-do-the-ismailis-followers-of
-aga-khan/Ismaili.net. Sermons can be found at Ismaili.net, 4 June 2015, http://ismaili
.net/heritage/audio-waez-nodes. Also see Aga Khan University, http://www.aku.edu;
Aga Khan Development Fund, http://www.akdn.org; and Institute of Ismaili Studies,
http://www.iis.ac.uk.

132. Shaadi, https://www.shaadi.com.

133. Ismaili Muslims, Facebook, 6 June 2015, http://www.facebook.com/IsmailiMuslims.

134. FIELD-First Ismaili Electronic Library and Database, 7 June 2015, http://ismaili.net/heritage/audio_nodes_search.

135. The World Federation of Khoja Shia Ithna-Asheri Muslim Communities, http://www.world-federation.org.

136. Zainab Zulfikarali Alimohamed, "A Life Changing Experience: Madinah and Bab 2011," The World Federation of Khoja Shia Ithna-Asheri Muslim Communities, 14 March 2012, http://www2.world-federation.org/IslamicEducation/Articles/life_changing_experience_Madinah_Bab_2011.htm.

137. Babulilm Network, Facebook, http://www.facebook.com/babulilmnetwork; "Quran O Ahlebait Conference in Karachi Report," City21.tv, 26 March 2012, http://www.city21.tv/2012/03/26/quran-o-ahlebait-conference-in-karachi-report/; Babulilm Library, http://babulilmlibrary.com/.

138. Babulilm, http://www.babulilm.org.

139. Bani Hashim, http://www.banihashim.org/locationmaps.aspx.

140. Yohanan Friedmann, "Ahmadiyah," in The Oxford Encyclopedia of Islam and Politics, Oxford Islamic Studies Online, 2009, http://www.oxfordislamicstudies.com/article/opr/t342/e0082.

141. Al Islam: The Official Website of the Ahmadiyya Muslim Community, https://www.alislam.org/.

142. Hazrat Khalifatul Masih V, http://www.khalifaofislam.com; Al Islam, "AlislamKhutbaArchive," YouTube, 11 March 2017, https://www.youtube.com/user/AlislamKhutbaArchive/videos.

143. Michele Langevine Leiby, "Pakistan Official Consider Options for Filtering YouTube Videos," Independent, 10 November 2012, http://www.independent.co.uk/news/world/asia/pakistan-official-consider-options-for-filtering-youtube-videos-8303440.html.

144. Christopher S. Chivvis, Keith Crane, Peter Mandaville, and Jeffrey Martini, Libya's Post-Qaddafi Transition: The Nation-Building Challenge (Santa Monica: Rand Corporation, 2012).

145. Abdelhak Hamiche, "How to Respond to the Offensive Videos about Prophet Muhammad," Gulf Times, 9 October 2012, http://www.gulf-times.com/story/131626/How-to-respond-to-the-offensive-videos-about-Prophet-Muhammad.

146. "Sayyed Nasrallah Urges Muslim Ummah to Protest over Offensive Film," almanar.com.lb, 17 September 2012, http://www.almanar.com.lb/english/adetails.php?eid=68750&frid=23&seccatid=14&cid=23&fromval=1.

147. Bruce B. Lawrence, "YouTube Terrorism," Religion Dispatches, USC Annenberg, 13 September 2012, http://www.religiondispatches.org/archive/culture/6387/youtube_terrorism/.

CHAPTER 4

1. I first looked at these issues in Gary R. Bunt, Islam in the Digital Age: E-jihad, Online Fatwas and Cyber Islamic Environments (London: Pluto Press, 2003), 124–204.

2. Marcia Hermansen, "The Emergence of Media Preachers," in *Islam in the Modern World*, ed. Jeffrey T. Kenney and Ebrahim Moosa (New York: Routledge, 2014), 301–18.

3. *Surah al-Furqan* (Surah 25:33), *The Holy Qur'an: Text, Translation and Commentary*, trans. Abdullah Yusuf Ali (Jeddah: Islamic Education Centre, 1946).

4. *Encyclopaedia of Islam* CD-ROM ed. 1.0., 1999, s.v. "idjtihad" (Leiden: E. J. Brill).

5. Kemal A. Faruki, *Islamic Jurisprudence* (Karachi: Pakistan Publishing House, 1962), 288.

6. Gary R. Bunt, "Decision Making and Idjtihad in Islamic Environments: A Comparative Study of Pakistan, Malaysia, Singapore and the United Kingdom" (PhD diss., University of Wales, Lampeter, 1996).

7. The transliterated plural of fatwa is *fatawa*. Given that the term has been anglicized, "fatwa" will be applied in the remainder of this chapter in the singular and "fatwas" in the plural when appropriate.

8. *Surah Al-Ma'ida* (Surah 5:102-3), *The Qur'an*, trans. Muhammad A. S. Abdel Haleem (Oxford: Oxford University Press, 2004).

9. M. Muhsin Khan, *The Translation of the Meanings of Sahih Al-Bukhar* (New Delhi: Kitab Bhavan, 1984), vol. 9, no. 392, 29.

10. Abdul Hamid Siddiqi, *Sahih Muslim: Being Traditions of the Sayings and Doings of the Prophet Muhammad as Narrated by His Companions and Compiled under the Title Al Jami'-Us-Sahih by Imam Muslim* (Lahore: Sh. Muhammad Ashraf Publishers, 1977; 1986), vol. 4, CMLXXXV, no. 5818, 1257.

11. Siddiqi, *Sahih Muslim*, no. 5822, 1257.

12. Khan, *Translation of the Meanings of Sahih Al-Bukhar*, vol. 9, no. 281, 212.

13. Wael B. Hallaq, *A History of Islamic Legal Theories: An Introduction to Sunni Usul al-Fiqh* (Cambridge: Cambridge University Press, 1997).

14. Stephanie Garlock, "Debating Sharia Law, Digitally," *Harvard Magazine*, May–June 2015, http://harvardmagazine.com/2015/05/debating-sharia-law-digitally.

15. "Thousands Take Part in Muharram Discourses in City," *Times of India*, 1 December 2011, http://timesofindia.indiatimes.com/city/mumbai/Thousands-take-part-in-Muharram-discourses-in-city/articleshow/10937363.cms.

16. Maqpal Mukankyzy and Farangis Najibullah, "Kazakh Mullahs Get Web-Savvy," Radio Free Europe/Radio Liberty, 22 November 2013, http://www.rferl.org/content/kazakhstan-islam-Internet-youth/25176864.html.

17. Today's Zaman, "Greece Muslims," MuslimPopulation.com, 24 October 2010, http://www.muslimpopulation.com/Europe/Greece/Greek Muslims New.php.

18. Zakir Naik, "Is Using Internet Haram or Halal from Islamic Point of View?," Facebook, 22 June 2014, https://www.facebook.com/permalink.php?story_fbid=7159390 98466273&id=715933681800148.

19. Ustadha Zaynab Ansari, "Blurred Lines: Women, 'Celebrity' Shaykhs, and Spiritual Abuse," Muslim Matters, 27 May 2015, http://muslimmatters.org/2015/05/27/blurred-lines-women-celebrity-shaykhs-spiritual-abuse/.

20. "US Imam Sets Muslim Role Model," OnIslam.net, 3 December 2011, http://www.onislam.net/english/news/3338/454886.html [link deleted].

21. Gulandam Zaripova, "iMulla: Tatarstan Citizens Were Offered to Invite Imam by One Click," Realnoe Vremya, 29 June 2016, https://realnoevremya.com/articles/524.

22. Amr Khaled, "From Podcasts and Friday Sermons, a New Start for Yemen," *National*, 28 November 2010, http://www.thenational.ae/the-national-conversation/news/comment/from-podcasts-and-friday-sermons-a-new-start-for-yemen; "A Call for Muslims in the West to Serve Their Societies," interview with Amr Khaled, Qantara.de, 11 November 2010, https://en.qantara.de/content/interview-with-amr-khaled-a-call-for-muslims-in-the-west-to-serve-their-societies. Khaled is profiled in Aaron Rock, "Amr Khaled: From Da'wa to Political and Religious Leadership," *British Journal of Middle Eastern Studies* 37, no. 1 (2010): 15–37.

23. Sarah A. Topol, "Cairo's Revered Al Azhar University Now Overshadowed by TV Imams," *Christian Science Monitor*, 9 April 2010, http://www.csmonitor.com/World/Middle-East/2010/0409/Cairo-s-revered-Al-Azhar-University-now-overshadowed-by-TV-imams.

24. "Qaradawi: Marriage after Meeting over Net Permissible," Peninsula Qatar, 10 April 2011, http://www.thepeninsulaqatar.com/qatar/148429-qaradawi-marriage-after-meeting-over-net-permissible.html [link deleted].

25. "Al-Qaradawi: Freedom Takes Priority over Islamic Law," *Egypt Independent*, 12 February 2011, http://www.egyptindependent.com/al-qaradawi-freedom-takes-priority-over-islamic-law/.

26. Yahya Michot, "Qaradawi's Anti-Gaddafi Fatwa: Scholarly Analysis," OnIslam.net, 29 March 2011, http://www.onislam.net/english/shariah/shariah-and-humanity/miscellaneous/451624-the-fatwa-of-sheikh-al-qaradawi-against-gaddafi.html.

27. Alexander Smoltczyk, "Islam's Spiritual 'Dear Abby': The Voice of Egypt's Muslim Brotherhood," Spiegel Online, 15 February 2011, http://www.spiegel.de/international/world/islam-s-spiritual-dear-abby-the-voice-of-egypt-s-muslim-brotherhood-a-745526.html. See the profile in Ian Johnson, "Our Secret Connections with the Muslim Brotherhood," *New York Review of Books*, 11 March 2011, http://www.nybooks.com/articles/archives/2011/mar/10/our-secret-connections-muslim-brotherhood/.

28. "Who Are the Most Prominent Qatar-Linked Figures in New Terror Designated List?," Al Arabiya News, 9 June 2017, http://english.alarabiya.net/en/features/2017/06/09/Who-are-the-most-prominent-Qatar-linked-figures-in-new-terror-designated-list-.html.

29. Andrea Elliott, "Why Yasir Qadhi Wants to Talk about Jihad," *New York Times*, 17 March 2011, http://www.nytimes.com/2011/03/20/magazine/mag-20Salafis-t.html?_r=2&hp=&pagewanted=all.

30. Dale F. Eickelman and James Piscatori, *Muslim Politics* (Princeton: Princeton University Press, 1996); Jakob Skovgaard-Petersen and Bettina Gräf, eds., *The Global Mufti: The Phenomenon of Yusuf Al-Qaradawi* (London: C. Hurst, 2008); Dale F. Eickelman and Jon W. Anderson, eds., *New Media in the Muslim World* (Bloomington: Indiana University Press, 2003); Peter Mandaville, *Global Political Islam* (New York: Routledge, 2007); Charles Hirschkind, *The Ethical Soundscape: Cassette Sermons and Islamic Counterpublics* (New York: Columbia University Press, 2006).

31. Deborah L. Wheeler, *Digital Resistance in the Middle East: New Media Activism in Everyday Life* (Edinburgh: Edinburgh University Press, 2017); Gary R. Bunt, "Mediterranean Islamic Expression and Web 2.0," in *Arab Society in Revolt: The West's*

Mediterranean Challenge, ed. Olivier Roy and Cesare Melini (New York: Brookings Institution Press, 2012), 76–95; Philip N. Howard, *The Digital Origins of Dictatorship and Democracy: Information Technology and Political Islam* (Oxford: Oxford University Press, 2010).

32. Charles Allers, *Anwar Ibrahim: Evolution of a Muslim Democrat* (New York: Peter Lang, 2013).

33. Anwar Ibrahim (@anwaribrahim), Twitter, https://twitter.com/anwaribrahim; BebasAnwar (@bebasanwar), Twitter, https://twitter.com/BebasAnwar.

34. Wan Azizah Wan Ismail (@drwanazizah), Twitter, https://twitter.com/drwanazizah; Wan Azizah Wan Ismail (@drwawi), Facebook, https://www.facebook.com/drwawi.

35. Anthony R. Byrd and Richard C. Martin, "From Isfahan to the Internet: Islamic Theology in the Global Village," in *Islam in the Modern World,* ed. Jeffrey T. Kenney and Ebrahim Moosa (New York: Routledge, 2014), 91; Abdol Karim Soroush, http://drsoroush.com.

36. Ahmad Sadri and Mahmoud Sadri, "Soroush, Abdolkarim," in *Oxford Encyclopedia of Islam and Politics,* Oxford Islamic Studies Online, http://www.oxfordislamicstudies.com/article/opr/t342/e0432; Valla Vakili, "Abdolkarim Soroush and Critical Discourse in Iran," in *Makers of Contemporary Islam,* ed. John L. Esposito and John O. Voll, 2001, Oxford Islamic Studies Online, http://www.oxfordislamicstudies.com.

37. Annabelle Sreberny and Gholam Khiabany, *Blogistan* (London: I. B. Tauris, 2010); Gholam Khiabany, *Iranian Media: The Paradox of Modernity* (London: Routledge, 2010).

38. Yasuyuki Matsunaga, "Human Rights and New Jurisprudence in Mohsen Kadivar's Advocacy of 'New-Thinker' Islam," *Die Welt des Islams* 51, nos. 3–4 (2011): 358–81; Mohsen Kadivar, http://kadivar.com.

39. Yousefi Eshkevari, http://yousefieshkevari.com.

40. Tariq Ramadan (@TariqRamadan), Twitter, https://twitter.com/tariqramadan; Tariq Ramadan (@official.tariqramadan), Facebook, https://www.facebook.com/official.tariqramadan; Tariq Ramadan, YouTube channel, https://www.youtube.com/user/tariqramadanvideo; Tariq Ramadan, "Tariq Ramadan," https://tariqramadan.com.

41. Tariq Ramadan (@TariqRamadan), " 'Comprendre la Voie: équilibre entre la règle, l'éthique et les objectifs' en direct depuis Bassam, Côte d'Ivoire," Twitter, 13 August 2017, https://twitter.com/TariqRamadan/status/896703524989538304.

42. Margot Badran, "Political Islam and Gender," in *Oxford Handbook of Islam and Politics,* ed John L. Esposito and Emad El-Din Shahin, 2013, Oxford Islamic Studies Online, http://www.oxfordislamicstudies.com; Valentine M. Moghadam and Namrata Mitra, "Women and Gender in the Muslim World," in *Islam in the Modern World,* ed. Jeffrey T. Kenney and Ebrahim Moosa (New York: Routledge, 2014), 151–76; Anne-Sofie Roald, *Women in Islam: The Western Experience* (London: Routledge, 2001); Leila Ahmed, *Women and Gender in Islam: Historical Roots of a Modern Debate* (New Haven: Yale University Press, 1992); Shadaab Rahemtulla, *Qur'an of the Oppressed: Liberation Theology and Gender Justice in Islam* (Oxford: Oxford University Press, 2017).

43. miriam cooke and Bruce B. Lawrence, "Introduction," in *Muslim Networks from Hajj to Hip Hop,* ed. miriam cooke and Bruce B. Lawrence (Chapel Hill: University of North Carolina Press, 2005), 10–13.

44. Amina Wadud (@dr.aminawadud2), Facebook, https://www.facebook.com/dr.aminawadud2/; Amina Wadud (@aminawadud), Twitter, https://twitter.com/aminawadud.

45. Hermansen, "Emergence of Media Preachers," 313–14.

46. Farhat Hashmi, "Quran in Hand," al-Huda, http://www.farhathashmi.com/alhuda-apps/.

47. Faiza Mushtaq, "A Controversial Role Model for Pakistani Women," *South Asia Multidisciplinary Academic Journal Online* 4 (2010), https://samaj.revues.org/3030.

48. Women Living under Muslim Laws Solidarity Network (@WLUML), Facebook, https://www.facebook.com/WLUML/.

49. Muslim Women's Council (@MWC_Bradford), Twitter, https://twitter.com/MWC_Bradford.

50. Lallab (@AssoLallab), Facebook, 24 August 2017, https://www.facebook.com/AssoLallab.

51. James M. Dorsey, "A Battle of the Fatwas," Qantara.de, 8 December 2010, http://www.qantara.de/webcom/show_article.php/_c-478/_nr-1137/i.html.

52. Saudi Gazette, "Wrong Interpretations of Dreams Cause Family Chaos: Grand Mufti," Sauress, 7 October 2011, http://www.sauress.com/en/saudigazette/110111.

53. "Seminar on Dawa Sites on the Internet," *Arab News*, 7 September 2011, arabnews.com; "Kingdom Is Safeguarding Children from Internet Abuse," *Saudi Gazette*, 14 April 2011, http://64.65.60.109/index.cfm?method=home.regcon&contentid=2011041498266.

54. Express News Service, "Use Technology to Spread Message of Religion: Imam of Grand Mosque in Mecca," *Indian Express*, 27 March 2011, http://indianexpress.com/article/cities/delhi/use-technology-to-spread-message-of-religion-imam-of-grand-mosque-in-mecca/.

55. "Religious Leaders Outshine Lady Gaga in Twitter Popularity," Al Arabiya News, 5 June 2012, http://english.alarabiya.net/articles/2012/06/05/218752.html.

56. "Mujtahidd: A Tweeting Thorn in the Side of Al Saud," Al-Akhbar English, 20 February 2012, http://english.al-akhbar.com/content/mujtahid-tweeting-thorn-side-al-saud. Also see "Twitter Is a Platform for Promoting Lies: Saudi Mufti," Emirates 24/7, 29 January 2012, http://www.emirates247.com/news/region/twitter-is-a-platform-for-lies-saudi-grand-mufti-2012–01–29–1.439921.

57. Jonathan Schanzer and Steven Miller, "Facebook Fatwa: Saudi Clerics, Wahhabi Islam, and Social Media," The Foundation for Defense of Democracies, 2012, http://www.defenddemocracy.org/stuff/uploads/documents/facebook_fatwa_low_res_2.pdf.

58. Mohamad al-Arefe (@MohamadAlarefe), Twitter, 4 September 2017, https://twitter.com/mohamadalarefe.

59. Hassan Hassan, "New Saudi Policy Will Ensure Clerics Fall in Line," *National*, 13 September 2017, https://www.thenational.ae/opinion/new-saudi-policy-will-ensure-clerics-fall-in-line-1.628123; Margherita Stancati, "Saudi Arabia Detains Two Prominent Clerics," *Wall Street Journal*, 12 September 2017, https://www.wsj.com/articles/saudi-arabia-detains-two-prominent-clerics-1505159358; "Saudi Arabia 'Arrests Clerics in Crackdown on Dissent,'" BBC News, 13 September 2017, http://www.bbc.co.uk/news/world-middle-east-41260543.

60. Muhammad As'ad, "'Kyai' Twitter: When Clerics Go Online," *Jakarta Post*, 3 February 2012 http://www.thejakartapost.com/news/2012/02/03/kyai-twitter-when-clerics-go-online.html.

61. Asharq Alawsat, "Saudi Telecom Shuts Websites Violating Fatwa Edict," Asharq Al-Awsat, 5 September 2010, https://english.aawsat.com/theaawsat/news-middle-east/saudi-telecom-shuts-websites-violating-fatwa-edict.

62. "Egypt: Fatwa Forbids Muslims from Facebook," ADN Kronos International, 5 February 2010, http://www.adnkronos.com/AKI/English/Religion/?id=3.0.4274275243.

63. Amro Hassan, "Al Azhar Denies Facebook Fatwa," *Babylon & Beyond* (blog), *Los Angeles Times*, 7 February 2010, http://latimesblogs.latimes.com/babylonbeyond/2010/02/egypt-azhar-denies-facebook-ban.html.

64. "Index," El-Hatef El-Islami, 2009, http://www.elhatef.com [link deleted].

65. Katerina Nikolas, "Egyptian Islamist denounces Internet as Major Sin," *Digital Journal*, 11 November 2012, http://www.digitaljournal.com/article/336902.

66. Sheikh Muhammad Hussein Yaqob, 5 January 2018, Yaqob.com, http://www.yaqob.com.

67. D. Danish Raza, "Can't a Muslim Who Hasn't Attended a Madrasa Speak for the Community?," First Post, 21 June 2012, http://www.firstpost.com/india/cant-a-muslim-who-hasnt-attended-a-madrasa-speak-for-the-community-351816.html.

68. Statistic Brain Research Institute, "Attention Span Statistics," Statistic Brain, 14 July 2015, http://www.statisticbrain.com/attention-span-statistics/.

69. StreetDawa.com, http://www.streetdawa.com.

70. Radical Middle Way, "iKhutbah," YouTube channel, https://www.youtube.com/user/radicalmiddleway.

71. Negar Azimi, "Islam's Answer to MTV," *New York Times*, 13 August 2010, http://www.nytimes.com/2010/08/15/magazine/15Pop-t.html.

72. "In Islamic Iran Prayer Sellers' Trade Is Booming," Reuters, 28 January 2010, http://in.reuters.com/article/idINTRE65R1UO20100628.

73. Varjavand [pseud.], "'Quran Misconstrued': The Quran Should Be Interpreted by Unbiased Experts in a Positive, Constructive Way," *Iranian*, 5 February 2010, https://iranian.com/main/2010/feb/quran-misconstrued.html.

74. Zakaria Lyousoufi, cited in Martijn van Tol, "'Sheikh Google' Confuses Young Muslims," Radio Netherlands Worldwide, 11 August 2010, http://www.rnw.nl/english/article/sheikh-google-confuses-young-muslims. A similar point is made by Sheikh Ali Gomaa, Grand Mufti of Egypt. Rym Ghazal, "Grand Mufti Calls for Dialogue about the Internet," *National*, 20 February 2012, http://www.thenational.ae/news/uae-news/grand-mufti-calls-for-dialogue-about-the-Internet.

75. John Thorne, "'The Fatwa Show': Moroccan Journalist Tells Clerics to Just Have Some Fun," *Christian Science Monitor*, 10 April 2013, http://www.csmonitor.com/World/Middle-East/2013/0410/The-Fatwa-Show-Moroccan-journalist-tells-clerics-to-just-have-some-fun.

76. "The Fatwa Show," FreeArabs.com, 1 March 2014, http://www.freearabs.com/index.php/fun-stuff/fatwa-show. Also see "Islamic Cleric Bans Women from Touching Bananas," *Times of India*, 7 December 2011, http://timesofindia.indiatimes

.com/world/mad-mad-world/Islamic-cleric-bans-women-from-touching-bananas/
articleshow/11020659.cms. Widely cited in varied online media, this topic was also
utilized by sites with anti-Islam agendas as a means of ridiculing Islam and Muslims as a
whole.

77. "A Muslim's Guide to Facebook Arguments (and Online Ridiculousness in
General)," Muslim Matters, 19 March 2012, http://muslimmatters.org/2012/03/
19/a-muslims-guide-to-facebook-arguments-and-online-ridiculousness-in-general/.

78. "When Madrassa Pedagogy Meets Technology," Muslimology, 14 April 2010
http://muslimology.wordpress.com/2010/04/13/when-madrassa-pedagogy-meets
-technology/.

79. Fatima Sidaya, "Opinion Divided on TV, Online Fatwa Services," Arab News, 1
September 2009, http://www.arabnews.com/node/327599.

80. Brian Whitaker, "Conflicting Fatwas Are Good for Muslims," Guardian, 16
August 2010, http://www.guardian.co.uk/commentisfree/2010/aug/16/fatwas
-saudi-king-islam.

81. Greta Riemersma and Martijn van Tol, "It's Raining Fatwas in Morocco This
Summer," Radio Netherlands Worldwide, 7 August 2010, http://www.rnw.nl/english/
article/it%E2%80%99s-raining-fatwas-morocco-summer.

82. "Divorcing via E-mail or SMS Message: Valid?," OnIslam.net, 21 February 2014,
http://www.onislam.net/english/ask-the-scholar/family/divorce/175379-divorcing
-ones-wife-via-e-mail-or-cell-phone-text-message.html [link deleted].

83. "What Is It Like to Be in a Polygamous Marriage?," OnIslam.net, 21 February
2014, http://www.onislam.net/english/family/special-coverage/491235-what-is-it-like
-to-be-in-a-polygamous-marriage-f.html [link deleted].

84. "I Hate the Look of My Fat Husband," OnIslam.net, 12 August 2015, http://www
.onislam.net/english/family/husbands-and-wives/491301-i-hate-the-look-of-my-fat
-husband-advice-.html [link deleted].

85. Yasir Qadhi, "Coffee Is Haram? How to Deal with Strange Fatwas," OnIslam
.net, 9 August 2015, http://www.onislam.net/english/shariah/shariah-and-humanity/
shariah-and-life/469967-fatwa-haram-fiqh-islam-sheikh-scholar-imam-west.html [link
deleted].

86. For example, see "Online Relationship: Does It Have a Future?," OnIslam
.net, 11 August 2015, http://www.onislam.net/english/ask-the-counselor/virtual
-relations/491221-online-relationship-does-it-have-a-future.html [link deleted].

87. "The Top 500 Sites on the Web—Religion and Spirituality/Islam," Alexa
.com, 9 September 2016, http://www.alexa.com/topsites/category/Top/Society/
Religion_and_Spirituality/Islam.

88. AlMunajjidWhats, "WhatsApp, Sheikh al-Munajjid," http://www
.almunajjidwhats.com [link deleted].

89. "Saudi Arabia: Sheikh [Imam] Al-Munajjid Forgives His Son's Killer," Discover
the Truth, 20 April 2014, http://discover-the-truth.com/2014/04/20/saudi-arabia
-sheikh-imam-al-munajjid-forgives-his-sons-killer/; "Killing Mickey Mouse: Sheikh
Al-Munajid Responds," YouTube, 12 October 2008, https://www.youtube.com/
watch?v=yjD6rUyESuk.

90. Muhammad al-Munajjid (@almonajjid), Twitter, https://twitter.com/almonajjid; Muhammad al-Munajjid (@IslamQA), Twitter, http://twitter.com/islamqa_en.

91. Muhammad Saalih al-Munajjid, YouTube channel, https://www.youtube.com/channel/UCEtzpou7x4iq1r8PxSAcZxQ.

92. Ibid., "Values," 5 August 2015, https://youtu.be/iHmW6exTjtI?t=3m52s.

93. "Saudi Blocks Scholar Website after Fatwa Control Decree: Report," Xinhuanet .com, 3 September 2010, http://news.xinhuanet.com/english2010/world/2010–09/03/c_13477495.htm. Also see Abdullah Al Ayed, "Saudi Arabia Blocks Islam Q&A of Sheikh Munajid," Al Arabiya News, 17 October 2010, http://www.alarabiya.net/articles/2010/09/03/118350.html. Also see Christopher Boucek, "Saudi Fatwa Restrictions and the State-Clerical Relationship," Carnegie Endowment for International Peace, 27 October 2010, http://carnegieendowment.org/2010/10/27/saudi-fatwa-restrictions-and-state-clerical-relationship/6b81.

94. Reuters, "Saudi Cleric Issues Fatwa on Snowmen," *Guardian*, 12 January 2015, http://www.theguardian.com/world/2015/jan/12/saudi-arabia-snowmen-winter-fatwa; Martin Beckford, "Mickey Mouse Must Die, Says Saudi Arabian Cleric," *Telegraph*, 15 September 2008, http://www.telegraph.co.uk/news/worldnews/middleeast/saudiarabia/2963744/Mickey-Mouse-must-die-says-Saudi-Arabian-cleric.html.

95. Thembisa Fakude, "Al Jazeera Studies, Arab World Journalist in a Post-Beheading Era," Al Jazeera Centre for Studies, 10 December 2014, http://studies.aljazeera.net/en/reports/2014/12/2014121095622836950.html.

96. Al-Manhaj, 10 December 2014, http://www.manhaj.com/manhaj.

97. "Our Attitude towards Rumours and News on the Internet," Islam Question and Answer, 29 January 2002, https://islamqa.info/en/22878.

98. "He Makes Some Useful Contributions on the Internet and Sometimes He Checks Out Haraam Things, Should He Stay There or Leave?," Islam Question and Answer, 6 September 2009, https://islamqa.info/en/130645.

99. Ebrahim Moosa, *What Is a Madrasa?* (Chapel Hill: University of North Carolina Press, 2015).

100. Irena Akbar, "Inside the Fatwa Lab," *Indian Express*, 23 May 2010, http://www.indianexpress.com/news/inside-the-fatwa-lab/621879/0. For examples of these opinions, see "Fatwa Factory: Black Hair Dye, Women Receptionists, 'un-Islamic'!," *Rediff News*, 12 December 2012, http://www.rediff.com/news/slide-show/slide-show-1-fatwa-factory-no-yoga-insurance-veena-malik-tv/20121212.htm.

101. "Index," Deoband, 9 August 2015, http://www.deoband.org.

102. "Fatwas Are Not Necessarily Binding on Muslims: Islamic Scholars," *Indian Express*, 9 December 2012, http://www.indianexpress.com/news/fatwas-are-not-necessarily-binding-on-muslims-islamic-scholars/1042692.

103. For a discussion on the conflict between Deobandi and Barewli followers and its origins, see Moosa, *What Is a Madrasa?*

104. Darul Uloom Deoband India, http://darululoom-deoband.com.

105. Innes Bowen, *Medina in Birmingham, Najaf in Brent: Inside British Islam* (Oxford: Oxford University Press, 2014), 11.

106. Haq Islam, http://haqislam.org.

107. Al Kawthar Academy, http://www.akacademy.eu.

108. Darul Ifta, http://www.daruliftaa.com.

109. "Grand Ayatollah Sistani," Sistani.org, 4 June 2015, http://www.sistani.org. See my early discussion on Sistani.org in Bunt, *Islam in the Digital Age*, 190–92.

110. "Following a Mujtahid (Taqlid)," Sistani.org, 10 August 2015, http://www .sistani.org/english/book/48/2116/.

111. "Taharat & Najasat: Ritual Purity & Impurity » General Rules," Sistani.org, http://www.sistani.org/english/book/46/2029/.

112. "Index," Imam Ali Foundation–London, 9 August 2015, http://www.najaf.org/ english/.

113. "Index," Aalulbayt Information Centre, 2 March 2017, http://www.al-shia.org

114. AlSistani Office (@AlSistaniOffice), Twitter, 2 March 2017, http://twitter.com/ alsistanioffice?lang=en.

115. Sistani.org (@sayyedsistani), Facebook, 2 March 2017, http://facebook.com/ sayyedsistani/.

116. Astan Quds Razavi, "Virtual Pilgrimage of the Holy Shrine of Imam Reza (A. S.)," http://photo.aqr.ir/UserFiles/File/Multi%20Media/dtree/index-en.htm; Astan Quds Razavi, "Android and iOS App," http://razavitv.aqr.ir/en/page/36/Download -Android-and-iOS-app-of-www.razavi.tv; Astan Quds Razavi, http://aqr.ir.

117. Golnar Motevalli, "The World Needs to Watch Iran's Election," *Bloomberg*, 12 May 2017, https://www.bloomberg.com/news/features/2017–05–12/iran-s -election-is-a-chance-for-angry-hardliners-to-win-back-power.

118. Stefano Allievi and Jorgen S. Nielsen, *Muslim Networks and Transnational Communities in and across Europe* (Boston: Brill, 2003); Mustafa Draper, Jorgen S. Nielsen, and Galina Yemelianova, "Transnational Sufism: The Haqqaniyya," in *Sufism in the West*, ed. Jamal Malik and John Hinnells (London: Routledge, 2006), 103–14; Gary R. Bunt, "#Islam, Social Networking and the Cloud," in *Islam in the Modern World*, ed. Jeffrey T. Kenney and Ebrahim Moosa (New York: Routledge, 2014), 187–91.

119. Taher Siddiqui, "Dream: regarding Grand Shaykh Dagestani R. A [*sic*]," eShaykh.com, May 12, 2011, http://eshaykh.com/dreams/regarding-grand-shaykh -dagestani-r-a/.

120. eShaykh.com, http://eshaykh.com.

121. "Marriage Partner," eShaykh.com, 9 August 2015, http://eshaykh .com/?s=marriage+partner.

122. "Lost Love," eShaykh.com, 9 August 2015, http://eshaykh.com/tag/lost-love/.

123. SufiLive, http://sufilive.com.

CHAPTER 5

1. An earlier version of aspects of this opening discussion can be found in Gary R. Bunt, *Islam in the Digital Age: E-jihad, Online Fatwas and Cyber Islamic Environments* (London: Pluto Press, 2003), 25–36.

2. See Martin Lings, *Muhammad: His Life Based on the Earliest Sources* (London: George Allen and Unwin, 1983); F. E. Peters, *A Reader on Classical Islam* (Princeton: Princeton University Press, 1994), 154–65; Rudolph Peters, "Jihād," in *The Oxford*

Encyclopedia of the Islamic World, ed. John L. Esposito, Oxford Islamic Studies Online, 2009, http://www.oxfordislamicstudies.com; Sohail H. Hashmi, "jihad," in *Encyclopedia of Islam and the Muslim World*, ed. Richard C. Martin (New York: Macmillan Reference USA, 2004).

3. Thomas Hegghammer, "Jihadi-Salafis or Revolutionaries: On Religion and Politics in the Study of Militant Islamism," in *Global Salafism: Islam's New Religious Movement*, ed. Roel Meijer (London: C. Hurst, 2009), 244–66; Rüdiger Lohlker, "The Forgotten Swamp Revisited," in *New Approaches to the Analysis of Jihadism: Online and Offline*, ed. Rüdiger Lohlker (Vienna: Vienna University Press, 2012), 124–39; Henri Lauzière, *The Making of Salafism: Islamic Reform in the Twentieth Century* (New York: Columbia University Press, 2015).

4. Ömer Taspınar, "Fighting Radicalism, not 'Terrorism': Root Causes of an International Actor Redefined," *SAIS Review* 29, no. 2 (2009): 75–86, 75.

5. Khouwaga Yusoufzai and Franziska Emmerling, "Explaining Violent Radicalization in Western Muslims: A Four Factor Model," *Journal of Terrorism Research* 8, no. 1 (2017): 68–80, http://doi.org/10.15664/jtr.1292.

6. Peter Neumann, "The Trouble with Radicalization," *International Affairs* 89, no. 4 (2013): 873–93.

7. Marc Sageman, *Understanding Terror Networks* (Philadelphia: University of Pennsylvania Press, 2004). Also see Scott Atran, "A Failure of Imagination (Intelligence, WMDs, and 'Virtual Jihad')," *Studies in Conflict and Terrorism* 29 (2006): 263–78; and Gabriel Weimann, "Social Media's Appeal to Terrorists," Insite Blog on Terrorism and Extremism, 3 October 2014, http://news.siteintelgroup.com/blog/index.php/entry/295-social-media%E2%80%99s-appeal-to-terrorists.

8. Kamaldeep Bhui, Maria Joao Silva, Raluca A. Topciu, and Edgar Jones, "Pathways to Sympathies for Violent Protest and Terrorism," *British Journal of Psychiatry* 209, no. 6 (2016): 483–90. On the possible stigmatization on people with mental health issues, also see Kamaldeep Bhui, Adrian James, and Simon Wessely, "Mental Illness and Terrorism," *British Medical Journal* 354 (2016): i4869.

9. Emily Dugan, "Radicalised Muslims in UK More Likely to Be Born in Britain, Rich and Depressed," *Independent*, 24 September 2014, http://www.independent.co.uk/news/uk/politics/radicalised-muslims-in-uk-more-likely-to-be-well-heeled-9754062.html. Also see Frank Cilluffo, Gregory Saathoff, Jan Lane, Sharon Cardash, and Andrew Whitehead, *NETworked Radicalization: A Counter-Strategy*, special report by the George Washington University Homeland Security Policy Institute and the University of Virginia Critical Incident Analysis Group, 2007, https://cchs.gwu.edu/sites/cchs.gwu.edu/files/downloads/HSPI_Report_11.pdf, 9.

10. See the case of Rasheed Benyahia, discussed in Dominic Casciani, "An Extremist in the Family," BBC News, 21 November 2016, http://www.bbc.co.uk/news/magazine-37973246.

11. Olivier Roy, "Jihad and Death (le djihad et la mort), book introduction," MEDirections EUI, YouTube, 12 December 2016, https://youtu.be/hv3KMUVrhyM. This is discussed in detail in Olivier Roy, *Jihad and Death: The Global Appeal of Islamic State*, trans. Cynthia Schoch (London: C. Hurst, 2017).

12. Nico Prucha, "The 'Who's Who' of the Most Important Jihadi Accounts on Twitter," Jihadica, 20 August 2013, http://www.jihadica.com. Also see Abdelasiem El

Difraoui, *Al-Qaida par l'image. La prophétie du martyre* (Paris: Presses Universitaires de France, 2013).

13. Japheth Omojuwa, "How Boko Haram May Benefit from Using Social Media," Naij.com, 2015, http://www.naij.com/394084-how-boko-haram-may-benefit-from-using -social-media.html; BBC Monitoring, "Is Islamic State Shaping Boko Haram Media?," BBC News, 4 March 2015, http://www.bbc.co.uk/news/world-africa-31522469.

14. "Jihad Advocates Focus on Young Muslims in West-Czech BIS," ČeskéNoviny.cz, 28 August 2012, http://www.ceskenoviny.cz/news/zpravy/jihad-advocates -focus-on-young-muslims-in-west-czech-bis/831245 [link deleted]; Samuel Jaberg, "Growing Threat: Tracking Jihadists in Switzerland," SwissInfo.ch, 4 July 2012, http:// www.swissinfo.ch/eng/politics/foreign_affairs/Tracking_jihadists_in_Switzerland .html?cid=33034934; Dutch General Intelligence and Security Service (AIVD), "Online Jihadism Important Driving Force behind Global Jihad Movement," 14 February 2012, https://english.aivd.nl/latest/news/2012/02/14/online-jihadism-important-driving -force-behind-global-jihad-movement; "Dutch Secret Service Ran Islam Website," Netherlands Information Service News, 10 August 2010, http://www.nisnews.nl/ public/100810_2.htm [link deleted].

15. Home Affairs Committee, "Nineteenth Report. Roots of Violent Radicalisation," www.parliament.uk, 31 January 2012, http://www.publications.parliament.uk/pa/ cm201012/cmselect/cmhaff/1446/144602.htm; Lorenzo Vidino, "The Evolution of Jihadism in Italy: Rise in Homegrown Radicals," CSS, 12 December 2013, http://isnblog .ethz.ch/international-relations/the-evolution-of-jihadism-in-italy-rise-in -homegrown-radicals.

16. Özlem Gezer, "How German Islamists Recruit Young Men for Jihad," Spiegel Online, 23 August 2012, http://www.spiegel.de/international/germany/how-german -islamists-recruit-young-men-for-jihad-a-851393.html; Christoph Sydow, "German Jihadists Target Youth on the Internet, Study Finds," Spiegel Online, 1 November 2012, http://www.spiegel.de/international/germany/german-jihadists-target-youth-on -the-internet-study-finds-a-864797.html; "German Jihadists Targeting NATO Troops," Deutsche Welle, 21 April 2010, http://www.dw-world.de/dw/article/0,,5487772,00.html.

17. See an earlier discussion in Gary R. Bunt, *Virtually Islamic: Computer-Mediated Communication and Cyber Islamic Environments* (Cardiff: University of Wales Press, 2000), 67–73; and Tufail Ahmad, "The Afghan Taliban's Internet Media Empire—Hosted in Malaysia, Singapore, America," MEMRI, 25 March 2013, http://www.memri.org/ report/en/0/0/0/0/0/0/7102.htm.

18. Danny Schechter, "Opinion: When the Taliban Calls, Pick Up," Al Jazeera, 3 October 2010, http://english.aljazeera.net/indepth/opinion/2010/10/ 20101011228373058z.html.

19. Abdulhadi Hairan, "A Profile of the Taliban's Propaganda Tactics," *Huffington Post*, 1 February 2010, http://www.huffingtonpost.com/abdulhadi-hairan/a-profile-of -the-talibans_b_442857.html.

20. Akhtar Jamal, "Afghan Taliban Rejects Peace Talks," *Pakistan Observer*, 25 October 2010, http://pakobserver.net [link deleted].

21. Usman Sharifi, "Taliban Offer Question-and-Answer Service Online," *AFP/ Express Tribune*, 27 March 2012, https://tribune.com.pk/story/356353/taliban -offer-online-questions-and-answers/.

22. Bashir Ahmad Gwakh, "The Taliban's Internet Strategy," Radio Free Europe/ Radio Liberty, 10 September 2011, http://www.rferl.org/content/the_talibans _internet_strategy/24323901.html.

23. Austin Bodetti, "From WhatsApp to Hawala, How the Taliban Moves Money Around," Motherboard, 15 November 2016, https://motherboard.vice.com/ en_us/article/from-whatsapp-to-hawala-how-the-taliban-moves-money-around; Sune Engel Rasmussen, "Afghan Taliban Create Smartphone App to Spread Their Message," *Guardian*, 3 April 2016, https://www.theguardian.com/world/2016/apr/03/ afghan-taliban-create-smartphone-app-spread-message.

24. Ibn Siqilli [pseud.], "Afghan Taliban Photography Magazine, *In Fight* No. 12, December 2009 Issue," *Views from the Occident* (blog), http://occident2.blogspot .com/2010/01/afghan-taliban-photography-magazine-in.html.

25. "Taliban Magazine 'Azan' Calls for Jihad to Retake Andalus," MEMRI, 24 August 2013, http://www.memri.org/report/en/0/0/0/0/0/0/7195.htm.

26. Robert Fisk, "Glossy New Front in Battle for Hearts and Minds," *Independent*, 2 April 2010, http://www.independent.co.uk/opinion/commentators/fisk/robert-fisk -glossy-new-front-in-battle-for-hearts-and-minds-1934020.html.

27. Susan Sachs, "Taliban Embrace Information Age with Twitter, English Websites," *Globe and Mail*, 8 May 2011, http://www.theglobeandmail.com/news/world/asia-pacific/ taliban-embrace-information-age-with-twitter-english-websites/article2014590/.

28. Bashir Ahmad Gwakh, "Taliban Employs Modern Weapons in 'War of Words,'" Radio Free Europe/Radio Liberty, 16 March 2011, http://www.rferl.org/content/ taliban_employs_modern_weapons_in_war_of_words/2340644.html.

29. Austin Wright, "U.S. Twitter War vs. Taliban Flares," Politico, 18 June 2012, http://www.politico.com/news/stories/0612/77524.html.

30. Bodetti, "From WhatsApp to Hawala, How the Taliban Moves Money Around."

31. Jon Swaine, "Al-Shabaab's American Recruitment Drive: 'Betray the US and Join "the real Disneyland" of African jihad,'" *Telegraph*, 25 September 2013, http://www .telegraph.co.uk/news/worldnews/africaandindianocean/kenya/10335139/Al-Shabaabs -American-recruitment-drive-Betray-the-US-and-join-the-real-Disneyland-of-African -jihad.html.

32. Jenny Cuffe, "My Brother and the Deadly Lure of al-Shabab Jihad," BBC News, 2 November 2010, http://www.bbc.co.uk/news/uk-11667690.

33. "Somalia's Militants Group al-Shabab Joins al-Qaida, Qaida Leader Says in Video," *Australian*, 9 February 2012, http://www.theaustralian.com.au; "8 Reasons Why al-Shabaab Killed al-Amriki," *Sahan Journal*, 28 September 2013, http://sahanjournal .com/al-shabaab-killed-al-amriki-omar-hammami/#.Vh4YqqId75w.

34. Christopher Anzalone, "The Rapid Evolution of Al-Shabab's Media and Insurgent 'Journalism,'" OpenDemocracy.net, 16 November 2011, http://www .opendemocracy.net.

35. Jason Burke, "Al-Shabab's Tweets Won't Boost Its Cause," *Guardian*, 16 December 2011, http://www.guardian.co.uk/commentisfree/2011/dec/16/al-shabab-tweets-terrorism-twitter?newsfeed=true.

36. "Al-Shabaab Says Smartphones Used 'to Spy on Muslim People,'" SaahiOnline.com, 14 November 2013, http://sabahionline.com [link deleted].

37. Ghaith Abdul-Ahad, "How Somalia's Civil War Became New Front in Battle against al-Qaida," *Guardian*, 7 June 2010, http://www.theguardian.com/world/2010/jun/07/somalia-civil-war-al-qaida.

38. Rebecca Chao, "The Western Voices of al-Shabaab's Twitter Account," TechPresident.com, 24 September 2013, http://techpresident.com/news/wegov/24366/western-voices-al-shabaab-twitter. Also see "Tweets Stream in over Kenya's Westgate Mall Shooting," *Mail and Guardian*, 23 September 2013, http://mg.co.za/article/2013-09-23-social-media-hope-for-kenya.

39. Cited in Henry Austin, "Interpol Issues 'Red Notice' for Britain's Terror Widow on Behalf of Kenyan Authorities," NBC News, 26 September 2013, http://www.nbcnews.com/news/other/interpol-issues-red-notice-britains-terror-widow-behalf-kenyan-authorities-f8C11263385.

40. AFP, "Twitter Pulls Shebab Accounts as Group Boasts of Kenya Attack," Raw Story, 19 November 2013, http://www.rawstory.com/rs/2013/11/19/twitter-pulls-shebab-accounts-as-group-boasts-of-kenya-attack/.

41. Daveed Gartenstein-Ross, "Critical Questions Regarding the Role of Foreign Fighters in Shabaab," Threat Matrix, 27 September 2010, http://www.longwarjournal.org/threat-matrix/archives/2010/09/critical_questions_regarding_t.php.

42. "Somalia: Al-Amriki and Foreign Fighters in Showdown with Al-Shabaab Leader," AllAfrica.com, 30 April 2013, http://allafrica.com/stories/201305010475.html.

43. "Al-Amriki Pleads for Intervention to Resolve 'Friction' within al-Shabaab," SabahiOnline.com, 30 October 2012, http://sabahionline.com [link deleted].

44. "US-Born 'Jihadist Rapper' Omar Hammami Reportedly Killed in Somalia," *Guardian*, 12 September 2013, http://www.theguardian.com/world/2013/sep/12/jihadist-rapper-omar-hammami-killed.

45. Prucha, "'Who's Who' of the Most Important Jihadi Accounts on Twitter."

46. Lara Setrakian, "'Osama Bin Laden' Facebook Page Shut Down," ABC News, 17 April 2010, http://abcnews.go.com/International/Blotter/osama-bin-laden-facebook-page-shut/story?id=10402921.

47. Department of Homeland Security, "Terrorist Use of Social Networking Sites: Facebook Case Study," Public Intelligence, 2010, https://publicintelligence.net/ufouoles-dhs-terrorist-use-of-social-networking-facebook-case-study/.

48. AHN, "Congress Tries to Counter Terrorist Social Media Propaganda," GantDaily.com, 5 December 2011, http://gantdaily.com/2011/12/05/congress-tries-to-counter-terrorist-social-media-propaganda/ [link deleted].

49. Damien McElroy, "Al-Qaeda Plans Cartoon to Fight the West," *Telegraph*, 20 July 2011, http://www.telegraph.co.uk/news/worldnews/al-qaeda/8649907/Al-Qaeda-plans-cartoon-to-fight-the-West.html.

50. "A New Role for Jihadi Media," Investigative Project on Terrorism, 11 January 2011, http://www.investigativeproject.org/2487/a-new-role-for-jihadi-media.

51. Yassin Musharbash, Marcel Rosenbach, and Holger Stark, "Al-Qaida Threatens Terror Attacks in Germany after Election," Spiegel Online, 18 September 2009, http://www.spiegel.de/international/germany/0,1518,649987,00.html.

52. "Al-Qaeda Fighter Bekkay Harrach 'Killed in Afghanistan,'" BBC News, 20 January 2011, http://www.bbc.co.uk/news/world-europe-12241462.

53. Jarret Brachman, "Bekkay Harrach: Al-Qaida's Epistemological Ambassador," JarretBrachman.net,19 September 2009, http://jarretbrachman.net/?p=1041 [link deleted].

54. Abdulsattar Hatitah, "Is Al Qaeda's 'internet generation' their most dangerous?," Asharq Alawsat, 15 January 2011, http://aawsat.com/english/news.asp?section =3&id=23774 [link deleted].

55. Thomas Hegghammer, "Stockholm," Jihadica, 12 December 2010, http://www .jihadica.com/stockholm/.

56. Ibn Siqilli [pseud.],"Tribute Facebook Page Dedicated to Stockholm, Sweden Kamikaze, Bomber Taymour Abdel Wahhab al-Abdaly," Views from the Occident (blog), 13 December 2010, http://occident.blogspot.com/2010/12/in-pictures-tribute-facebook -page.html [link deleted].

57. Andrew Brown, "Sweden's Problem Isn't Immigrants, It's the Internet," Foreign Policy, 22 December 2010, http://www.foreignpolicy.com/articles/2010/12/22/ sweden_s_problem_isn_t_immigrants_it_s_the_internet.

58. "Cops Fear Footage of Terror in Toulouse Will Surface," Australian, 23 March 2012, http://www.theaustralian.com.au/news/world/cops-fear-footage-of-terror-in -toulouse-will-surface/story-e6frg6so-1226308576975.

59. Ibn Siqilli [pseud.], "Cyber Jihadi-Takfiri Video Dedicated to Muhammad Merah," Views from the Occident (blog), 25 March 2012, http://occident.blogspot .co.uk/2012/03/cyber-jihadi-takfiri-video-dedicated-to.html [link deleted].

60. Bunt, Virtually Islamic, 96–98.

61. "RFE, Militant Website Confirms Buryatsky's Death," Radio Free Europe/Radio Liberty, 7 March 2010, http://www.rferl.org/content/Militant_Website_Confirms _Buryatskys_Death/1976923.html; Murad Batal al-Shishani, "The New Ideologues of the North Caucasus Jihadists," Terrorism Monitor 8, no. 38 (2010), http://www .jamestown.org/programs/gta/single/?tx_ttnews%5Btt_news%5D=37057&tx_ ttnews%5BbackPid%5D=26&cHash=745d832dad.

62. "Online Jihadis Tweet Footage of U.S. Marines Arriving in Yemen, along with a Call to Target Them: 'An Opportunity for the Mujahideen to Taste . . . White Meat,'" MEMRI, 9 July 2012, http://www.memri.org/report/en/0/0/0/0/0/0/6503.htm.

63. Nelly Lahoud, "Beware of Imitators: Al-Qa'ida through the Lens of Its Confidential Secretary," Combatting Terrorism Center, 4 June 2012, https://www.ctc .usma.edu/posts/beware-of-imitators-al-qaida-through-the-lens-of-its -confidential-secretary.

64. Ibn Siqilli [pseud.], "Abu Yahya al-Libi's New Book: Jihad & the Battle of Uncertainty/Vagueness/Doubt," Views from the Occident (blog), 25 June 2010, http:// occident2.blogspot.com/2010/06/abu-yahya-al-libis-new-book-jihad.html.

65. Kim Pilling, "Jihadi Terror Obsession Led to Pair's Conviction," Independent, 23 June 2010, http://www.independent.co.uk/news/uk/crime/jihadi-terror-obsession-led -to-pairs-conviction-2008115.html.

66. Yaakov Lappin, "Al-Qaida Affiliated Gaza Group Issues Hebrew Revenge Threat," *Jerusalem Post*, 18 November 2010, http://www.jpost.com/MiddleEast/Article.aspx?id=195878.

67. For example, see "Two More German GIMF Online Jihadis Arrested," Jawa Report, 25 November 2008, http://mypetjawa.mu.nu/archives/195137.php.

68. Ibn Siqilli [pseud.], "Al-Qa'ida in the Arabian Peninsula: 'Toward a Dignified Life,'" *Views from the Occident* (blog), 24 February 2010, http://occident.blogspot.com/2010/02/al-qaida-in-arabian-peninsula-toward.html.

69. Reuters, "Brazen Islamic Militants Showed Strength before Benghazi Attack," Defence Web, 17 October 2012, http://www.defenceweb.co.za/index.php?option=com_content&view=article&id=28112:insight-brazen-islamic-militants-showed-strength-before-benghazi-attack&catid=54:Governance&Itemid=118.

70. AFP, "Al Qaeda Advertises for Suicide Bombers on the Web," NDTV, 7 June 2012 http://www.ndtv.com/article/world/al-qaeda-advertises-for-suicide-bombers-on-the-web-228301.

71. "North Africa: AQIM Creates Twitter Account," AllAfrica.com, 4 April 2013, http://allafrica.com/stories/201304050023.html.

72. "Lashkar-e-Taiba Resumes Online Jihad," *Hindu*, 14 June 2012 http://www.thehindu.com/news/national/article3529067.ece.

73. "Lashkar's Own Skype Frazzles Indian Intelligence," *Times of India*, 30 April 2012, http://articles.timesofindia.indiatimes.com/2012–04–30/india/31506381_1_lashkar-men-voip-muridke.

74. Steven Stalinsky, "Al-Qaeda's Embrace of Encryption Technology: 2007–2011," MEMRI, http://www.memri.org/report/en/0/0/0/0/0/0/5457.htm.

75. Hunter Walker, "Can the Jihadi Geek Squad Secure the Web for Al Qaeda?," TPM, 20 May 2013, http://tpmdc.talkingpointsmemo.com/2013/05/the-jihadi-geek-squad.php.

76. Aaron Y. Zelin, "New magazine Released: 'Magazine of Supporters of the Technical Base for Information Security and Hacking #1,'" Jihadology, 29 May 2011, http://jihadology.net/2011/05/29/new-magazine-released-magazine-of-supporters-of-the-technical-base-for-information-security-and-hacking-1/.

77. "How Islamist Extremists Quote the Qur'an," ASU Center for Strategic Communication, 9 July 2012, http://csc.asu.edu/2012/07/09/how-islamist-extremists-quote-the-quran/.

78. John Hudson, "Jihadis Create Retro 2-D Shooter Video Game," Foreign Policy, 12 March 2013, http://www.foreignpolicy.com/posts/2013/03/12/jihadis_create_retro_2_d_shooter_video_game.

79. Danny Sullivan, "The Death of Osama Bin Laden, Live Tweeted," Storify.com, http://storify.com/dannysullivan/the-death-of-osama-bin-laden-live-tweeted; AFP, "Blogger 'Tweets' Attack on Osama bin Laden," Dawn, 2 May 2011, https://www.dawn.com/news/625472.

80. "Bin Laden Praised Arab Uprising," *New York Times/Sydney Morning Herald*, 10 May 2011, http://www.smh.com.au/world/bin-laden-praised-arab-uprising-20110519-1euuu.html [link deleted].

81. Aaron Y. Zelin, "The bin Laden Aftermath: The Internet Jihadis React," *Foreign Policy*, 2 May 2011, http://afpak.foreignpolicy.com/posts/2011/05/02/the_bin_laden_aftermath_the_internet_jihadis_react.

82. "Osama bin Laden Was Blind in One Eye, Says al-Qaida Leader," *Guardian*, 27 September 2012, http://www.guardian.co.uk/world/2012/sep/27/osama-bin-laden-blind-eye?newsfeed=true.

83. Spencer Ackerman, "Watch: Osama's Blooper Reel, Courtesy of the Navy SEALs," *Wired*, 7 May 2011, http://www.wired.com/dangerroom/2011/05/watch-osamas-blooper-reel-courtesy-of-the-navy-seals/?pid=425; J. M. Berger, "New Osama bin Laden Videos: More Questions Than Answers," IntelWire.com, 7 May 2011, http://news.intelwire.com/2011/05/new-osama-bin-laden-videos-more.html.

84. Frank Gardner, "Tracking Key Terror Suspects," BBC News, 13 May 2011, http://www.bbc.co.uk/news/uk-13366706.

85. Mathew J. Schwartz, "Cracking Bin Laden's Hard Drives," InformationWeek.com, 5 May 2011, http://www.informationweek.com/news/security/encryption/229402923.

86. "Bin Laden's Letters Reveal a Terrorist Losing Control," CNN, 4 May 2012, http://edition.cnn.com/2012/05/03/us/bin-laden-documents/.

87. "Bin Laden's Porn Has Been Found," Foreign Policy, http://blog.foreignpolicy.com/node/799941 [link deleted].

88. "Bin Laden's Bookshelf," Office of the Director of National Intelligence, 2017, https://www.dni.gov/index.php/resources/bin-laden-bookshelf?start=11.

89. 9/11 Commission, *The 9/11 Commission Report: Final Report of the National Commission on Terrorist Attacks upon the United States, Official Government Edition* (Washington: National Commission on Terrorist Attacks upon the United States, 2004). Also see U.S. Senate Committee on Homeland Security and Governmental Affairs, "Violent Islamist Extremism, the Internet, and the Homegrown Terrorist Threat," 2008, www.hsgac.senate.gov/public/_files/IslamistReport.pdf.

90. "Facebook Bows to 'Israel' Deletes 'Third Palestinian Intifada' Page Unjustly," ArabCrunch.com, 30 March 2011 http://arabcrunch.com/2011/03/while-obama-is-calling-for-violence-facebook-bowes-to-israel-deletes-third-palestinian-intifada-page.html [link deleted].

91. Ask Hamas (@HamasInfoEn), Twitter, 4 August 2014, http://twitter.com; Gilad Lotan, "Israel, Gaza, War and Data—The Art of Personalizing Propaganda," Global Voices, 4 August 2014, http://globalvoicesonline.org/2014/08/04/israel-gaza-war-data-the-art-of-personalizing-propaganda/.

92. Al-Fateh, http://www.al-fateh.net; Yohanan Manor and Ido Mizrahi, "Hamas's Web School for Suicide Bombers," *Middle East Quarterly*, Spring 2010, 31–40, http://www.meforum.org/2675/hamas-web-school-suicide-bombers.

93. Ben Hubbard, "Hamas Releases Cartoon about Captured Israeli," *San Diego Union-Tribune*, 25 April 2010, http://www.sandiegouniontribune.com/sdut-hamas-releases-cartoon-about-captured-israeli-2010apr25-story.html.

94. Will Ward, "Social Media and the Gaza Conflict," *Arab Media and Society*, 21 January 2009, http://www.arabmediasociety.com/?article=701.

95. "Pro-Palestinian Hackers Apologise for Cyber Attack on Haaretz Newspaper Website," *National*, 27 January 2012, http://www.thenational.ae/news/world/middle -east/pro-palestinian-hackers-apologise-for-cyber-attack-on-haaretz-newspaper-website.

96. "Group Anonymous Attacks Israeli Websites to Retaliate against Bombing of Gaza," Al Arabiya News, 16 November 2012, http://english.alarabiya.net/articles/ 2012/11/16/250005.html

97. Adnan Abu Amer, "Hamas Vows Crackdown on Collaborators with Israel," Al-Monitor, 29 January 2013, http://www.al-monitor.com/pulse/originals/2013/01/ palestinian-israeli-intelligen-1.html.

98. "Israeli and Palestinian Officials Exchange War of Words via Social Media," Global News, 15 November 2012, http://www.globaltvedmonton.com/israeli+and +palestinian+officials+exchange+war+of+words+via+social+media/6442754590/ story.html [link deleted]; Miriyam Aouragh, *Palestine Online: Transnationalism, the Internet and the Construction of Identity* (London: I. B. Tauris, 2011).

99. Al Jazeera English, "Gaza under Attack—The Stream," Al Jazeera, 14 November 2012, http://login.stream.aljazeera.com/story/gaza-under-attack-0022404.

100. Free Aafia, http://freeaafia.org/.

101. Ibn Siqilli [pseud.], "Battle of 'Aafia Siddiqui': Al-Qa'ida Central Releases Video of Attack on Pakistani Military Post in Landi Kotel," *Views from the Occident* (blog), 24 September 2010, http://occident.blogspot.org. [link deleted].

102. Mohammed Hanif, "How Pakistan Responded to Salmaan Taseer's Assassination," *Guardian*, 6 January 2011, http://www.guardian.co.uk/world/2011/jan/06/ pakistan-salman-taseer-assassination?INTCMP=SRCH; Kala Kawa, 6 January 2011, http://kalakawa.wordpress.com/2011/01/06/ghuttan/.

103. Carla Power, "Can a Fatwa against Terrorism Stop Extremists?," *Time*, 12 March 2010, http://www.time.com/time/world/article/0,8599,1969662,00.html.

104. Alex Rodriguez, "Taliban Flogging Video May Show Different Girl, but Message Is the Same," *Los Angeles Times*, 29 April 2010, http://articles.latimes.com/2010/ apr/29/world/la-fg-pakistan-flogging-20100429.

105. Riaz Ahmad, "Bannu Attack: Taliban Release Video of Brazen Jailbreak," *Express Tribune*, 16 May 2012, http://tribune.com.pk/story/379408/bannu-attack-taliban -release-video-of-brazen-jailbreak/.

106. Bill Roggio, "Taliban, IMU Form Ansar al Aseer to Free Jihadist Prisoners," *FDD's Long War Journal*, 5 February 2013, http://www.longwarjournal.org/archives/ 2013/02/taliban_imu_form_ans.php.

107. Jon Boone and Jason Burke, "Pakistan Attacks: At Least 30 Dead in Terror Raid at Bacha Khan University," *Guardian*, 20 January 2016, https://www.theguardian.com/ world/2016/jan/20/bacha-khan-university-explosions-heard-as-gunmen-attack-pakistan.

108. "2012: A Year of Revolt and Social Change in Francophone Countries: Part 1 of 2," Global Voices, 11 January 2013, http://globalvoicesonline.org/2013/01/11/2012-a-year -of-revolt-and-social-change-in-francophone-countries-part-1-of-2/.

109. John Thorne, "In Timbuktu, a Giant Task of Reconnecting a Remote City to the World," *MinnPost*, 30 January 2013, http://www.minnpost.com/ christian-science-monitor/2013/01/timbuktu-giant-task-reconnecting-remote -city-world.

110. "Timbuktu Destruction: Internet Buzzes with Debate," Radio Netherlands Worldwide, 13 July 2012, http://www.rnw.nl/africa/article/timbuktu-destruction-internet-buzzes-debate.

111. "Exclusive Video: Man with Bloodied Hands Speaks at Woolwich Scene," ITV News, 22 May 2013, http://www.itv.com/news/update/2013-05-22/exclusive-video-man-with-bloodied-hands-speaks-at-woolwich-scene/.

112. "Bungling Plotters 'Were the Real Deal,' " *Standard*, 21 February 2013, http://www.standard.co.uk/news/crime/bungling-plotters-were-the-real-deal-8505242.html.

113. "Birmingham Terror Cell: A Forlorn Fight against Extremism in the Balti Triangle," *Independent*, 21 February 2013, http://www.independent.co.uk/news/uk/crime/birmingham-terror-cell-a-forlorn-fight-against-extremism-in-the-balti-triangle-8505045.html.

114. "Extradited Briton Babar Ahmad Admits Terrorism Offences," BBC News, 10 December 2013, http://www.bbc.co.uk/news/uk-25322782; "UK Terror Suspect Babar Ahmad Returns Home from US," Al Jazeera, 19 July 2015, http://www.aljazeera.com/news/2015/07/uk-terror-suspect-babar-ahmad-150719042048971.html.

115. Her Majesty's Government, "Terrorism Act 2000," http://www.legislation.gov.uk/ukpga/2000/11/section/58.

116. "Student in al-Qaida Raid Paid £20,000 by Police," *Guardian*, 14 September 2011, http://www.guardian.co.uk/uk/2011/sep/14/police-pay-student-damages-al-qaida.

117. "Law Student Convicted over Terror Videos," *Independent*, 24 February 2011, http://www.independent.co.uk/news/uk/crime/law-student-convicted-over-terror-videos-2224708.html.

118. Raffaello Pantucci, "Bringing London's 'Christmas Bombers' to Trial," Jamestown Foundation, 16 December 2011, https://jamestown.org/program/bringing-londons-christmas-bombers-to-trial/.

119. Brendan Hughes, "Court Hears of Cardiff Family's Extensive Links with Terrorism," Wales Online, 15 March 2013, http://www.walesonline.co.uk/news/wales-news/court-hears-cardiff-familys-extensive-2494380.

120. "Muslim Couple Guilty of Anti-Jewish Bomb Plot," *Yorkshire Post*, 19 July 2012, http://www.yorkshirepost.co.uk/news/at-a-glance/main-section/muslim-couple-guilty-of-anti-jewish-bomb-plot-1-4756169.

121. "Sarkozy Vows Crackdown on Islamic Indoctrination," *The World Today*, ABC, 23 March 2012, http://www.abc.net.au/worldtoday/content/2012/s3461911.htm.

122. "Eight Convicted in Belgium for Recruiting Terrorists for al-Qaeda," *Earth Times*, 10 May 2010, http://www.earthtimes.org/articles/show/322974,eight-convicted-in-belgium-for-recruiting-terrorists-for-al-qaeda.html. Also see AFP, "Three Leaders of Al Qaeda Cell Jailed in Belgium," Dawn, 11 May 2010, http://www.dawn.com/wps/wcm/connect/dawn-content-library/dawn/the-newspaper/front-page/three-leaders-of-al-qaeda-cell-jailed-in-belgium-150.

123. "Shooting Suspect Admits Killing US Airmen," Yahoo! News, 31 August 2011, https://www.yahoo.com/news/frankfurt-shooting-suspect-admits-killing-us-airmen-watching-094233186.html.

124. "16-Months Prison Term for German Who Posted Islamic Terror Videos on the Internet," Associated Press, 4 March 2011, http://www.google.com/hostednews

/ [link deleted]; "Five Years Jail for Qaeda Internet Recruiter: German Court," Expatica, 22 March 2012, http://www.expatica.com/news/local_news/five-years-jail-for-qaeda -Internet-recruiter-german-court_216736.html.

125. "Quebecker Gets Life Sentence in Internet Bomb Plot," *Globe and Mail*, 18 March 2010, http://www.theglobeandmail.com/news/national/quebecker-gets -life-sentence-in-internet-bomb-plot/article1366210/.

126. Michael May, "Keyboard Jihadist," Prospect, 14 May 2012, http://prospect. org/article/keyboard-jihadist. Also see Andy Worthington, "Tarek Mehanna's Powerful Statement as He Received 17-Year Sentence Despite Having Harmed No One—OpEd," EurasiaReview.com, 14 April 2012, http://www.eurasiareview.com/14042012-tarek -mehannas-powerful-statement-as-he-received-17-year-sentence-despite-having-harmed -no-one-oped/.

127. "Mehanna Friend Said to Seek Camps for Training," *Boston Globe*, 16 November 2011, http://bostonglobe.com/metro/2011/11/16/mehanna-friend-said-seek-camps -for-training/Xtg5EQTfJNj8RqUHConrRL/story.html; AP, "US Man Convicted on Terrorism Charges for Conspiring to Aid al-Qaida," *Guardian*, 20 December 2011, https://www.theguardian.com/world/2011/dec/20/tarek-mehanna-terrorism-charges -al-qaida; "Mehanna Defense Focuses on Language in Terror Case," *Boston Globe*, 14 December 2011, http://www.bostonglobe.com/metro/2011/12/14/mehanna-defense -focuses-language-terror-case/A8TyqH7Ts2hfnnwiMiWJZO/story.html. Also see Adam Serwer, "Does Posting Jihadist Material Make Tarek Mehanna a Terrorist?," *Mother Jones*, 16 December 2011, http://motherjones.com/politics/2011/12/tarek-mehanna-terrorist; and Mark Joseph Stern, "Translating Terrorism: Is Publishing Radical Islamic Texts on the Internet a Crime?," *Slate*, 3 September 2014, http://www.slate.com/articles/ technology/future_tense/2014/09/mehanna_at_the_supreme_court_is_translating _jihad_texts_a_crime.html.

128. Dan Goodin, "Suburban Woman Accused of Using Net to Recruit Terrorists," *Register*, 10 March 2010, http://www.theregister.co.uk/2010/03/10/jihadjane _indictment/. Also see Reuters Investigates, "Jihad Jane: From Abused Child to American Jihadist," Reuters, 9 December 2012, http://uk.reuters.com/article/video/ idUKBRE8B804620121209?videoId=239757442.

129. For example, see Jarret Brachman, "2 More Web Jihadists Announced Dead," 1 February 2010, http://jarretbrachman.net/?p=458 [link deleted].

130. Joby Warrick, "The 'App of Choice' for Jihadists: ISIS Seizes on Internet Tool to Promote Terror," *Washington Post*, 23 December 2016, https://wpo.st/aQwe2.

131. Murad Batal Al-Shishani, "Taking al-Qaeda's Jihad to Facebook," Jamestown Foundation, 5 February 2010, https://jamestown.org/program/taking-al-qaedas -jihad-to-facebook.

132. Joas Wagemakers, "A Crash Course in Jihadi Theory (Part 1)," Jihadica, 21 September 2010, http://www.jihadica.com/a-crash-course-in-jihadi-theory-part-1.

133. Abdullah al-Dani, "Extremist Sites Winning Battle of the Web," *Saudi Gazette*, 18 October 2010, http://www.saudigazette.com.sa/index.cfm?method=home .regcon&contentID=2010101685431.

134. Yasir Qadhi, "The Lure of Radicalism and Extremism among Muslim Youth," Muslim Matters, 18 October 2010, http://muslimmatters.org/2010/10/18/yasir-qadhi

-the-lure-of-radicalism-among-muslim-youth/. Also see Mind Body Soul, "Yasir Qadhi Misses the Boat on Radicalism," Yursil.com, 18 October 2010, http://www.yursil.com/blog/2010/10/yasir-qadhi-misses-the-boat-on-radicalism/.

135. Salah Uddin Shoaib Choudhury, "Al Qaeda Eyes on Bangladesh," *Sri Lanka Guardian*, 29 June 2010, http://www.srilankaguardian.org/2010/06/al-qaeda-eyes-on-bangladesh.html.

136. Veli Sirin, "Radical Islam in Germany: The Convert as Missionary," Gatestone Institute, 11 July 2011, https://www.gatestoneinstitute.org/2253/radical-islam-germany.

137. "Internet and Terrorist Propaganda," Ennahar Online, 2 August 2010, http://www.ennaharonline.com/en/news/4450.html; Siham Ali in Rabat and Mawassi Lahcen, "Morocco at a Crossroad," *Morocco World News*, 4 April 2013, https://www.moroccoworldnews.com/2013/04/85649/morocco-at-a-crossroad/.

138. William Maclean, "Interview: UK Islamist Says Like-Minded U.S. Groups Expanding," Reuters, 2 September 2010, http://www.reuters.com/article/idUSTRE68067F20100902.

139. Quilliam Foundation, http://www.quilliamfoundation.org; "New Quilliam Report Published," Quilliam Foundation, 27 September 2010, http://www.quilliamfoundation.org/index.php/component/content/article/700; Mohammed Ali Musawi, "Cheering for Osama," Quilliam Foundation, 2010, https://www.quilliaminternational.com/shop/e-publications/cheering-for-osama-how-jihadists-use-internet-forums-2/.

140. "Spy Agencies in Covert Push to Infiltrate Virtual World of Online Gaming," *Guardian*, 9 December 2013, http://www.theguardian.com/world/2013/dec/09/nsa-spies-online-games-world-warcraft-second-life.

141. AFP, "Norway Killer Anders Behring Breivik Tells Terror Trial al-Qaeda Inspired Him, Would Repeat Attacks If He Could," *National Post*, 17 April 2012, http://news.nationalpost.com/2012/04/17/norway-killer-anders-behring-breivik-tells-terror-trial-al-qaeda-inspired-him-would-repeat-attacks-if-he-could/.

142. "Nokhba Jihadi Media Releases Jihadist-Produced First Aid Booklet," SITE Intelligence Group, 21 March 2011, https://news.siteintelgroup.com/Jihadist-News/nokhba-jihadi-media-releases-jihadist-produced-first-aid-booklet.html.

143. "'Jihad Cosmo': An al Qaeda Women's Magazine," *Week*, 15 March 2011, http://theweek.com/article/index/213158/jihad-cosmo-an-al-qaeda-womens-magazine.

144. "Weapons and Explosives Expert Publishes First Issue of 'Al-Qaeda Airlines' Magazine, Dedicated Entirely to Home Manufacture of Chloroform," MEMRI, 10 April 2012, http://www.memri.org/report/en/0/0/0/0/0/0/6267.htm; "Al-Qaeda Releases English-Language Jihad Manual, Encourages Attacks in the West," ABC News, 16 May 2012, http://abcnews.go.com/Blotter/expect-expecting-jihadi/.

145. "Al Qaeda Home-Delivers Magazine in Pak: Report," NDTV, 9 January 2012, http://www.ndtv.com/article/world/al-qaeda-home-delivers-magazine-in-pak-report-165068.

146. Greg Miller, "Muslim Cleric Aulaqi Is 1st U.S. Citizen on List of Those CIA Is Allowed to Kill," *Washington Post*, 7 April 2010, http://www.washingtonpost.com/wp-dyn/content/article/2010/04/06/AR2010040604121.html.

147. Murad Batal Al-Shishani, "The Radical Source for Non-Arabic Speaking Muslims: Anwar al-Awlaki," *Terrorism Monitor* 8, no. 2 (2010), https://jamestown.org/program/the-radical-source-for-non-arabic-speaking-muslims-anwar-al-awlaki/.

148. Sara Carter, "Web Jihad Inaction-Jihadists Use US Servers to Spread Terror Message," *Washington Guardian*, 21 May 2013, http://www.washingtonguardian.com/web-jihad-inaction [link deleted].

149. A version of the first edition was hacked by British intelligence and replaced with cake recipes.

150. "Opinion, Awlaki's Killing No Interest for Arabs," OnIslam.net, 3 October 2011, http://www.onislam.net/english/news/middle-east/454169-awlakis-killing-no-interest-for-arabs.html [link deleted].

151. "Amazon.com Sells Sermons, Inspirational Islamic Teachings of Dead Al-Qaeda Leader Yemeni-American Sheikh Anwar Al-Awlaki; Available For Kindle Too," MEMRI, 20 December 2012, http://www.memri.org/report/en/0/0/0/0/0/0/6886.htm; "Anwar Al-Awlaki: Books," Amazon, 21 July 2014, http://www.amazon.com.

152. Steven Stalinsky and R. Sosnow, "'Inspire' Magazine Issue XI—First Issue Released Via Twitter," MEMRI, 11 June 2013, http://www.memri.org/report/en/0/0/0/0/0/0/7226.htm.

153. Aaron Y. Zelin, "American Jihadi: The Death of Samir Khan in Yemen Marks the End of a Key Figure in the Internet Jihad," Foreign Policy, 30 September 2011, http://www.foreignpolicy.com/articles/2011/09/30/samir_khan_dead_inspire_magazine.

154. AP, "My Son the Terrorist: One Mother's Grief at How Her Privately-Educated American Son Met a Violent End in Pakistan's Al Qaeda Badlands," *Daily Mail*, 18 January 2012, http://www.dailymail.co.uk/news/article-2088399/Moeed-Abdul-Salam-From-US-boarding-school-student-al-Qaeda-terrorist.html.

155. "Al-Qaeda Magazine That Gives Tips on How to Kill Americans Was Smuggled into Guantanamo Bay," *Daily Mail*, 18 January 2012, http://www.dailymail.co.uk/news/article-2088606/Al-Qaedo-magazine-smuggled-Guantanamo-Bay-terror-suspect.html.

156. "Stephen Timms Stabbing: How Internet Sermons Turned Quiet Student into Fanatic," *Telegraph*, 2 November 2010, http://www.telegraph.co.uk/news/uknews/crime/8105516/Stephen-Timms-stabbing-how-internet-sermons-turned-quiet-student-into-fanatic.html.

157. "Luton 'Terror Plotters' Planned Sending Toy Car Bomb into Territorial Army Centre," *Huffington Post*, 15 April 2013, http://www.huffingtonpost.co.uk/2013/04/15/terror-plotters-luton-zahid-iqbal-mohammed-ahmed-_n_3084783.html?utm_hp_ref=uk.

158. Scott Shane and Souad Mekhennet, "Anwar al-Awlaki—From Condemning Terror to Preaching Jihad," *New York Times*, 9 May 2010, http://www.nytimes.com/2010/05/09/world/09awlaki.html.

159. Bill Roggio, "US-Born Cleric Awlaki 'Proud' to Have Taught al Qaeda Operatives," *FDD's Long War Journal*, 27 April 2010, http://www.longwarjournal.org/archives/2010/04/usborn_cleric_awlaki.php.

160. Richard Spencer, "How al-Qaeda Cleric Anwar al-Awlaki Told the 'Underpants Bomber' to Pray," *Telegraph*, 9 December 2015, http://www.telegraph.co.uk/news/worldnews/al-qaeda/12042126/How-al-Qaeda-cleric-Anwar-al-Awlaki-told-the-underpants-bomber-to-pray.html.

161. "Web Post by Fort Hood Gunman Major Nidal Malik Hasan Could Shed Light on Motives," *Times Online*, 6 November 2009, http://www.timesonline.co.uk/tol/news/world/us_and_americas/article6905958.ece.

162. AP, "Feds: Boston Marathon Suspect Had Bomb-Making Instructions, Jihad Literature Available Online," Fox News, 28 June 2013, http://www.foxnews.com/us/2013/06/28/feds-boston-marathon-suspect-had-bomb-making-instructions-jihad-literature.html. Also see Shira Schoenberg, "Dzhokhar Tsarnaev Trial: Jihadi Videos, Photos of Bloodied Muslim Children on Brother's Computer," MassLive.com, 28 April 2015, http://www.masslive.com/news/boston/index.ssf/2015/04/dzhokhar_tsarnaev_trial_tamerl.html; Richard Valdmanis, "Boston Bomber's Lawyers Focus on Brother's Obsession with Islam," Yahoo! News, 28 April 2015, http://news.yahoo.com/boston-bombers-lawyers-probe-tsarnaevs-troubled-history-110517940.html.

163. J. M. Berger, "Al Qaeda's American Dream Ends," Politico, 23 April 2015, http://www.politico.com/magazine/story/2015/04/al-qaeda-adam-gadahn-isis-rebirth-americans-recruited-to-isil-117285.html. Also see "American al-Qaeda Spokesman Urges Attacks in US," *Al Arabiya News*, 28 October 2010, https://www.alarabiya.net/articles/2010/10/23/123381.html.

164. Reports suggested that the perpetrator, Mohamed Lahouaiej Bouhlel, had searched Islamic State content online. See Elena Berton and Kim Hjelmgaard, "Paris Prosecutor: Nice Attacker Searched Online for Islamic State," *USA Today*, 18 July 2016, http://www.usatoday.com/story/news/world/2016/07/18/nice-attackers-link-islamic-state-puzzles-investigators/87239960/.

CHAPTER 6

1. See the discussion in "Should We Ditch Islamic State in Favour of Daesh?," Channel 4 News, 3 July 2015, https://www.channel4.com/news/islamic-state-isis-isil-daesh-bbc-cameron-grayling.

2. Glenn E. Perry, "Caliph," in *The Oxford Encyclopedia of the Islamic World*, Oxford Islamic Studies Online, 2009, http://www.oxfordislamicstudies.com/article/opr/t236/e0131; Andrew Rippin, *Muslims: Their Religious Beliefs and Practices* (London: Routledge, 2012), 67–68.

3. "Qaradawi Says 'Jihadist Caliphate' Violates Sharia," Al Arabiya News, 5 July 2014, http://english.alarabiya.net/en/News/middle-east/2014/07/05/Qaradawi-says-jihadist-caliphate-violates-sharia-.html.

4. J. M. Berger, "The Islamic State vs. al Qaeda—Who's Winning the War to Become the Jihadi Superpower?," Foreign Policy, 2 September 2014, http://www.foreignpolicy.com/articles/2014/09/02/islamic_state_vs_al_qaeda_next_jihadi_super_power.

5. "Inside Mosul: Why Iraqis Are Celebrating Islamic Extremists' Takeover of Their City," Niqash, 12 June 2014, http://www.niqash.org/articles/?id=3458.

6. Roula Khalaf and Sam Jones, "Selling Terror: How Isis Details Its Brutality," *Financial Times*, 17 June 2014, http://www.ft.com. Also see Tyler Durden, "ISIS Stunner: Terrorist Organization's Annual Reports Unveiled; Reveal Full 'Investment Highlights,'" ZeroHedge.com, 17 June 2014, http://www.zerohedge.com/news/2014-06–17/isis-stunner-terrorist-organizations-annual-reports-unveiled-reveal-full-investment-.

7. Lori Hinnant, "ISIS Revamps Recruitment, with Savvy, Professional Broadcasts," Rudaw.net, 1 June 2015, http://rudaw.net/english/world/010620153.

8. Gilad Shiloach, "ISIS Issues Sign Language Propaganda in New Video," Vocativ, 8 March 2015, http://www.vocativ.com/world/isis-2/isis-sign-language-propaganda/ [link deleted].

9. "Shocking Video: ISIS Dumps Bodies of Executed Rivals in Deep Gorge," Al Arabiya News, 25 June 2014, http://english.alarabiya.net/en/webtv/reports /2014/06/25/ISIS-publicly-execute-men-and-dump-their-bodies-1783.html.

10. Jack Moore, "The Ginger Jihadist of Mosul: Omar al-Shishani the Chechen 'General,'" *International Business Times*, 11 June 2014, http://www.ibtimes.co.uk/ ginger-jihadist-mosul-omar-al-shishani-chechen-general-1452232.

11. Rajia Aboulkheir, "Meet Islam Yaken, a Cosmopolitan Egyptian Who Turned into ISIS Fighter," Al Arabiya News, 3 August 2014, http://english.alarabiya.net/en/ variety/2014/08/03/Meet-Islam-Yaken-a-cosmopolitan-Egyptian-who-turned-into -ISIS-fighter-.html.

12. "British 'Recruiter' Jihadist Allegedly Killed in Iraq," Al Arabiya News, 16 July 2014, http://english.alarabiya.net/en/News/middle-east/2014/07/16/British-recruiter -Jihadist-allegedly-killed-in-Iraq-.html; "Cardiff Jihadist Reyaad Khan, 21, Killed by RAF Drone," BBC News, 7 September 2015, http://www.bbc.co.uk/news/uk-wales-34176790.

13. Louisa Loveluck, "'Moron' Militant's Selfie Leads to US Air Raid on Isil Unit," *Telegraph*, 4 June 2015, http://www.telegraph.co.uk/news/worldnews/islamic -state/11652942/Moron-militants-selfie-leads-to-US-air-raid-on-Isil-unit.html.

14. Jamie Bartlett, "Telegram, Isis and Their So-Called Social Media Genius," *Telegraph*, 29 June 2014, http://blogs.telegraph.co.uk/technology/jamiebartlett/ 100013899/isis-and-their-so-called-social-media-genius/.

15. "Iraq Conflict Breeds Cyber-War among Rival Factions," BBC News, 22 July 2014, http://www.bbc.co.uk/news/technology-28418951.

16. Robert Fisk, "Propaganda War of Islamic Extremists Is Being Waged on Facebook and Internet Message Boards, Not Mosques," *Independent*, 13 October 2014, http://www.independent.co.uk/voices/comment/robert-fisk-beware-of-the-role-of-the -laptop-in-our-addiction-to-politics-and-war-9790093.html.

17. "Isis's Teenage Austrian Poster Girl Jihadi Brides 'Have Changed Their Minds and Want to Come Home,'" *Independent*, 12 October 2014, http://www.independent .co.uk/news/world/middle-east/isiss-austrian-poster-girl-jihadi-brides-have-changed -their-minds-and-want-to-come-home-9789547.html.

18. "A Facebook Interview with One of Austria's Foreign Fighters," oe24.at, 1 September 2014, http://www.oe24.at/oesterreich/chronik/wien/ISIS-Krieger -Firas-H-droht-jetzt-Oesterreich/156294052.

19. Simona Foltyn, "Austrian Youth Flocking to ISIL," Al Jazeera, 10 October 2014, http://www.aljazeera.com/indepth/features/2014/10/austrian-youth-flocking -isil-2014108101425255506.html.

20. "Analyst Group: Colorado Teens Spoke with Top Islamic State Terrorists," *Denver Post*, 29 October 2014, http://www.denverpost.com/news/ci_26823939/ analyst-group-colorado-teens-spoke-top-islamic-state.

21. "Three British Teenage Jihadi Brides Are Now on the Run from Isis," *Daily Mail*, 13 May 2015, http://www.dailymail.co.uk/news/article-3078579/Three-British -teenage-Jihadi-brides-married-militants-Iraq-run-Isis-escaping.html; Nabeelah Jaffer, "The Secret World of Isis Brides: 'U dnt hav 2 pay 4 ANYTHING if u r wife of a martyr,'" *Guardian*, 24 June 2015, http://www.theguardian.com/world/2015/jun/24/isis-brides -secret-world-jihad-western-women-syria

22. Rukmini Callimachi, "ISIS and the Lonely Young American," *New York Times*, 28 June 2015, http://www.nytimes.com/2015/06/28/world/americas/isis-online-recruiting -american.html.

23. Erin Marie Saltman and Melanie Smith, *Till Martyrdom Do Us Part: Gender and the ISIS Phenomenon*, Institute for Strategic Dialogue, 2015, http://www .strategicdialogue.org/wp-content/uploads/2016/02/Till_Martyrdom_Do_Us _Part_Gender_and_the_ISIS_Phenomenon.pdf; Jamaal Abdul-Alim, "ISIS 'Manifesto' Spells Out Role for Women," *Atlantic*, 8 March 2015, http://www.theatlantic.com/ education/archive/2015/03/isis-manifesto-spells-out-role-for-women/387049/; "'Watch Out for Satanic Earrings!' IS Publishes Women's Manifesto," Radio Free Europe/Radio Liberty, 5 February 2015, http://www.rferl.org/content/islamic-state-womens -manifesto/26832051.html; Carolyn Hoyle, Alexandra Bradford, and Ross Frenett, *Becoming Mulan? Female Western Migrants to ISIS*, Institute for Strategic Dialogue, 2015, http://www.strategicdialogue.org/wp-content/uploads/2016/02/ISDJ2969_Becoming _Mulan_01.15_WEB.pdf.

24. Thomas Seymat, "How Nasheeds Became the Soundtrack of Jihad," Euronews, 8 October 2014, http://www.euronews.com/2014/10/08/nasheeds-the-soundtrack -of-jihad.

25. Steve Rose, "The Isis Propaganda War: A Hi-Tech Media Jihad," *Guardian*, 7 October 2014, http://www.theguardian.com/world/2014/oct/07/isis-media -machine-propaganda-war.

26. Islam Sakka, "Slaying, Slaughtering, and Burning: ISIS, the Cinematic Caliphate," Al-Akhbar English, 5 February 2015, http://english.al-akhbar.com/content/ slaying-slaughtering-and-burning-isis-cinematic-caliphate.

27. "Fox News under Fire for Showing Uncut ISIS Video," Al Arabiya News, 5 February 2015, http://ara.tv/zqx74.

28. "Clerics Denounce Burning Alive of Pilot as Un-Islamic," Al Arabiya News, 4 Feburary 2015, http://english.alarabiya.net/en/News/middle-east/2015/02/04/Clerics -denounce-burning-alive-of-pilot-as-un-Islamic.html.

29. "ISIS Execute Two Imams and Four Civilians for Condemning Pilot's Death," *Daily Mail*, 5 February 2015, http://www.dailymail.co.uk/news/article-2940990/ISIS -beheads-four-Syrians-took-Facebook-condemn-burning-Jordanian-pilot-death-two -Muslim-clerics-criticised-murder-shot-firing-squad.html.

30. "'An Attack upon the Nests of Fornication, Vice and Disbelief in God': ISIS's Chilling Words after Tunisian Massacre Which Killed 38 as They Warn 'Worse Is to Follow,'" *Daily Mail*, 27 June 2015, http://www.dailymail.co.uk/news/article- 3141379/Face-killer-ISIS-releases-picture-man-claims-carried-slaughter-38 -tourists-Tunisia.html.

31. Deborah Hastings, "France Terror Suspect Sent Selfie with Severed Head: Officials," *New York Daily News*, 27 June 2015, http://www.nydailynews.com/news/world/france-terror-suspect-selfie-severed-head-report-article-1.2273446.

32. Suman Varandani, "ISIS Releases Audio Clip Purporting to Be of Kuwait Shiite Mosque Bomber," *International Business Times*, 25 June 2015, http://www.ibtimes.com/isis-releases-audio-clip-purporting-be-kuwait-shiite-mosque-bomber-1987390.

33. "ISIS Killer 'Found Accomplice Online' Despite Being on Terror List," *Daily Mail*, 28 July 2016, http://www.dailymail.co.uk/news/article-3711739/The-Facebook-Jihadis-Priest-killer-recruited-accomplice-internet-despite-terror-list.html.

34. "ISIS Supporters Mourn Death of 'Youngest Fighter,' " Al Arabiya News, 9 October 2014, http://english.alarabiya.net/en/News/middle-east/2014/10/09/ISIS-supporters-mourn-death-of-youngest-fighter-.html.

35. "Dewsbury Teenager Is 'UK's Youngest Ever Suicide Bomber,' " BBC News, 14 June 2015, http://www.bbc.co.uk/news/uk-england-leeds-33126132.

36. "Cardiff Student Pleads Guilty to Terror Charge," BBC News, 17 June 2015, http://www.bbc.co.uk/news/uk-wales-south-east-wales-33166540.

37. "Iraqi Woman Dubbed 'the Twitter Terrorist' Is Jailed," *Daily Mail*, 11 June 2015, http://www.dailymail.co.uk/news/article-3120226/Iraqi-woman-dubbed-Twitter-terrorist-posted-45-000-messages-encouraging-violent-jihad-one-al-Qaeda-s-favourite-tweeters-jailed.html.

38. "Hyderabad Techie Arrested for Allegedly Trying to Join the Islamic State," Firstpost, 29 October 2014, http://www.firstpost.com/india/hyderabad-techie-arrested-allegedly-trying-join-islamic-state-1778237.html.

39. Phoebe Hurst, "ISIS Is Trying to Lure British Recruits with Cappuccinos," Vice.com, 20 May 2015, http://munchies.vice.com/articles/isis-is-trying-to-lure-british-recruits-with-cappuccinos.

40. Ben Taub, "Journey to Jihad," *New Yorker*, 1 June 2015, http://www.newyorker.com/magazine/2015/06/01/journey-to-jihad; Ellie Hall, "Gone Girl: An Interview with an American in ISIS," BuzzFeed News, 17 April 2015, http://www.buzzfeed.com/ellievhall/gone-girl-an-interview-with-an-american-in-isis; Anna Erelle, "Skyping with the Enemy: I Went Undercover as a Jihadi Girlfriend," *Guardian*, 26 May 2015, http://www.theguardian.com/world/2015/may/26/french-journalist-poses-muslim-convert-isis-anna-erelle; Yiswaree Palansamy, "Lonely Women Are Potential Islamic State Recruits, Minister Says," *Malay Mail Online*, 16 April 2015, http://www.themalaymailonline.com/malaysia/article/lonely-women-are-potential-islamic-state-recruits-minister-says.

41. "Mothers Living under ISIS Share Photos of Children Posing with Guns," *Daily Mail*, 18 March 2015, http://www.dailymail.co.uk/news/article-3000271/Keeping-jihadis-Mothers-living-ISIS-post-photographs-children-newborn-babies-guns-social-media-sickening-game-one-upmanship.html.

42. "60,000 Pro-IS Twitter Accounts Set Up since May," Sky News, 5 September 2014, http://news.sky.com/story/1329640/60000-pro-is-twitter-accounts-set-up-since-may; Tom Cheshire, "Armchair Jihad," Medium.com, 4 September 2014, https://medium.com/sky-news/armchair-jihad-the-data-aff69388c6b0. Also see " 'Thugs Wanted—Bring Your Own Boots': How Isis Attracts Foreign Fighters to Its Twisted

Utopia," *Guardian*, 9 March 2015, http://www.theguardian.com/world/2015/mar/09/how-isis-attracts-foreign-fighters-the-state-of-terror-book; and J. M. Berger and Jessica Stern, *Isis: The State of Terror* (New York: HarperCollins, 2015).

43. "Jihadists Appear Caught Offguard by Release of Steven Sotloff Video," *Telegraph*, 2 September 2014, http://www.telegraph.co.uk/news/worldnews/middleeast/iraq/11071496/Jihadists-appear-caught-offguard-by-release-of-Steven-Sotloff-video.html.

44. Adam Senft, Jakub Dalek, Helmi Noman, and Masashi Crete-Nishihata, "Monitoring Information Controls in Iraq in Reaction to ISIS Insurgency," The Citizen Lab, 20 June 2014, https://citizenlab.org/2014/06/monitoring-information-controls-in-iraq/.

45. "Islamic State 'Help Desk' Helps Members Avoid Internet Surveillance," *Telegraph*, 11 February 2016, http://www.telegraph.co.uk/technology/2016/02/11/islamic-state-help-desk-helps-members-avoid-internet-surveillanc/.

46. Aaron Brantly and Muhammad al-'Ubaydi, "Extremist Forums Provide Digital OpSec Training," Counter Terrorism Centre, 28 May 2014, https://www.ctc.usma.edu/posts/extremist-forums-provide-digital-opsec-training.

47. Gilad Shiloach, "ISIS Opens Its Own Social Network," Vocativ, 8 March 2015, http://www.vocativ.com/world/isis-2/isis-opens-its-own-social-network/.

48. Gilad Shiloach, "The Islamic State Is Starting a TV Channel," Vocativ, 14 January 2015, http://www.vocativ.com/world/isis-2/isis-tv-channel/. [link deleted].

49. "Islamic State Uses Downloadable Apps to Hide Attack Plans, Recruit Followers," *Washington Times*, 28 June 2015, http://www.washingtontimes.com/news/2015/jun/28/islamic-state-uses-downloadable-apps-to-hide-attac/.

50. "Global Cyber-Strategy Needed to Confront 'IS' and Other Terror Groups," Deutsche Welle, 28 May 2015, http://www.dw.de/global-cyber-strategy-needed-to-confront-is-and-other-terror-groups/a-18481090.

51. Stilgherrian, "Islamic State Has 'Best Cyber Offence' of Any Terrorist Group," ZDNet, 5 June 2015, http://www.zdnet.com/article/islamic-state-has-best-cyber-offence-of-any-terrorist-group/.

52. Washington Post, "The Islamic State May Be Trying to Raise Funds Using Bitcoin," AstroAwani.com, 10 June 2015, http://english.astroawani.com/world-news/islamic-state-may-be-trying-raise-funds-using-bitcoin-62110.

53. "First Footage of Islamic State Grooming HQ," Sky News, 28 May 2015, http://news.sky.com/story/1492005/first-footage-of-islamic-state-grooming-hq.

54. Mohammed A. Salih, "Mosul under ISIL: 'No Internet, No Shaving,'" Al Jazeera, 29 March 2015, http://www.aljazeera.com/news/2015/03/mosul-isil-internet-shaving-150323061307541.html.

55. AFP, "Jihadists Increasingly Wary of Internet, Experts Say," ABC, 31 January 2015, http://www.abc.net.au/news/2015–01–31/jihadists-increasingly-wary-of-internet-experts-say/6059604.

56. Thomas Hegghammer, "Sample Messages from #CalamityWillBefallUS Twitter Campaign," Storify.com, 2014, https://storify.com/hegghammer/calamitywillbefallus.

57. Kurt Nimmo, "ISIS Releases Global Takeover Map," Infowars, 27 June 2014, http://www.infowars.com/war-propaganda-the-isis-five-year-plan/.

58. Supriya Jha, "'Thank God for Twitter'—Militants Tweet after Taking Iraq's Mosul," Zee News, 11 June 2014, http://zeenews.india.com/news/world/thank-god-for-twitter-militants-tweet-after-taking-iraq-s-mosul_938707.html.

59. David Mack, "ISIS Threatens Twitter Founder and Employees over Blocked Accounts," BuzzFeed News, 1 March 2015, http://www.buzzfeed.com/davidmack/isis-twitter-threat.

60. Stacy Meichtry and Sam Schechner, "How Islamic State Weaponized the Chat App to Direct Attacks on the West," Wall Street Journal, 20 October 2016, https://www.wsj.com/articles/how-islamic-state-weaponized-the-chat-app-to-direct-attacks-on-the-west-1476955802. Also see "Analyzing How Islamic State Recruits through Social Media," Eurasia Review, 17 June 2016, http://www.eurasiareview.com/17062016-analyzing-how-islamic-state-recruits-through-social-media/.

61. Cole Bunzel, "'Come Back to Twitter': A Jihadi Warning against Telegram," Jihadica, 18 July 2016, http://www.jihadica.com/come-back-to-twitter/.

62. Ghuraba18 (@ghuraba18), "This Is Our Call of Duty and We Respawn in Jannah," 21 January, 2014 http://twitter.com.

63. "Friday Sermon Wants Jihad on Internet Falsehood," MalaysiaKini.com, 29 May 2015, https://www.malaysiakini.com/news/300082.

64. Thalia Beaty, Kristopher Brant, and Maggy Donaldson, "More—Not Less—Religion Needed to Fight Extremism, Imam Director Says," PBS News Hour, 20 May 2015, http://www.pbs.org/newshour/rundown/extremism-fight/.

65. Sara Hussein, "Hackers Stole from Syrian Rebels by Posing as Women," Your Middle East, 3 February 2015, http://www.yourmiddleeast.com/news/hackers-stole-from-syrian-rebels-by-posing-as-women_29647.

66. "The Fake Battle That Fooled IS Supporters—and Their Opponents," BBC News, 15 June 2015, http://www.bbc.co.uk/news/blogs-trending-33111934.

67. "Vanguard Unit of Hacktivists Anonymous Meets 'Islamic State' on Cyberfront," Deutsche Welle, 5 June 2015, http://www.dw.de/vanguard-unit-of-hacktivists-anonymous-meets-islamic-state-on-cyberfront/a-18498998.

68. "Anonymous Reveals List of ISIS-Linked Twitter Accounts," Al Arabiya News, 16 March 2015, http://english.alarabiya.net/en/media/digital/2015/03/16/Anonymous-reveals-list-of-ISIS-linked-Twitter-accounts.html.

69. Lorenzo Franceschi-Bicchierai, "How Anonymous and Other Hacktivists Fight ISIS Online," Motherboard, 1 November 2016, https://motherboard.vice.com/en_us/article/how-anonymous-and-other-hacktivists-fight-isis-online-5886b7589848b145c38b4589.

70. Oliver Gee, "France to Enlist Hackers to Tackle Jihadists," The Local, 29 May 2015, http://www.thelocal.fr/20150529/france-to-hire-hackers-to-tackle-jihadists.

71. "Schools Monitoring Pupils' Web Use with 'Anti-radicalisation Software,'" Guardian, 10 June 2015, http://www.theguardian.com/uk-news/2015/jun/10/schools-trial-anti-radicalisation-software-pupils-internet.

72. "U.S. Muslims Take On ISIS' Recruiting Machine," New York Times, 20 February 2015, http://www.nytimes.com/2015/02/20/us/muslim-leaders-in-us-seek-to-counteract-extremist-recruiters.html.

73. "Twitter Suspends Almost 250,000 Accounts with 'Terror' Links," Middle East Eye, 18 August 2016, http://www.middleeasteye.net/news/twitter-suspends-almost -250000-accounts-terror-links-403822918; Sharon Gaudin, "How to Keep Facebook, Twitter from Being Terrorists' Hunting Grounds," Computerworld, 3 August 2016, http://www.computerworld.com/article/3104087/security/how-to-keep-facebook -twitter-from-being-terrorists-hunting-grounds.html.

74. Sirwan Kajjo and Mehdi Jedinia, "US, Private Sector Join Forces in Anti-IS Social Media Project," VOA, 8 September 2016, http://www.voanews.com/a/us-private -sector-anti-islamic-state-social-medai-project/3499396.html; Andy Greenberg, "Google's Clever Plan to Stop Aspiring ISIS Recruits," Wired, 7 September 2016, https:// www.wired.com/2016/09/googles-clever-plan-stop-aspiring-isis-recruits/.

75. Average Mohamed, "A Muslim in the West," YouTube, 5 October 2015, https:// youtu.be/umY5GezsOQ4; Average Mohamed, "Be Like Aisha," YouTube, 19 October 2015, https://youtu.be/1N8WIQqK9UI; Average Mohamed, "What Does Islam Have to Say about Slavery?," YouTube, 20 October 2015, https://youtu.be/C_4HSzYDnJ8. Also see the discussion in Tanya Silverman, Christopher J. Stewart, Zahed Amanullah, and Jonathan Birdwell, The Impact of Counter-Narratives, Institute for Strategic Dialogue, 2016, http://www.strategicdialogue.org/wp-content/uploads/2016/08/Impact-of-Counter -Narratives_ONLINE.pdf.

76. "Iranian Cartoon Contest Lampoons IS, Alleged Backers," Radio Free Europe/ Radio Liberty, 26 May 2015, http://www.rferl.org/content/iran-islamic-state-cartoon -contest-blames-us-israel-saudis/27038156.html.

77. Open Your Eyes, http://www.openyoureyes.net.

78. "Saudi TV Series Uses New Weapon against ISIS: Satire," CNN, 22 June 2015, http://www.cnn.com/2015/06/22/middleeast/anti-isis-satire/index.html.

79. "Syria's Nine-Year-Old YouTube Storyteller," BBC News, 16 October 2014, http://www.bbc.co.uk/news/av/magazine-29633815/bbctrending-syria-s-nine-year -old-youtube-storyteller.

80. Frank Gardner, "Inside Jordan's Fight against Home-Grown Extremism," BBC News, 26 May 2015, http://www.bbc.co.uk/news/world-middle-east-32782439.

81. Active Change Foundation, "#NotInMyName: ISIS Do Not Represent British Muslims," YouTube, 10 September 2014, https://youtu.be/wfYanI-zJes.

82. "Haqiqah—What Is the Truth behind ISIS?," ImamsOnline.com, March 2015, http://imamsonline.com/blog/haqiqah-what-is-the-truth-behind-isis/.

83. "Saudi Grand Mufti Urges Muslims to Use Internet to Fight Terror," Al Arabiya News, 9 March 2015, http://english.alarabiya.net/en/News/middle-east/2015/03/09/ Saudi-Grand-Mufti-urges-Muslims-to-use-internet-to-fight-terror.html.

84. Iman Research, "Pondok Manusiawi #1—Syurga di Bawah Kilauan Pedang?," YouTube, 16 August 2016, https://youtu.be/oCdFeGmVOmM. Discussed in "Research Outfit Starts Online 'Pondok' to Counter Radicalism," Malay Mail Online, 18 August 2016, http://www.themalaymailonline.com/malaysia/article/research-outfit-starts -online-pondok-to-counter-radicalism.

85. Katherine Rushton, "Google's Bid to Ban IS Footage: Internet Giant Hires Arabic Speaker to Help Crackdown on Jihadi Groups Using YouTube to Radicalise Recruits,"

Daily Mail, 5 February 2015, http://www.dailymail.co.uk/news/article-2940403/Google
-s-bid-ban-footage-Internet-giant-hires-Arabic-speaker-help-crackdown-jihadi-groups
-using-YouTube-radicalise-recruits.html.

86. "EU Plans to Target Cyber-Terrorism," BBC News, 12 March 2015, http://www
.bbc.co.uk/news/technology-31851119; "Ministers Look to Strip Online Jihad's 'Glamour,' "
Euractiv.com, 19 January 2015, http://www.euractiv.com/section/justice-home-affairs/
news/ministers-look-to-strip-online-jihad-s-glamour/.

87. "Russia Bans Wayback Machine Internet Archive over Islamic State Video,"
Moscow Times, 26 October 2014, http://www.themoscowtimes.com/news/article/
russia-bans-wayback-machine-internet-archive-over-islamic-state-video/510074.html.

88. TerrorMonitor (@Terror_Monitor), "#IslamicState (#ISIS) Terror Group
Claims Responsibility for #ParisAttacks," 14 November 2015, https://twitter.com/
Terror_Monitor.

89. "Sharia4Belgium Trial: Belgian Court Jails Members," BBC News, 11 February
2015, http://www.bbc.co.uk/news/world-europe-31378724.

90. Matthew Dalton and Margaret Coker, "How Belgium Became a Jihadist-
Recruiting Hub," *Wall Street Journal*, 28 September 2014, http://www.wsj.com/articles/
how-belgium-became-a-jihadist-recruiting-hub-1411958283.

91. Gary R. Bunt, "From Mosque to YouTube: Cyber Islamic Networks in the
UK," in *Postcolonial Media Cultures*, ed. Ros Brunt and Rinella Cere (London: Palgrave
Macmillan, 2011), 68–81.

92. Ahmed Elumami, "Manchester Bomber Radicalised in Britain in 2015—Tripoli
Counter-Terrorism Force," Reuters, 8 June 2017, https://uk.reuters.com/article/uk
-britain-security-manchester-libya-idUKKBN18Z1CR. Also see "Manchester Attack: 22
Dead and 59 Hurt in Suicide Bombing," BBC News, 23 May 2017, http://www.bbc.co.uk/
news/uk-england-manchester-40010124.

93. Shekhar Bhatia, "American Hate Preacher Who 'Inspired' London Attacker
Posed as a Jihadi, Glorified bin Laden, Told Followers to Kill Non-Muslims—and
Has Now Fled Home So Fast He Left His Flip Flops Behind," *Daily Mail*, 6 June 2017,
http://www.dailymail.co.uk/news/article-4578458/U-S-hate-preacher-inspired
-London-attacker.html. Also see Aleem Maqbool, "Influential Radical Imam 'a
Nuisance' in Dearborn's Muslim Community," Michigan Radio, 9 June 2017, http://
michiganradio.org/post/influential-radical-imam-nuisance-dearborn-s-muslim
-community

94. "London Bridge: Third Attacker Named as Youssef Zaghba," *Guardian*, 6 June
2017, https://www.theguardian.com/uk-news/2017/jun/06/london-bridge-attack
-third-attacker-named-in-italy-as-youssef-zaghba.

95. Bethan McKernan, "Isis Supporters Celebrate Barcelona Attack after the Terror
Group Claim Responsibility," *Independent*, 18 August 2017, http://www.independent
.co.uk/news/world/middle-east/isis-barcelona-attack-terror-group-responsibility-las
-ramblas-islamists-islamic-state-a7899406.html; "ISIL Claims Responsibility for Van
Attack in Barcelona," Al Jazeera English, 18 August 2017, http://www.aljazeera.com/
news/2017/08/isil-claims-responsibility-van-attack-barcelona-170817193535815.html.

96. Javier Negre, "El Presunto Terrorista Moussa Oukabir: 'Mataría a todos los
infieles, sólo dejaría a los musulmanes que siguiesen la religión,'" *El Mundo*, 18 August

2017, http://www.elmundo.es/cataluna/2017/08/18/5996ab4aca474100368b460d
.html.

97. *Rumiyah*, issues 1–9, September 2016–May 2017.

98. "Tehran Attacks," *Independent*, 7 June 2017, http://www.independent.co.uk.

99. Daniel L. Byman, "Comparing Al Qaeda and ISIS: Different Goals, Different Targets: Prepared Testimony before the Subcommittee on Counterterrorism and Intelligence of the House Committee on Homeland Security," Brookings, 2015, https:// www.brookings.edu/testimonies/comparing-al-qaeda-and-isis-different-goals-different -targets/; Raphael Gluck (@einfal), "Do ISIS & Al Qaeda Ever Issue Competing Claims for Same Attack? Just Happened!," Twitter, 5 September 2017, https://twitter.com/einfal/ status/905084157277155328.

CONCLUSION

1. A digital divide still sees less than half of the global population having Internet access: "The International Data Corporation (IDC) estimates that 3.2 billion people, or 44 percent of the world's population, will have access to the Internet in 2016. Of this number, more than 2 billion will be using mobile devices to do so." The same report projected a 2 percent yearly increase in Internet access until 2020. The zones of population currently with limited or no internet access inevitably include regions with substantial Muslim populations. "Mobile Internet Users to Top 2 Billion Worldwide in 2016, According to IDC," International Data Corporation, 17 December 2015, http://2016 .idciotforum.com/articles/article02.

2. "Islamic State 'Help Desk' Helps Members Avoid Internet Surveillance," *Telegraph*, 11 February 2016, http://www.telegraph.co.uk/technology/2016/02/11/islamic -state-help-desk-helps-members-avoid-Internet-surveillanc/.

3. For example, see Javier Lesaca, "On Social Media, ISIS Uses Modern Cultural Images to Spread Anti-modern Values," Brookings, 24 September 2015, http://www .brookings.edu/blogs/techtank/posts/2015/09/24-isis-social-media-engagement; and Cori E. Dauber and Mark Robinson, "ISIS and the Hollywood Visual Style," Jihadology, 6 July 2015, http://jihadology.net/2015/07/06/guest-post-isis-and-the -hollywood-visual-style/.

4. Imam Suhaib Webb (@imamsuhaibwebb), Snapchat, 2 April 2016. See the discussion in Nushmia Khan, "This Imam Delivers Eight-Second Snapchat Sermons," *Quartz*, 25 March 2016, http://qz.com/646902/this-imam-delivers-eight-second -snapchat-sermons/.

5. Talabetoday (@Talabetoday), Instagram, 3 April 2016, https://www.instagram .com/p/BCe7RuQpnuO/?taken-by=talabetoday. Also see BBC Trending, "Instagram Imams Are Unlikely Online Hit," BBC News, 1 February 2016, http://www.bbc.co.uk/ news/blogs-trending-35439946.

6. "Iran to Spend $36 Million on Internet 'Smart Filtering,' to No Avail," Payvand .com, 25 February 2016, http://www.payvand.com/news/16/feb/1137.html.

7. Terrormonitor.org (@Terror_Monitor), "#TTP Splinter Group Jamaat-ul-Ahrar Releases Picture of #Lahore Suicide Bomber," Twitter, 28 March 2016, https://twitter .com/Terror_Monitor/.

8. Bloomberg, "Taliban Develop Smartphone App to Advance Propaganda Efforts," *South China Morning Post*, 2 April 2016, http://www.scmp.com/news/world/article/1933411/taliban-develops-smartphone-app-advance-propaganda-efforts.

9. Wales does have distinct Muslim communities, in particular in Cardiff, Swansea, and Newport.

#Glossary

adhān: Call to prayer.

ahl al-bayt: People of the House (of the Prophet Muḥammad); associated
　　with descendants of the Prophet (Shiʻa and Sunni).

al-arkān (al-Islām): Pillars or foundations (of Islam) [marked with an * in
　　this glossary]; sing. *rukn*.

al-Azhar: University located in Cairo; literally "the brilliant one."

ʻālim: A scholar; pl. *ʻulamā'*.

Allāh: God.

ʻĀshūrā: The tenth day of Muḥarram, when Muḥammad's grandson
　　Husayn ibn Ali was martyred during the Battle of Karbala, 680 CE.

āya: Verse from the Qur'an, meaning "sign"; pl. *āyat*. See *sūra*.

āyatullāh: Literally meaning the "sign of God," within Shiʻa Islam; this
　　can denote the rank of a highly qualified interpreter of Islamic
　　jurisprudence.

daʻwa: The call or invitation to Islam, associated with propagation of the
　　religion.

dhikr: Remembrance or ritual invocation (of God) in prayer and ritual acts,
　　often associated with Sufi practices.

Eid al-Adha, ʻĪd al-Aḍḥā: The Feast of Sacrifice.

Eid al-Fitr, ʻĪd al-Fiṭr: The concluding feast of Ramadan.

fatwā: The opinions of specific contemporary imams and ayatollahs; pl.
　　fatāwā.

fiqh, fikh: Islamic "jurisprudence."

ḥādīth: A traditional saying or report of the actions of Muhammad; pl.
　　aḥādīth.

*ḥadjdj, hajj: The major pilgrimage to Mecca.

haḍra: "Presence"; Sufi ritual acts of devotion.

ḥāfiz: A title denoting one who has learned the Qur'an by heart.

ḥalāl: A term applied to denote that which is considered appropriate or
　　permitted within the bounds of Islam.

ḥijāb: A covering, such as a veil; a traditional female body covering.

Hezbollah: "Party of God"; also transliterated as Ḥizb Allāh or Hizbollah, prominent in Lebanon.

Ibrāhīm: Abraham.

ijtihād: Independent judgment based on Islamic sources; a striving for the pragmatic interpretation of Islamic primary sources in the light of contemporary conditions. The term can be synonymous with "renewal" and "reform."

al-Ikhwān al-Muslimūn: The Muslim Brotherhood, a "reformist" movement originating in Egypt in 1928 that spread elsewhere in the Muslim world.

imām: The term *imām* (pl. *a'imma*) usually refers to one who leads the prayers, not necessarily to one "qualified" in the sense of trained clergy. In Shi'a Islam, *imām* has associations with religious leadership and continuity of spiritual authority.

imsāk: Abstention during Ramadan.

Islām: "Submission" to God.

Ismā'īlī: A form of Shi'a Islam, which itself formed disparate branches including the Fatimids, the Nizaris, the Assassins, and the Bohoras.

isnād: Chain of authority (of *ḥadīth*, transmission).

Ithnā 'Asharīs: The "Twelvers," a form of Shi'a Islam following a line of twelve imams descended from Muhammad.

jihād: "Striving" to attain an Islamic objective; the term has either spiritual or militaristic connotations or both.

jihād bil-sayf: Jihad "with the sword."

jihādi: An advocate of jihad.

Ka'bah: The "holy house" (in Mecca).

khalīfa: Caliph, "vice-regent," "successor" (to Muhammad).

Koran: A variant spelling of Qur'an.

madhhab: A "school" of Islamic interpretation, such as the broad Ḥanafī, Ḥanbalī, Mālikī, and Shaf'ī; pl. *madhāhib*.

masdjid: Mosque, place of prayer.

mawlid: Birthday of Muhammad or the anniversary of "saints."

minbar: In a mosque, the equivalent of a pulpit.

mudjtahid: An "interpreter" (of Islam, especially Islamic jurisprudence); a practitioner of *ijtihād*.

Muḥammad: Muḥammad ibn 'Abd Allāh, the Prophet of Islam, c. 570–632 CE (active c. 610–632).

Muḥarram: First month of the Muslim calendar, associated in particular
with fasting, especially for Shi'a Muslims during Āshūrā.

murīd: A person on a spiritual path or a seeker of religious knowledge,
often applied in the context of Sufi beliefs.

murshid: A person who provides guidance to those on the spiritual path.
See murīd.

najis: Ritually unclean.

nashīd: Genre ranging from "sung" ahādīth to prayers and popular
"Islamic" music.

pīr: See murshid.

qibla/ḳibla: Direction of Muslim prayer (toward Mecca).

Qur'an: Revelation received by the Prophet Muhammad from God via the
angel Gabriel.

rak'a: A sequence within salāt.

Ramaḍān: Month of fasting and the month in which the Qur'an was
revealed.

ribā: Capital interest, usury.

salafi: (1) "Pious ancestors," applied in terms of Muhammad's companions
and the "early" Muslim community, representing an exemplar to
follow; (2) used by Muslim "reformist" movement(s), such as al-
Ikhwān al-Muslimūn ; and (3) applied by a number of platforms,
especially in contemporary contexts, indicating their intention to
"return" to the principles of Muhammad and his community.

*salāt: Prayer.

*ṣawm: Fasting during Ramadan.

*shahāda: The principle of proclaiming a belief in a One God whose Final
Prophet is Muhammad.

shahīd: A "witness," frequently used in the sense of a "martyr."

sharī'a: The body of Islamic law based on the "source" of the Qur'an (and
other Islamic sources); divine "law," as revealed to Muhammad.

shaykh: Religious leader; leader of a tarīqa. Also see murshid.

Shī'a: "Party" or "sect"; the followers of the line of Ali ibn Abi Talib.

Ṣūfī: Muslim "mystic." The term has broad connotations and definitions
within disparate branches of Sufism.

sunna: The customary practice of Muhammad. Cf. ḥadīth.

Sunnī: "Orthodox" Islam, based on the sunna.

sūra: A chapter within the Qur'an; pl. *suwar*. Cf. *āyāt*.

tablīgh: Communication. Cf. *daʿwa*.

tadjwīd: recitation styles of the Qur'an, according to specific rules.

tafsīr: Commentary on or exegesis of the Qur'an.

ṭahīr: Purity (in ritual).

taḳlīd: The imitation primarily of the practice of the Prophet Muhammad and secondarily of his companions and his successors. See *salafi*.

ṭalāq: Pronouncement of divorce; title of Sura 65.

tarīqa: A "path"; generally a term associated with Sufi orders.

ṭawāf: A ritual associated with *hajj* involving the circumambulation of the Kaʿba.

ummah: Muslim community.

ʿumra: The "lesser" pilgrimage to Mecca.

*zakāt: Annual alms taxation.

zaouiya, zāwiya: Religious educational institution or school, frequently associated with West and North African contexts; Sufi lodge.

#Index

Tatarstan, Russian Federation, 72
technology, 64, 92, 147, 149
Tehran, Iran, 137
telecommunications industry, 47
telegram, 20, 30, 31, 104, 117, 131, 138, 141
Texas, 58, 109, 120
al-Tidjani, Sidi 'Ahmad, 55
Tidjaniya Sufi Order, 55
Timbuktu, Mali, 114–15
Timms, Stephen, 120
Tokio, Dina, 53
Tor, 26
Toulouse, France, 109
Tsarnaev brothers, 109, 120
Tumblr, 39, 84
Tunisia, 21, 27, 109, 129
Turkey, 25, 127
Twitter, 19, 20, 22, 25, 26, 27, 28, 32, 39, 46,
    49, 65, 71, 78, 81, 84, 87, 93, 96, 97, 105, 107,
    110, 111, 112, 113, 120, 127, 129, 130, 131, 133,
    138; Periscope, 46, 75

'ulama'. See 'alim
ummah, 139
umrah, 45
United Arab Emirates, 1, 21, 24,
    33, 48, 59, 73
United Kingdom, 76, 80, 103, 109, 115–16,
    126, 129, 133; *Terrorism Act 2000*, section
    58, 116
United States, 31, 115, 116–17, 119, 121,
    130, 132, 134; African American
    issues in, 121; U.S. Army Medical
    Corps, 120
Urdu, 89–91, 92, 104
Utøya, Norway, 118
Uzbek, 42

Velayatmardan, 32
video conferencing, 73,
Vimeo, 111
virtual reality, 147
Voice of Jihad (online magazine), 104
Voice of Shariah (online magazine), 104

Wadud, Amina, 76
Wales, 1, 148, 202n9
Warriors of Imam Mahdi, 57
Waziristan, Pakistan, 116
web design, 101
Webb, Suhail, 142
Westminster, University of, 126
WhatsApp, 19, 22, 30, 31, 50, 86, 87, 104, 117,
    131, 138
Whole Earth 'Lectronic Link, 13
Wikipedia, 54, 83
Women Living under Muslim Laws, 76
World of Warcraft (video game), 118

Yaken, Islam, 126
Yaqob, Muhammad Hussein, 79
Yazdi, Agya Pooya, 44
Yazdi, Mesbah, 163n3
Yemen, 21, 58, 61, 72, 116–17, 119–21
Yorkshire, England, 116
youth, 18
YouTube, 25, 26, 27, 39, 49, 55, 60, 71, 75, 82,
    88, 91, 111, 114, 116, 119–21, 129, 134

Zamani, Hamed, 57
Zanzibar-style mourning ritual, 58
al-Zawahiri, Ayman, 105, 109, 111
Zaydi Shi'a, 56
Zemzami, Abdelbari, 83
Zoroastrianism, 92

#Islamic Civilization and Muslim Networks

Gary R. Bunt, *Hashtag Islam: How Cyber-Islamic Environments Are Transforming Religious Authority* (2018).

Ahmad Dallal, *Islam Without Europe: Traditions of Reform in Eighteenth-Century Islamic Thought* (2018).

Irfan Ahmad, *Religion as Critique: Islamic Critical Thinking from Mecca to the Marketplace* (2017).

Scott Kugle, *When Sun Meets Moon: Gender, Eros, and Ecstasy in Urdu Poetry* (2016).

Kishwar Rizvi, *The Transnational Mosque: Architecture, Historical Memory, and the Contemporary Middle East* (2015).

Ebrahim Moosa, *What Is a Madrasa?* (2015).

Bruce Lawrence, *Who Is Allah?* (2015).

Edward E. Curtis IV, *The Call of Bilal: Islam in the African Diaspora* (2014).

Sahar Amer, *What Is Veiling?* (2014).

Rudolph T. Ware III, *The Walking Qur'an: Islamic Education, Embodied Knowledge, and History in West Africa* (2014).

Sa'diyya Shaikh, *Sufi Narratives of Intimacy: Ibn 'Arabī, Gender, and Sexuality* (2012).

Karen G. Ruffle, *Gender, Sainthood, and Everyday Practice in South Asian Shi'ism* (2011).

Jonah Steinberg, *Isma'ili Modern: Globalization and Identity in a Muslim Community* (2011).

Iftikhar Dadi, *Modernism and the Art of Muslim South Asia* (2010).

Gary R. Bunt, *iMuslims: Rewiring the House of Islam* (2009).

Fatemeh Keshavarz, *Jasmine and Stars: Reading More than "Lolita" in Tehran* (2007).

Scott Kugle, *Sufis and Saints' Bodies: Mysticism, Corporeality, and Sacred Power in Islam* (2007).

Roxani Eleni Margariti, *Aden and the Indian Ocean Trade: 150 Years in the Life of a Medieval Arabian Port* (2007).

Sufia M. Uddin, *Constructing Bangladesh: Religion, Ethnicity, and Language in an Islamic Nation* (2006).

Omid Safi, *The Politics of Knowledge in Premodern Islam: Negotiating Ideology and Religious Inquiry* (2006).

Ebrahim Moosa, *Ghazālī and the Poetics of Imagination* (2005).

miriam cooke and Bruce B. Lawrence, eds., *Muslim Networks from Hajj to Hip Hop* (2005).

Carl W. Ernst, *Following Muhammad: Rethinking Islam in the Contemporary World* (2003).